OCEAN!

DK | Penguin Random House

Senior Editor Jenny Sich
Senior Art Editor Stefan Podhorodecki
Editors Kelsie Besaw, Annie Moss,
Vicky Richards, Anna Streiffert Limerick
US Editor Jennette ElNaggar
Art Editors Mik Gates, Renata Latipova,
Gregory McCarthy, Lynne Moulding, Rob Perry
Jacket Design Development Manager Sophia MTT
Jacket Designer Tanya Mehrotra
Production Editor Robert Dunn
Production Controller Sian Cheung
Managing Editor Francesca Baines
Managing Art Editor Philip Letsu
Publisher Andrew Macintyre
Associate Publishing Director Liz Wheeler
Art Director Karen Self
Publishing Director Jonathan Metcalf

Written by Derek Harvey,
Nicola Temple, John Woodward

Consultants Derek Harvey, Professor Dorrik Stow

Illustrators Andrew Beckett @ Illustration Ltd,
Adam Benton, Peter Bull, Barry Croucher / The Art Agency,
Jean-Michel Girard / The Art Agency, Gary Hanna, Jason Harding,
Jon @ KJA, Arran Lewis, Peter Minister, Sofian Moumene,
Stuart Jackson-Carter – SJC Illustration, Simon Tegg

First American Edition, 2020
Published in the United States by DK Publishing
1450 Broadway, Suite 801, New York, NY 10018

Copyright © 2020 Dorling Kindersley Limited
DK, a Division of Penguin Random House LLC
21 22 23 24 10 9 8 7 6 5 4
015–316688–Sep/2020

A catalog record for this book
is available from the Library of Congress.
ISBN 978-1-4654-9147-3

DK books are available at special discounts when purchased in bulk
for sales promotions, premiums, fund-raising, or educational use.
For details, contact: DK Publishing Special Markets,
1450 Broadway, Suite 801, New York, NY 10018
SpecialSales@dk.com

Printed and bound in UAE

For the curious
www.dk.com

Smithsonian
THE SMITHSONIAN

Established in 1846, the Smithsonian is the world's
largest museum and research complex, dedicated to
public education, national service, and scholarship in the
arts, sciences, and history. It includes 19 museums and galleries
and the National Zoological Park. The total number of artifacts, works of art,
and specimens in the Smithsonian's collection is estimated at 155.5 million.

MIX
Paper from
responsible sources
FSC™ C018179

This book was made with Forest Stewardship
Council™ certified paper – one small step
in DK's commitment to a sustainable future.
For more information go to
www.dk.com/our-green-pledge

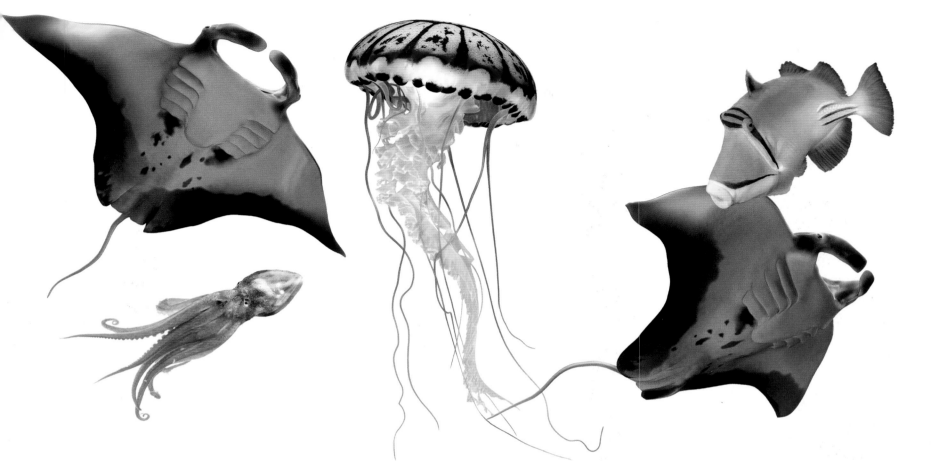

DK SMITHSONIAN
OCEAN!

CONTENTS

SEASHORES

OCEANS AND US

OCEAN MAPS

POLAR OCEANS

Scales and sizes

The data box for each animal includes a scale drawing to indicate its size. These are based on the height of an average adult human male and the hand and thumb tip shown below. The sizes given in this book are **typical maximums**. Unless otherwise stated, the sizes given are the length of the animal, from the front of the head or tip of the beak, to the rear of the body—or tip of the tail or tentacles, where the animal has these. Some animals have shapes that mean width is a more useful measurement than length, so this is given instead.

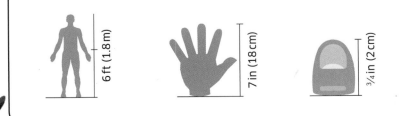

6ft (1.8m)   7in (18cm)   3/4in (2cm)

OCEAN SCIENCE

Earth's oceans are almost as old as the planet itself. Formed more than four billion years ago, they have been evolving ever since. Their waters are constantly on the move–flowing in currents around the globe, pulled in a daily cycle of tides, and rising and falling as waves that crash on the shores.

OCEAN WATERS

The vast majority of the planet's water is contained within the oceans, filling these huge basins up to several miles deep. Ocean water is salty—in contrast with the fresh water found in rivers and lakes—and varies in temperature around the globe, from the balmy tropics to the freezing poles. Water continually moves between the oceans, air, and land, in the global water cycle.

WHAT IS WATER?

Water is made up of molecules far too small to see, even with the most powerful microscope. There are more than a billion trillion of them in a single drop. Each molecule of water is made up of a single oxygen atom and two hydrogen atoms joined by strong chemical bonds.

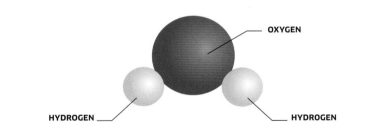

OXYGEN

HYDROGEN

HYDROGEN

SALTY WATER

On average, ocean water contains about 1.2 oz (35 g) of salt in every quart (liter). This salt is made up of a mixture of chemicals. More than 80 percent of salt is made up of just two types of chemicals called sodium and chloride. These make up sodium chloride—the salt we use for flavoring food. But ocean salt also contains other chemicals, in smaller amounts.

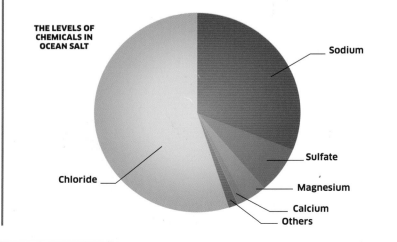

THE LEVELS OF
CHEMICALS IN
OCEAN SALT

Sodium

Sulfate

Magnesium

Calcium

Others

Chloride

HOW MUCH WATER?

Seen from space, Earth's vast expanses of water give it its nickname—the blue planet. More than 300 million cubic miles (1.3 billion cubic km) of salty water covers most of Earth's surface. The average ocean basin extends to depths of around 3.7 miles (6 km) in depth. Compared to this, all other water sources, such as rivers, lakes, and inland seas, hold only very small amounts.

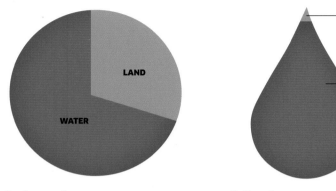

FRESH WATER

LAND

SALT WATER

WATER

Surface water
More than 70 percent of Earth's surface is covered by water. If all the water on Earth's surface was put together, it would dominate the globe.

Salt water
Ninety-seven percent of the planet's water is the salt water in the oceans. The other 3 percent is the fresh water in ice, under the ground, and in lakes and rivers.

WHY IS THE OCEAN BLUE?

Water is colorless and transparent, so sunlight can penetrate through it. But the sunlight we perceive as white is actually a mixture of all the different colors of the rainbow. Each color can penetrate to different depths. Blue light can get much deeper than the others, traveling down to 330 ft (100 m), which is why the sunlit part of the ocean appears blue. But below this, no light can penetrate, so at deeper depths, the ocean looks dark.

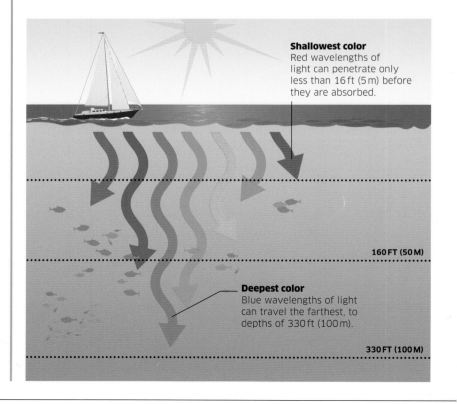

Shallowest color
Red wavelengths of light can penetrate only less than 16 ft (5 m) before they are absorbed.

160 FT (50 M)

Deepest color
Blue wavelengths of light can travel the farthest, to depths of 330 ft (100 m).

330 FT (100 M)

HOT AND COLD SEAS

Ocean temperature varies around the globe. Heat from sunshine is more intense in the areas around the equator, so the ocean's surface is warmer there and gets colder toward the poles. But oceans everywhere get cooler with depth, too, and the water at the ocean floor is always cold, even at the tropics.

Heat mapping
The map uses color to show how surface ocean temperature varies around the world—red indicating warm water and blue, cold water.

90°F — 30°C
70°F — 20°C
50°F — 10°C
30°F — 0°C

Tropical seas
These warm waters near the equator remain hot throughout the year.

Temperate seas
On either side of the tropical equatorial regions, these bands of ocean are still warm but have distinct seasons where temperatures can change.

Polar seas
Closest to the poles at the north and south of Earth, these seas are much colder.

THE WATER CYCLE

Since Earth was formed 4.5 billion years ago, the amount of water it contains has stayed about the same. However, this water constantly moves around and constantly changes state—between liquid, gaseous vapor, and solid ice. This process is called the water cycle and is driven by the sun. Water evaporates from the ocean surface due to the sun's warmth and eventually falls as rain, which then returns to the oceans.

Water vapor forms clouds
As rising water vapor cools, it turns to liquid drops. These are small enough to hang in the air as fluffy clouds.

Water falls as rain
Over time, the small droplets join with other droplets. They become big and heavy and fall to Earth as rain or snow. About 78 percent of this precipitation happens over the oceans, but some falls on land.

Water evaporates from rivers and lakes on land as well as the oceans

Water evaporates
The sun's heat warms the ocean water, making some of it change state into a gas (water vapor)—a process called evaporation.

Water flows into the ocean
Water that falls onto the land will eventually make its way back to the oceans, either running into rivers or seeping into the soil and through the rocks.

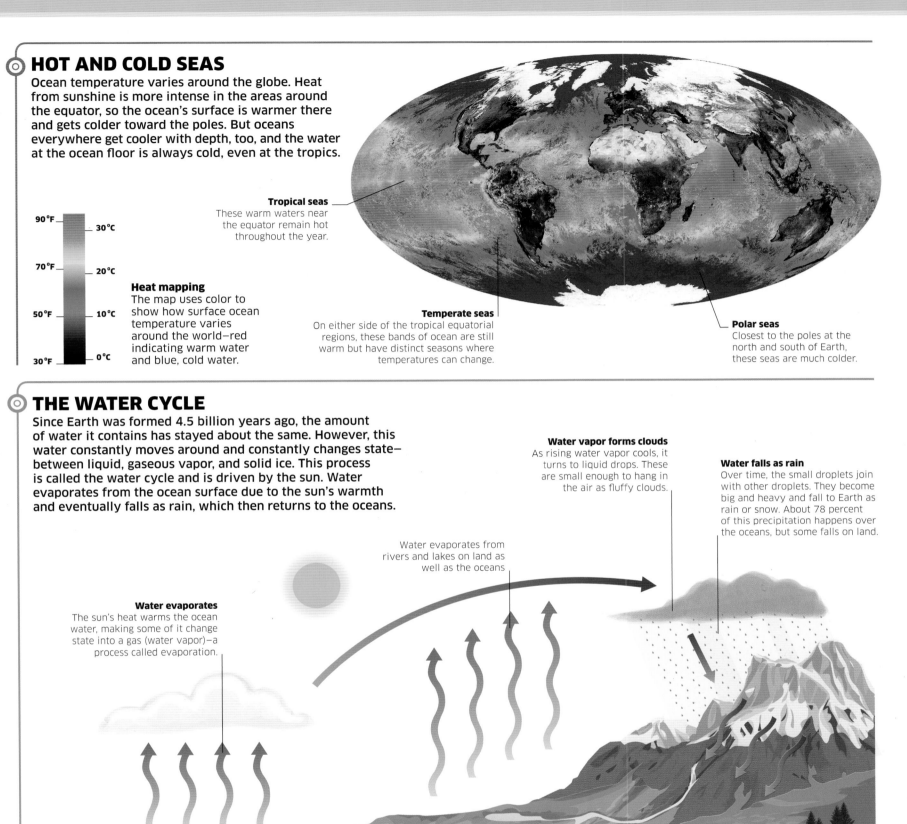

Molten surface
Hot molten rock flowed in huge streams before Earth's surface turned completely solid.

Shifting layers
Lighter rock floated to the surface, while heavier metals sank to form Earth's core.

1 4.54 billion years ago
Earth was formed as pieces of space rock and ice smashed together and gravity pulled these into a spherical planet. The energy of their collisions made conditions very hot, so much of early Earth's surface was covered with molten lava. Gases spewed out from volcanoes formed a layer around the planet that made up its atmosphere.

Craters
In this period the planet was bombarded with asteroids, leaving craters on the surface. Some theories suggest that much of Earth's water could have come from comet impacts.

2 4.4 billion years ago
As Earth cooled, the molten rock on the surface hardened into a crust. Then water vapor condensed from the atmosphere and began to fall as torrential rain. This filled the crust's rocky basins to create the very first bodies of water—the forerunners of the oceans today. Lighter rock settled on top of the ocean floor to become the first continents.

How Earth's Oceans Formed

Over billions of years, Earth's oceans have changed with our evolving planet, as seafloors shift, coastlines drift, and continents move around and break up.

The story of the oceans began when Earth was formed more than 4.5 billion years ago from colliding lumps of space rock and ice smashing together. In these fiery beginnings, ice turned to vapor and then condensed into liquid water as the newly formed planet began to cool. Rain fell and flooded the land, creating the very first seas. These early oceans would change many times over the next few billion years—growing and shrinking around new landmasses, and even freezing over when ice engulfed the globe.

The first single-celled life evolved
4 billion years ago,
most likely in the oceans.

The hot and fiery time period **when Earth was forming** is called the **Hadean Eon**, after Hades, the Greek god of the underworld.

4.375 billion years—the age of **zircon crystals** from Australia, **the oldest things found on Earth today**.

11

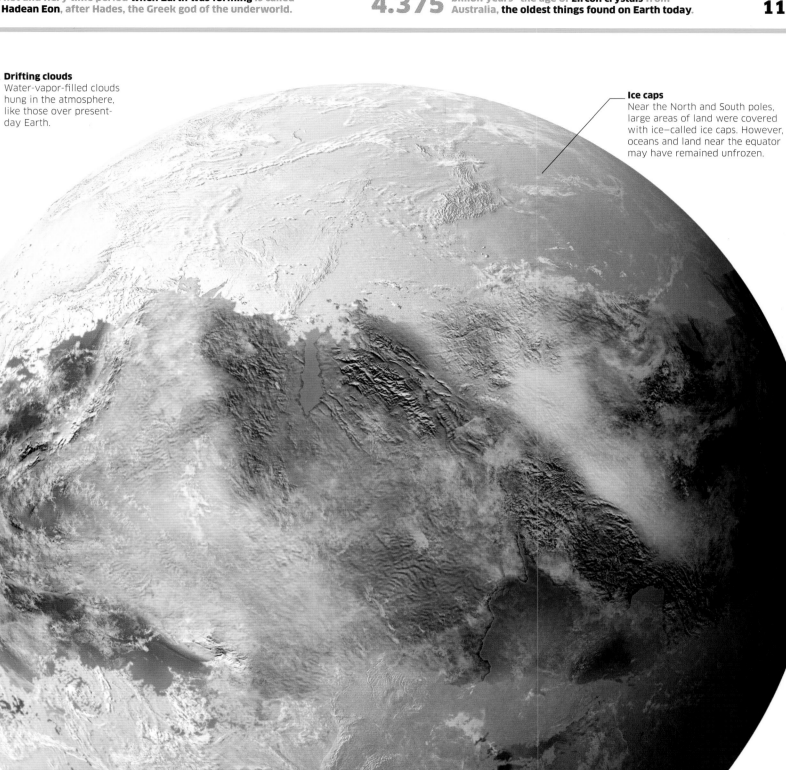

Drifting clouds
Water-vapor-filled clouds hung in the atmosphere, like those over present-day Earth.

Ice caps
Near the North and South poles, large areas of land were covered with ice—called ice caps. However, oceans and land near the equator may have remained unfrozen.

3 **2.3 billion years ago**
Soon after water appeared on the planet, life evolved. Some of these simple organisms used energy from sunlight to make food from carbon dioxide. As levels of carbon dioxide dropped in the atmosphere, the temperature dropped, too—freezing the oceans and plunging Earth into two ice ages—one after the other—that together lasted for nearly 100 million years.

Giant landmasses
Pangaea extended all the way from the North Pole to the South Pole.

Global ocean
A single global prehistoric ocean, called Panthalassa, surrounded the supercontinent of Pangaea.

4 250 million years ago
For billions of years after the planet's surface hardened, Earth's crust (the solid top layer) moved around, changing the geography of oceans and continents. About 250 million years ago, all the land was joined into a supercontinent called Pangaea. At this time, complex plants and animals were thriving, but disappearing coastlines, baking temperatures, volcanic eruptions, and changing ocean chemistry triggered a devastating mass extinction.

Tectonic plates

Earth's hard rocky crust broke into pieces soon after it was formed, like the shattered shell of a hard-boiled egg. These pieces are called tectonic plates. The movement of hot heavy rock below the plates moves them around, causing the seas and continents to shift.

5 150 million years ago
About 100 million years after the Pangaea mass extinction, life had recovered and was flourishing, and the oceans were filled with giant reptiles. Continents were splitting up, creating more seas and adding to the extent of the planet's coastlines. This provided more habitats for marine life, such as coral reefs.

Early Atlantic Ocean
New oceans were formed as continents moved away from each other, such as the Atlantic between South America and Africa.

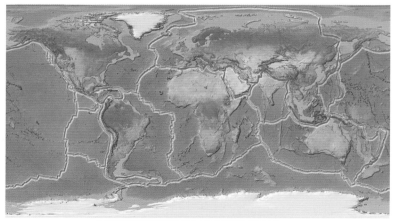

A MAP OF THE WORLD'S TECTONIC PLATES TODAY

The tectonic plate movements that cause continents to shift happen incredibly slowly—about as fast **as a fingernail grows.**

200 million years ago—**when the first waters of the Atlantic Ocean appeared**, as Pangaea began to split in two.

95 percent—the percentage of **ocean life wiped out by a mass extinction event** during the time of Pangaea.

13

Tethys Ocean
When Pangaea separated into northern and southern continents, a prehistoric ocean—the Tethys Ocean—opened up between them.

Mediterranean Sea
Today's Mediterranean Sea is all that remains of the prehistoric Tethys Ocean, which shrunk in size as the continents moved to the positions they hold today.

6 Modern-day Earth
As the continents moved to their current positions, they opened up the five modern oceans: the Atlantic, Indian, and Pacific straddling the equator and the ice-covered Arctic and Southern oceans around the poles. Today's oceans are still slowly changing, but human activity now also affects them—impacting sea levels and causing threats to ocean life.

Widening waters
The Atlantic Ocean continues to open wider even today, as new seafloor is created between America, Europe, and Africa as these continents slowly shift away from each other.

14 ocean science ○ HOW OCEAN LIFE EVOLVED

33 ft (10 m)—the length of *Dunkleosteus*, one of the biggest jawed predators to first appear in the oceans.

How Ocean Life Evolved

Billions of years ago, Earth's oceans were the birthplace of all the planet's life, which has been evolving ever since—from simple, tiny organisms to giant fish and mammals.

The oceans' first life forms were microscopic creatures made up of just a single cell. But from these simple ancestors came spectacular diversity, as organisms gradually changed by evolution over millions of generations, producing some of the biggest and most impressive animals ever to have lived on Earth. As landmasses and oceans moved and conditions on the planet changed, ocean life changed, too. Many of the animals that lived in prehistoric seas were vastly different from those we know today.

Chapters in animal evolution

Complex animal life has lived in the oceans for at least half a billion years, since an event called the Cambrian explosion, when many familiar animal groups evolved. Over hundreds of millions of years, descendants of these early creatures evolved into fast-swimming fish, giant reptiles, and filter-feeding whales. All these animals developed new adaptations to help them in their underwater lives, resulting in the huge variety of creatures in the oceans today.

Anomalocaris
A distant relative of shrimp, this creature was the biggest known predator of the Cambrian period.

Plourdosteus
Placoderms, such as *Plourdosteus*, were fish with skin protected by an armor of bone.

1 Simple life
Life is thought to have first appeared in the oceans 4 billion years ago, in the form of simple cells. The first ocean animals appeared much later, with fossils found from around 570 million years ago. Living mainly on the seabed, these Precambrian creatures had soft bodies often round and symmetrical or leaflike in shape.

Funisia
Some animals living in the Precambrian period were so unlike those living today that scientists struggle to classify them. This *Funisia* might have been related to sponges or anemones.

2 Explosion of life
Around 545 million years ago, a diverse range of animals emerged in a period called the Cambrian explosion. These included the ancestors of many modern animal groups, and many were small creatures with hard shells. Most lived on the seabed, but some swam in open water.

Ottoia
This creature had a mouth with hooks that it probably used to grab other seafloor animals as prey—like some predatory worms today.

3 Age of the fish
Around 400 million years ago, the oceans were teeming with many different types of fish. Armored prehistoric fish called placoderms had strong biting jaws and were some of the most ferocious predators of their day.

10,000 The **number of ammonite species that have been discovered** in the fossil record.

75 percent–the **proportion of ocean species that went extinct with the dinosaurs** 66 million years ago.

15

Evidence of prehistoric life

We know about the kinds of animals that lived in the prehistoric past from fossils. These are the traces or remains of their bodies left in rocks. By studying the rocks surrounding a fossil, scientists can estimate the fossil's age and determine how different kinds of animals came and went over the history of life on Earth.

Cast fossils
Many fossils that formed in prehistoric seas came from ammonites. These creatures left impressions on the seabed, which then fossilized and preserved their shape. Ammonites were related to squid and octopus but lived in hard coiled shells.

Hard fossils
Sharks have a skeleton made from rubbery cartilage, which is more likely to rot away than bone. But their teeth are harder and preserve well. This *Megalodon* tooth is three times bigger than that of a great white.

Eusthenopteron
This fish had thick, fleshy fins and was related to animals that eventually evolved limbs for walking.

Cretoxyrhina
Sharks, such as *Cretoxyrhina*, evolved a skeleton made from light, buoyant cartilage, making them a top ocean predator.

Toxochelys
Giant turtles appeared around the time of the dinosaurs. They descended from land-dwelling animals.

Acrophoca
Some groups of land mammals evolved into new oceangoing forms. The first seals, such as *Acrophoca*, descended from doglike carnivores.

Piscobalaena
This prehistoric whale fed using baleen–hairy strips for filtering plankton. These whales grew huge to get bigger mouthfuls of plankton.

Pterygotus
This large meat-eating creature was a prehistoric ocean relative of scorpions and spiders. It had strong claws for grasping prey.

4 Age of the reptiles
By 100 million years ago, during the Cretaceous period, plants and giant animals were thriving on land. This was the time of the dinosaurs, and many of their distant reptilian cousins—including giant plesiosaurs, mosasaurs, and turtles—lived in the ocean.

Tylosaurus
One of the biggest ocean reptiles, *Tylosaurus* could grow up to 46 ft (14 m) long. It was a mosasaur–a distant prehistoric cousin of snakes.

5 Age of the mammals
After giant reptiles were wiped out in a mass extinction 66 million years ago, mammals ruled on land. Some of these then evolved in the oceans to become the first whales. Their huge size might have helped defend against giant sharks, which were the new super-predators of the deep.

Megalodon
This super-predator was a giant relative of today's great white shark. Because most of its fossil evidence comes from teeth, nobody is sure how big it grew, but estimates range from 33 ft (10 m) to 59 ft (18 m) long.

Continental shelf
Home to shallower waters, the continental shelf is the submerged edge of a piece of continental crust.

Continental slope
This steep slope stretches down toward the ocean plain.

Submarine canyon
When sediment flows off the continental shelf, deep canyons may form.

Island arc
Along an ocean trench, clusters of volcanoes form, some of which rise up to become new islands.

Continental rise
A gentler slope, piled high with sediment, marks the foot of the continental slope. It lies above the transition between continental and oceanic crust.

Lithosphere
The lithosphere is Earth's rigid outer shell. It is made up of the brittle outer crust and the solid uppermost part of the mantle.

Ocean trenches
These deep valleylike trenches in the ocean floor can reach incredible depths. This one has been formed by two oceanic plates colliding.

Abyssal plain
The flat regions of the ocean floor are known as the abyssal plain.

The Ocean Floor

An ocean is a giant rocky basin filled with water, but its sides and bottom are not smooth and even. Mountains, volcanoes, and deep trenches all mark the ocean floor.

The shallow coastal seas around the edges of the continents are where most life that we know of is concentrated. But most of the ocean floor is at least 20 times deeper. Made of dense oceanic crust, it is covered in a deep layer of mud and ooze. Many of the features of the deep ocean floor are caused by the slow movements of Earth's tectonic plates.

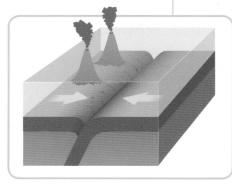

How trenches form
When plates push together, one slides below the other—a process called subduction—and a deep trench forms in the ocean floor. Magma pushing upward from the mantle causes a volcanic island arc to form on the upper plate.

1 mile (2 km)—the **height** of the tallest peaks of the **Mid-Atlantic Ridge** mountain range.

3.7 miles (6 km)—the **average thickness of oceanic crust**.

80 percent of all **volcanic eruptions** on Earth are thought to **take place in the ocean**.

17

Features of the floor

Tectonic plates are made up of 60-mile- (100-km-) thick slabs of hard rock, known as the lithosphere, and move around on semi-molten rock that is part of a layer called the mantle. When plates meet, they interact in different ways, causing parts of the ocean floor to sink down into deep trenches and new floor to rise up into underwater mountain ranges called ridges. Through these processes, ocean floor is constantly being created and destroyed.

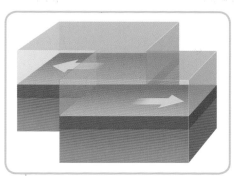

Shifting plates
Where plates grind past one another, they form massive gashes in Earth's crust called faults. These are very common at ridges. Sudden movement along these faults causes earthquakes.

Types of crusts

Earth's surface crust varies in thickness between continental crust, which makes up the land, and oceanic crust, which forms the seafloor. Continental crust is thicker but made of lighter rock, so it rises higher to form continents, while the thinner, heavier oceanic crust sinks to form ocean basins.

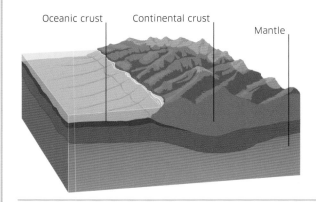

Oceanic crust   Continental crust   Mantle

Mariana Trench

The trenches formed by the subduction of oceanic crust mark the deepest parts of the world's oceans. Deepest of all is the Mariana Trench in the Pacific, which plunges 7 miles (11 km) below the surface— more than twice the average depth of the deep ocean plain. If the world's highest mountain, Mount Everest, was placed inside the Mariana Trench, its peak would not reach the water's surface.

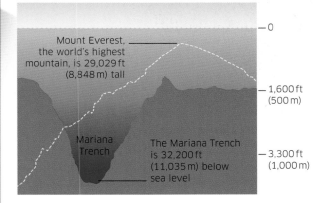

Mount Everest, the world's highest mountain, is 29,029 ft (8,848 m) tall

—0

—1,600 ft (500 m)

Mariana Trench

The Mariana Trench is 32,200 ft (11,035 m) below sea level

—3,300 ft (1,000 m)

Mapping the ocean

Scientists study the seafloor using sonar. They use ships to send pulses of sound down to the bottom and calculate the depth from the time it takes to receive the echo. These measurements are used to draw maps that show depth variations.

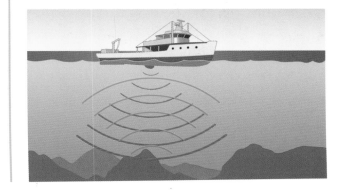

Ocean ridges
These underwater mountain ranges consist of many raised rocky peaks.

How ridges form
When plates move away from each other, molten volcanic rock rises up through Earth's crust to fill the gap. It flows up and spreads outward to harden into pointed ridges of new crust.

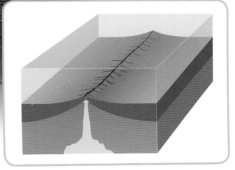

18 ocean science ∘ **VOLCANIC ISLANDS**

6 years–the age of the world's **youngest volcanic island Hunga Tonga-Hunga Ha'apai** in Tonga, which emerged in December 2014.

Island chain

The hard outer layer of Earth – made up of its brittle crust and the topmost part of the thick mantle layer – is called the lithosphere, and moves over the hot, moving mantle below. As it moves over a particularly fiery hot spot in the mantle, the molten rock pushing to the surface creates a chain of cone-shaped islands. Over millions of years, each island ages, cools, and sinks as the crust carries it further away from the hot spot where it was born.

1 Active volcano
As the plume from the hot spot rises, it melts through the crust and pushes the hot rock up, forming a volcano. Over a long period, this erupts many times, spewing lava that then solidifies to create a newborn rocky island– the youngest in the chain.

2 Thriving island
As the crust moves and carries the island away from the hot spot, the volcano becomes dormant and the land cools. The island and surrounding seas become home to a variety of wildlife.

Rising magma
When the rock of the crust and the mantle melts, it expands and pushes upward as liquid magma. Molten rock that erupts at the surface is called lava.

Plume head
When a hot spot reaches the crust, it spreads out to form a plume head.

Hot spot
A hot spot is a rising plume of molten rock that forms in one part of Earth's mantle.

Coral atolls

The rims of tropical oceanic islands–where the warm waters are bathed in sunlight–are perfect places for coral reefs (see pp.98-99) to grow, even as the island sinks below the water's surface.

Coral grows around the shore of the island

Coral continues to build up as the island sinks

A ring of coral remains

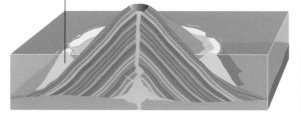

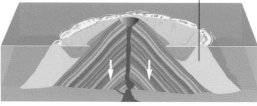

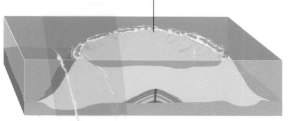

1 Fringing reef
Coral initially starts to grow on the rocky sides of the island around its coastline, in a formation called a fringing reef.

2 Barrier reef
As the reef grows bigger and the island gets eroded, a barrier reef is formed–a reef separated from the island by a deep channel.

3 Atoll
When the island disappears beneath the ocean, it leaves a ring of reef called a coral atoll, with a lagoon in the middle.

620 miles (1,000 km)—**how wide a plume head** can be.

32,800 ft (10,000 m)—**the height of Mauna Kea** from the seafloor, the world's **tallest mountain** and part of the Hawaiian island chain.

19

Volcanic Islands

At many points across Earth's vast oceans, volcanoes erupt from the ocean floor as enormous cones of rock. These cones can rise so high that they breach the water surface as islands.

Measured from their base on the seabed, these oceanic islands are the tallest mountainous peaks on Earth, with the biggest—Mauna Kea—more than 3,300 ft (1,000 m) higher than Mount Everest. They form over hot spots, places where plumes of molten rock break through the ocean floor.

Coastal communities
The coral reefs that grow around the island's coastline become an important habitat for ocean life.

3 Shrinking island
Over time, the island's rock erodes. The action of wind, rain, and waves wears its surface away, making it smaller and flatter.

Sheltered lagoon
As it is eroded, the island begins to collapse in the center, creating a new body of water separated from the ocean—a lagoon.

4 Seamount
Eventually, the top of the island becomes so worn it disappears beneath the ocean surface. The underwater peak that remains is called a seamount and will continue to be eroded over time.

Lithosphere
The upper part of the mantle makes up the lithosphere along with the crust.

Rocky mantle
The mantle is the layer of Earth that lies between the crust at the surface and the core at the centre. This part of the mantle, just below the lithosphere, is made of hot, moving rock.

Oceanic crust
This layer—never more than 6 miles (10 km) thick—is harder than the denser mantle below. It is much thinner than continental crust.

Shifting plates
Heat currents in the mantle drag the lithosphere along away from the hot spot. It moves several inches across the mantle surface each year.

The world's current most active volcano is Kilauea, which sits over a hot spot near Hawaii.
It erupted nonstop from 1983 to 2018.

The Seychelles

Unlike island chains formed by underwater hot spots, the islands of the Seychelles in the Indian Ocean are the broken-up pieces of an ancient supercontinent.

The Seychelles are a group of 115 islands that lie off the East Coast of Africa. But they used to be part of a giant landmass that broke apart millions of years ago, at the time of the dinosaurs, leaving fragments of land scattered between Madagascar and India. These fragments wore down to become small islands of gray granite rock covered in lush greenery and home to a diverse range of life. The Seychelles also include some coral islands with distinctive white sandy beaches.

Sinking water
When warm tropical water in the global conveyor reaches the colder seas of the North Atlantic, some of the water gets denser and heavier and sinks downward. This deepwater current travels all the way down the Atlantic Ocean.

Gyres
As winds blow across the water, they are deflected by the spinning Earth. This makes them veer in one direction, forming rotating circular patterns called gyres.

Most currents generated by wind extend no more than 164 ft (50 m) below the surface

Chilled water from the Atlantic is joined by more cold water from the Southern Ocean

Ocean Currents

The ocean's waters are constantly on the move, churned about by swirling currents that not only spread nutrients and oxygen but also affect the climate of the planet.

Wind blowing against the ocean surface over great distances pushes warm water from the tropics to cooler places, while chilly water from the poles eventually returns to replace it—much of it flowing deep along the ocean bed to get there. By cycling water in this way, the ocean currents help stop climates around the world from getting too hot or too cold. This is because the temperature of ocean water affects the air above it. Air warmed or cooled by the oceans moves across the land, regulating the temperature and climate of the whole globe.

Global currents

Ocean water moves in surface currents and deepwater currents. Surface currents are driven by the wind pushing against the water. The position of the continents and spinning of Earth determine their direction, creating circling patterns called gyres. At the same time, deepwater currents circulate water between the surface and the seabed, as cold dense water sinks and moves to warmer regions. This network is called the global conveyor.

Key

Cold surface currents   Warm surface currents   Global ocean conveyor

1,000 years—the **length of time it takes for ocean water** to complete the **circuit of the global ocean conveyor**.

Warm water flowing northward in **the Gulf Stream of the North Atlantic carries 150 times more water** than the Amazon River.

23

Gulf Stream
This fast-flowing current is one of the strongest in the world. It brings warm water up to northern Europe and is responsible for its mild climate.

Newly warm waters circulate around the globe

Rising water
In the North Pacific, and in the Indian Ocean, the cold deep water warms and rises upward, eventually replacing the surface water that sinks elsewhere.

The global ocean conveyor splits into two branches in the Southern Ocean

Wind blows out to sea

Water is pushed away from the shore

Water carrying nutrients rises up

Ocean gyres always flow clockwise in the Northern Hemisphere and **counterclockwise** in the Southern Hemisphere.

Coastal upwellings

On some parts of the coast, the movement of currents creates upwellings—nutrient-rich areas where ocean life can thrive. Winds blowing along coastlines get drawn out to sea by the spinning of Earth and push water away from the land. Deeper water rises up to replace it, bringing up nutrients from the seabed that sustain abundant coastal plankton and other animals.

24   ocean science ∘ **WAVES**

66 ft (20 m)—**the height of the biggest rogue waves**, though some are higher. They are more common in places such as **the coasts of South Africa and Japan and the Bay of Biscay.**

Structure of a wave
The water in each wave moves in a circular path, transferring energy forward. Only the wave—not the water itself—moves forward, which is why a floating object on the waves bobs up and down in one place. The top of each wave is called a crest, and the dip between two crests is a trough.

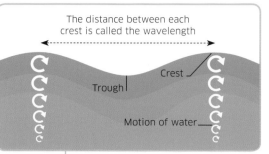

The distance between each crest is called the wavelength

Crest

Trough

Motion of water

Wave crest

Fetch
The area the winds blow across is called the fetch. The size of this area, as well as the strength of the winds and how long they blow for, determines how big the waves will be.

Ripples 1
Waves begin as gentle ripples on the ocean surface, caused by wind. These are very small and close together, like the ripples seen on ponds and smaller bodies of water.

Growing bigger 2
As more wind blows, the waves get bigger and gain more energy. The water in them moves in a circular path. This movement extends below the surface to a point called the wave base.

Wave base

Waves travel 3
The waves continue to grow, becoming larger and farther apart. They roll across the ocean toward shorelines.

Approaching the shore 4
In shallower water, waves get squashed up and closer together. As the wave base hits the seabed, it becomes slower than the crest, causing the waves to lean forward.

Waves break 5
As waves get closer to the shore, the crest of each wave becomes unstable and eventually topples forward—forming a wave called a breaker.

Breaking waves
Waves form out in the open ocean. They are visible as moving patterns of water on the surface, but their motion goes much deeper. As waves move toward a coastline, they become higher and more tightly bunched together. Eventually, the bottom of each wave hits the seabed and stops, but the top races on and spills over, making the wave break on the shore.

79 ft (24 m)—the **height of the biggest wave surfed**, off the coast of Portugal in 2017.

A research institute in **the Netherlands can create artificial waves of up to 15 ft (4.5 m)**, which are used to test the effectiveness of flood defenses.

25

Waves

Ocean waves can be powerful forces—reaching towering heights, traveling incredible distances, and eventually crashing down onto land when they reach the shore.

Waves are caused by wind that pushes against the ocean, creating ripples that grow bigger as more air blows across the surface. Once generated, waves can cover vast distances while losing only very little of their energy. They eventually break on shorelines—perhaps thousands of miles from where they began.

Rogue waves
Waves out in the open ocean can also reach huge heights. When strong winds cause two swells to come together, this rare event creates unusually big "rogue waves" that can throw ships around wildly and in some cases even sink them.

Growing waves
Waves grow higher as they travel, meaning the very highest ones have traveled great distances across the ocean.

Windsurfer
In some sports, such as surfing and windsurfing, participants ride the waves, using the energy of the waves to propel themselves forward.

Breaking wave
The breaking wave pushes water onto the shore into a region called the surf zone.

Swash and backwash
After a wave breaks on land, water rushes up the beach. This is called the swash. The water then runs back into the ocean pulled by gravity. This is called the backwash.

26 ocean science ○ **TROPICAL CYCLONE**

30 days—the duration of **Hurricane John**—the longest **sustained cyclone** on record, which formed in 1994.

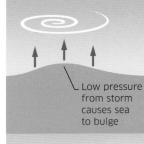 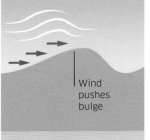 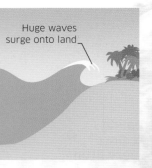

Huge waves surge onto land

Low pressure from storm causes sea to bulge

Wind pushes bulge

Storm surges

Low pressure in an ocean storm not only draws in air but also sucks in the water so the ocean bulges upward in a storm surge. As winds push this bulge toward the shore, tides and waves become higher than normal, flooding the land with the rising water.

Tropical Cyclone

Some of the worst weather happens over the oceans. Huge spiraling storms—called tropical cyclones—form far out to sea, and when they sweep over the land, torrential rain and gales often devastate anything in their path.

These extreme weather events are often seasonal, occurring at different times around the world. Storms over the ocean sometimes affect the land, causing surges of water that rush onto the shore. Earthquakes on the seabed can also generate another ocean hazard—enormous waves called tsunamis that flow far inland to cause destructive floods.

Ascending warm air
Air heated by warm ocean water rises upward through the storm.

Descending cool air
Colder air sinks back down between the cloud bands to the ocean surface.

Growth of a cyclone

Heavy storm clouds can form over the warm oceans of the tropics. As more moist air gets sucked upward through the storm, winds start to circle. This is a tropical cyclone—a spinning storm that is known as a hurricane when over the Caribbean and a typhoon over southeast Asia.

Fast-moving winds
Winds at this stage of the storm can range between 38 and 75 mph (61 and 120 km/h).

Key

→ Warm air

→ Cold air

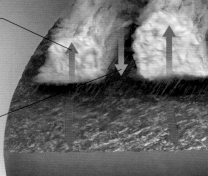

Warm, moist air is pulled in

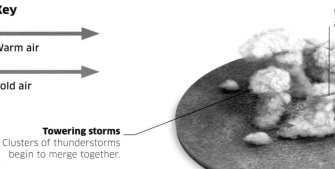

Towering storms
Clusters of thunderstorms begin to merge together.

2 Storms get bigger
The rising moisture-filled air leaves a pocket of low pressure underneath, called a depression. More moist air rushes into this pocket from the surrounding higher-pressure air. This makes the storm clouds grow and merge together.

3 Storms start to spin
The rotation of Earth helps make the winds spin, and they begin to form a large spiraling pattern. The clouds become taller and the winds faster. The storm system is now called a cyclone—meaning it revolves.

1 Storm clouds form
High temperatures in tropical oceans make lots of water evaporate from the ocean, filling the air with moist vapor. As warm air rises, it carries the vapor with it, which forms storm clouds and falls as rain.

Measuring 1,380 miles (2,220 km) across, the Pacific storm Typhoon Tip was **the largest cyclone** ever recorded anywhere in the world.

155 mph (250 km/h)–the minimum **wind speed of a category 5 cyclone**, the strongest grade of cyclone.

80 The average **number of cyclones formed each year** around the world.

27

Eye of the storm
The center, or the eye, of the storm is calm and cloud-free. Cool air sinks and warm air rises around it.

4 Monster cyclone
Building pressure pushes clouds farther out from the center, making the cyclone expand. The rising moist air forms spiraling bands of rain clouds delivering torrential rain. Between the bands, cooler, drier air sinks to replace the air rising up.

Surface winds
Winds spiral around into the storm. They are stronger the closer they are to the center of the cyclone.

Bands of clouds
Rising warm air creates long, spiraling bands of rain clouds inside the hurricane.

Tsunamis

Another deadly ocean phenomenon, tsunamis are large waves that can be caused by deep-sea earthquakes rather than storms. These earthquakes occur when the seafloor moves suddenly, such as when two plates of Earth's crust scrape against one another. A shock wave spreads out from this site, pushing the water and generating giant waves. As these travel toward coastlines, they reach great heights and can crash down on shores to wreak destruction.

Earthquake
As one tectonic plate sinks below another, it causes an earthquake.

Shock wave
Energy spreads out from the site of the earthquake pushing the water up.

Giant waves
As the waves move toward the shore, they become bigger.

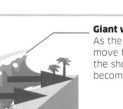

28 *ocean science* ○ **TIDES**

54 ft (16.3 m)—**the widest recorded range between high and low tide**, in the Bay of Fundy in Canada.

Tides

Along shorelines all around the world, the ocean's tides make water levels rise and fall in a daily cycle.

The tides mean that a spot on the shore can be high and dry one moment but submerged under deep water just a few hours later. In most places, there are roughly two high tides and two low tides in every 24-hour day. The cause lies far beyond our planet—the moon and the sun influence Earth's oceans with the strength of their gravity.

Life between the tides

Water levels rise and fall with the tides everywhere in the oceans, but the changing level is noticeable only where water meets land. Here, the rising tide brings a flood, so fish swim where, a few hours earlier, birds were walking over mud. On a typical shoreline, such as this one in eastern Australia, living things—from snails to seaweed—must survive being covered and uncovered by water.

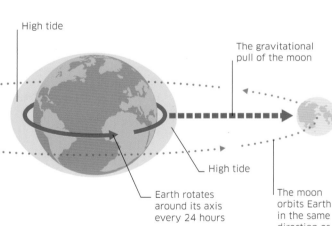

High tide

The gravitational pull of the moon

High tide

Earth rotates around its axis every 24 hours

The moon orbits Earth in the same direction as Earth spins on its axis

The effect of the moon

As Earth spins, different parts of its surface face the moon. The moon's gravity pulls on the ocean closest to it, which bulges outward to create a high tide. On the opposite side of Earth, a centrifugal force caused by Earth's spin pulls water away from the moon, creating a second bulge and a second high tide. There are roughly two tides every 24 hours.

Barnacles
At low tide, many ocean animals, such as the barnacles—small crustaceans related to crabs—that stick to the legs of this jetty, stop feeding and become inactive.

Limpets
Holding fast to the wood, these cone-shaped aquatic snails withdraw into their protective shells at low tide to prevent their soft bodies from drying out.

Australian pelican
Large birds rest on the mudflats between fishing trips.

Australian ibis
Birds use their long beaks to pick up invertebrate food.

Seaweed
These large, leafy marine algae have a slimy coating that helps keep them moist at low tide.

Pied oystercatcher
Wading birds take advantage of low tide by probing the mud for worms to eat.

LOW TIDE

3,000 gigawatts—the energy of tides worldwide, equivalent to **15 percent** of all energy released by **power plants**.

12 hours, 25 minutes—the average **time** between two high tides around the world.

29

Silver gull
Many seabirds swim as well as fly and wade, so they are adapted for wet and dry conditions.

When Earth was first formed more than 4.5 billion years ago, **the moon was closer**, so its pull was stronger and the tides rose higher than they do today.

Barnacles
At high tide, submerged barnacles extend their feathery legs into the water to catch plankton to eat.

Snapper
Rising waters help fish such as snapper range farther in to the shore, where they prey on crabs, shrimp, and smaller fish.

The effect of the sun
The sun is farther away from Earth than the moon but is much bigger, so its gravity has a tidal effect, too. When the orbiting moon aligns with the sun—something that happens twice a month—this makes the tides both higher and lower than usual. When the sun and the moon are at right angles, tides are less extreme.

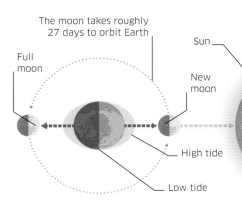

The moon takes roughly 27 days to orbit Earth

Full moon

Sun

New moon

High tide

Low tide

Extreme tides
The biggest tides happen just after every full and new moon, when the sun and the moon line up with Earth, reinforcing each other's gravitational pull. These are called spring tides, from the German word *springen*, meaning "to leap."

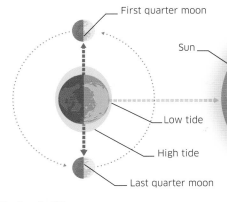

First quarter moon

Sun

Low tide

High tide

Last quarter moon

Moderate tides
The smallest tides happen during first quarter and last quarter moons, when the moon and the sun are at a right angle to Earth, partly canceling out each other's gravitational pull. These are called neap tides, meaning "lowest ebb."

HIGH TIDE

Seaweed
The fronds of seaweed are buoyed by water, exposing them to light and helping them make food by photosynthesis.

Limpets
When underwater, limpets and other ocean snails graze on algae and tiny organisms growing on rocks and wooden piles.

OPEN OCEAN

More than 80 percent of the inhabitable areas of our planet is the open ocean—deeper waters away from the shallow coastal seas. From its sunlit surface to its cold, dark floor, the open ocean is home to some of the most extraordinary animals known to science.

THE OPEN OCEAN

The majority of the ocean's water stretches beyond the coastal seas of the continental shelves and reaches down to the deepest parts of the ocean basins—an area called the open ocean. This is the single biggest habitat on Earth and contains more living things than anywhere else on the planet. But conditions at the surface are very different from those at the bottom.

OCEAN CONDITIONS

The surface of the ocean varies in temperature—from the warm tropics to the cold poles. But everywhere in the world, ocean conditions change dramatically with increasing depth, with temperature, pressure, and levels of light and oxygen all altering. Living things are adapted to live at different depths based on the conditions there.

Light
Sunlight shining on the surface is a vital part of most ocean food chains. But deeper down, light fades gradually until conditions become pitch-black.

Temperature
Heat from sunshine warms the ocean surface. But at depths of around 3,300 ft (1,000 m), little warmth penetrates, making temperatures drop steeply.

Pressure
The deeper you go, the more water there is pushing downward from above, which increases the pressure. At the bottom, there is enough pressure to crush a car.

Oxygen
Oxygen levels peak at the surface, where it is produced by algae, then drop as animals use it in respiration, before rising since there are fewer organisms to use it in deep waters.

DEPTH ZONES

The habitats of the open ocean change with depth. The surface layer—called the sunlit zone—is bright, warm, and has the most oxygen. Most ocean life lives in this layer. Beneath it, the twilight zone—dimmer, cooler, and with the lowest oxygen—extends down to 3,300 ft (1,000 m). The midnight zone is the darkest, coldest habitat, and its inhabitants are adapted to withstand its high pressures. The only deeper parts of the ocean are its deep-sea trenches, which make up the hadal zone.

Sunlit zone
0–660 ft (0–200 m)
This layer contains vast swarms of plankton, including algae that photosynthesize to make food.

Twilight zone
660–3,300 ft (200–1,000 m)
Food-producing algae cannot survive at this level, but the twilight zone still contains ocean animals. These are adapted to navigate in the dim light.

Midnight zone
3,300 ft–seabed (1,000 m–seabed)
This layer is pitch black because no sunlight can reach it and stretches all the way down to the seabed, which can be 9,800–19,700 ft (3,000–6,000 m) deep. Very few animals live here.

Hadal zone
Up to 32,800 ft (10,000 m)
This zone is made up of the ocean trenches that scar the seabed. These parts of the ocean have only rarely been explored by humans, and we know little about the animals that live there.

WHO LIVES WHERE

Life in the open ocean can be grouped according to how it gets around. The plankton (see pp.36–37) drift with the currents. Those that can swim from place to place, against the currents, are called the nekton. The benthos live right on the bottom, creeping or crawling along the seabed. A few animals, called the pleuston, live right at the surface.

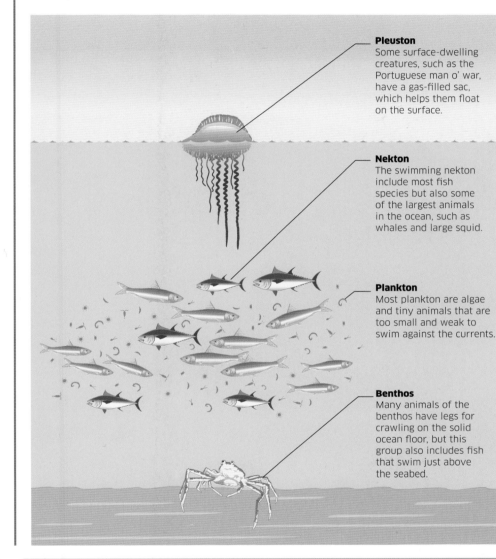

Pleuston
Some surface-dwelling creatures, such as the Portuguese man o' war, have a gas-filled sac, which helps them float on the surface.

Nekton
The swimming nekton include most fish species but also some of the largest animals in the ocean, such as whales and large squid.

Plankton
Most plankton are algae and tiny animals that are too small and weak to swim against the currents.

Benthos
Many animals of the benthos have legs for crawling on the solid ocean floor, but this group also includes fish that swim just above the seabed.

AVOIDING DETECTION

The open ocean can often be a difficult place for an animal to live, because there is nowhere to hide. But many animals have bodies that blend in with the open water. Clever camouflage can allow predators to get close enough to their prey to attack without being seen but also allows vulnerable species to avoid the attention of dangerous hunters.

Silver and blue coloring
Many fish in the open water, such as this mackerel, have silver or blue scales, which help camouflage them against the sunlit ocean near the surface by making their bodies highly reflective.

Countershading
Coloring that is darker above than below is called countershading. When viewed from below, the lighter underside blends in with the sunlit surface. When seen from above, the top side matches the darker deep waters.

Counterillumination
Some animals can produce tiny patches of light on the underside of their bodies. These make them blend in with the sunlit surface when viewed from below.

LIFE ON THE OCEAN FLOOR

The bottom of the ocean is the least explored and least understood habitat on Earth. Most of the animals that live here are scavengers that rely on eating the dead and waste material that sinks down from above. But some features on the ocean floor—such as hydrothermal vents (see pp.64–65) and cold seeps—can also create special conditions for organisms to make their own food.

Hydrothermal vents
Bacteria living around hydrothermal vents grow using energy from minerals and provide nourishment for many food chains.

Cold seeps
At these places on the seabed, methane gas erupts from the ocean floor. Some bacteria can use this to create food.

Dead creatures
The enormous carcasses of dead animals such as whales can attract lots of scavengers hungry for a meal.

Marine snow
Sinking particles of dead and waste matter, called marine snow, settle on the bottom and provide a source of food for scavengers.

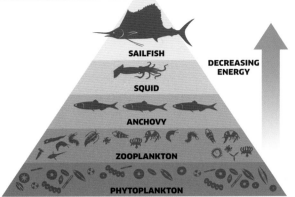

SAILFISH

DECREASING ENERGY

SQUID

ANCHOVY

ZOOPLANKTON

PHYTOPLANKTON

Pyramid of energy
The amount of energy passing through each level of an ocean food chain can be shown as a pyramid. As the animals at each level consume those from the one below, energy is transferred upward through the chain. However, a lot of food energy at each level is lost in waste and heat, leaving less energy to be consumed at the next level, which therefore supports fewer animals.

Fueled at the surface
Ocean food chains start in the sunlit upper layers of the ocean, where algae grow by photosynthesis. These provide the energy that flows up the chain to support other open-ocean life, from microscopic animals to much larger fast-swimming predators.

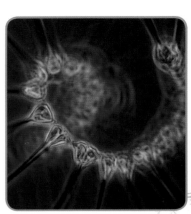

1 Phytoplankton
A bucket of seawater scooped from the surface of the ocean might contain 15 million single-celled algae. These minute organisms, known as phytoplankton, harness the energy from sunlight—they are the primary producers of this food chain.

Scavengers
Most of the deep ocean is too dark for photosynthesis, so the animals that live there rely on food that falls from above. Scavengers, such as this hagfish, feed on the bodies of dead animals that sink to the ocean floor.

Food Chains

All living things in the ocean are connected by food chains. They rely on each other for their food, and energy and nutrients pass from one species to another.

On land, food chains begin with leafy green plants, but in the ocean, microscopic algae, made of just one cell, start this off. There are trillions of them, floating just below the ocean surface, where sunlight can reach them. In a chemical process called photosynthesis, algae use the energy in light to turn carbon dioxide and water into the food they need for growth. The algae then become food for small animals, which in turn are hunted by meat-eating predators.

5 Sailfish
Top predators are the biggest, speediest consumers of all. The sailfish is the fastest fish in the ocean. It uses its long bill to slash and stab squid and fish. Only giant hunters such as orcas will prey on sailfish.

4 Squid
Shoals of anchovies provide food for many predators higher in the food chain. This neon flying squid is an example of a third-level, or tertiary, consumer. It has the speed and agility to catch darting little fish. The squid's huge eyes give it good vision in sunlit waters.

230 ft (70 m)—the width a shoal of European anchovies can stretch.

80 percent of Earth's oxygen is produced by photosynthesizing ocean algae.

68 mph (110 km/h)—the top speed of a sailfish hunting for prey.

35

2 Zooplankton
Mixed in with the phytoplankton are tiny animals called zooplankton, which include shrimp and the larvae of fish and other animals. These are the ocean's primary consumers; they eat the algae that thrive in the sunlight.

3 Anchovies
There is enough plankton to support huge shoals of anchovies. They have special rakers on their gills that trap plankton as water passes over them. Anchovies feed on phytoplankton and zooplankton, making them primary and secondary consumers.

36   open ocean   ○   **A DROP IN THE OCEAN**

100 trillion trillion—the estimated **number** **of cyanobacteria** in the world's oceans.

A Drop in the Ocean

A huge variety of life forms can be found in just a single drop of seawater, from plantlike algae to the ocean's tiniest herbivores and hunters.

These living things make up the plankton—the community of ocean drifters that are carried along with the currents because they are either too small or too weak to swim against them. Plankton exist everywhere in open water but are richest near the surface, where sunlight provides the energy for algae to make food.

Life in a droplet

Plankton are grouped into two main types: both can be seen in this large drop of seawater. Single-celled plantlike cyanobacteria and algae use the energy of sunlight to produce their own food in a process called photosynthesis. They are the phytoplankton. The plankton's animals, or zooplankton, graze on the phytoplankton like herbivores or hunt down other microscopic animals.

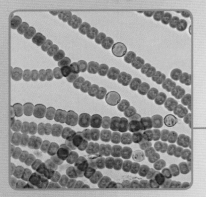

Bacteria
Cyanobacteria are bacteria that carry out photosynthesis. They are the tiniest planktonic organisms— visible only with a powerful microscope. Many kinds link together into long chains.

Copepod
These tiny crustaceans are less than 1/16 in (2 mm) long.

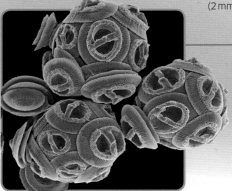

Algae
Sunlit waters may be filled with microscopic single-celled algae of all shapes. These spherical ones are called coccolithophores. They are encased in scales made of chalk.

Arrow worm
This predatory worm with a stiff dart-shaped body has biting jaws for catching other zooplankton.

75 percent of all zooplankton are **copepods**, making them the **most abundant animals in the ocean**.

55 billion tons (50 billion metric tons)—the amount of **carbon dioxide** used by **photosynthesizing phytoplankton** each year.

37

Spirulina
Some kinds of cyanobacteria, called spirulina, form threadlike filaments of cells that twist into tight coils.

Diatom
A type of algae, diatoms are surrounded by a stiff wall made from glasslike silica, which gives them distinct shapes: some are boxlike, others are like seeds or balls.

Crab larva
Many animals that live at the bottom of the ocean as adults, including crabs, spend their early life as tiny larvae swimming in the plankton.

Eggs
The eggs of fish and invertebrates are also plankton. Many of these eggs contain oil droplets that help them float near the surface.

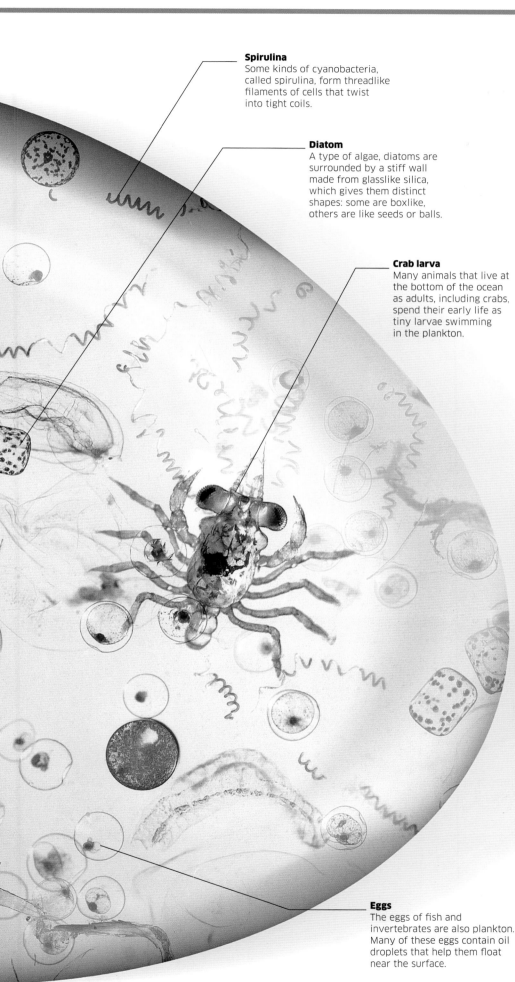

Giant plankton
The ocean sunfish, weighing up to a ton, is one of the biggest bony fish in the ocean. Most fish use their sweeping tails to propel themselves forward, but the ocean sunfish lacks a tail and must rely on weak flapping fins to move instead. So it drifts with the currents, technically making it one of the biggest members of the plankton.

Ancient remains
Foraminifera are single-celled plankton that produce shells made from chalky minerals. When they die, the shells build up on the ocean floor, and over millions of years they form limestone rock. Each kind has a distinctive shape, and studying their remains can tell us much about the age of the rock, past climates, and the environment.

Algal blooms
At certain times, conditions in the ocean can boost the numbers of planktonic algae. Nutrients that run off the land, or are blown out to sea on the wind, can fertilize the coastal waters, causing algae to grow so thickly they form colorful blooms. This aerial picture shows bright green blooms in the Baltic Sea.

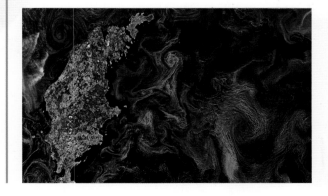

Flying rays

The giant manta ray is part of a group called mobula rays that share many similar behaviors. Sometimes they are seen jumping clear of the water, one after another. Why they do this is not completely understood. Some may breach (or break through) the water as part of a courtship ritual. Others may do it to dislodge parasites and other animals clinging to their skin.

Giant Manta Ray

It is not only small animals that feed on tiny plankton. Some plankton feeders are huge and can take massive mouthfuls, such as the giant manta ray—the biggest ray in the ocean.

Rays are fish with pectoral (shoulder) fins that stretch out like wings. The manta ray swims by flapping these fins slowly up and down, pushing against the water. Unlike most other rays, which mainly feed on the seabed, the manta ray feeds in open waters. As it swims gracefully forward, its wide mouth gapes open, channeling gallons of seawater through its gills, where special filters trap small prey.

Plankton-feeding giant

Twice as wide as it is long, the giant manta ray has a fin-span comparable to the length of a school bus. It cruises the open ocean, especially shallow, nutrient-rich coastal waters, where there are large populations of plankton to eat.

White underside
Contrasting with their dark top, the underside of the ray is pale with a distinct pattern of black patches.

Tail
Some rays have tails that carry sharp stingers, but the manta ray's tail is short and harmless.

Body disc
The flattened body of a ray is called a disc. Firm and muscular, it powers the pectoral fins.

Large fins
The long, triangular fins extend out to a point, giving them a big winglike surface for powering through the water.

Filter feeding

A manta ray is a ram feeder—it swims forward with its mouth open so that a continual stream of food-rich seawater passes into it. The water is strained as it passes through gill slits in the floor of the ray's mouth, trapping small animals. The animals are passed to the back of the ray's mouth and then swallowed.

Eyes
Widely separated on either side of the enormous head, the eyes have a wide range of vision.

Plankton are caught on gill rakers and then passed to the back of the mouth

Seawater enters mouth

Seawater exits through gills

Concentrated stream of plankton travels to the back of the throat

Giant manta rays possess
the largest brain of any ocean fish
and are thought to be very intelligent.

6,600 lb (3,000 kg)—the **record heaviest weight** of a giant manta ray.

39

Gill slits
These slits on the underside of the manta ray are the openings to the gills. Filtered ocean water flows out through the gill slits.

Gill arch
Angled struts, called gill arches, support the gills that sit between them. They are made of rubbery cartilage.

Hornlike fins
Front-facing curved fins help direct a current of plankton-rich seawater into the mouth.

Gills

Water flow

FISH

GIANT MANTA RAY

Mobula birostris

Location: Tropical oceans worldwide

Width: Up to 23 ft (7 m)

Diet: Small fish and planktonic animals

Gill rakers
On top of the manta ray's gills sit rows of comblike gill rakers. When water enters the mouth, it passes easily through them, but any animals are trapped and remain in the mouth. Below the gill rakers, feathery gills filter oxygen from the water.

Purple-striped Jellyfish

Despite lacking a head and a brain, a jellyfish is a deadly predator—able to deliver painful paralyzing stings from its trailing tentacles.

Circular in shape, a jellyfish has no front and back—only a top and bottom. Drifting with the currents, it pulsates its soft umbrella-like bell to propel itself upward, then slowly sinks lower when it relaxes. Beneath the bell is its mouth, which swallows any prey stunned motionless by the tentacles. Purple-striped jellyfish begin as tiny specks on the seabed, which then float into open water where they spend their entire lives.

Jellyfish life cycle

Male and female purple-striped jellyfish release their sperm and eggs into the water, where they come together to form fertilized eggs. These grow into microscopic larvae that settle on the seabed, where each develops into a tiny animal called a polyp. It can stay in this early stage of its life cycle for some time before its tip splits apart to release not just one but many new little jellyfish into the ocean waters.

5 Mature jellyfish
Out in the open ocean, the young jellyfish grows fast, nourished by plankton caught with its trailing tentacles. It increases dramatically in size, and as it gets older, the purple stripes on its bell get darker and bolder.

4 Ephyra
Each baby jellyfish that splits away from the mature polyp is called an ephyra. It is only ⅛ in (3 mm) across but can already use its bell to swim and tentacles to catch prey.

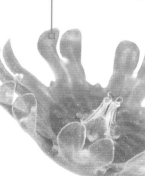

1 Larva
The flat oval larva that grows from a fertilized egg is barely 1/32 in (1 mm). It is covered in microscopic hairs that beat to help it swim as part of the clouds of ocean plankton.

2 Polyp forms
When the larva lands on the seabed or a rocky outcrop, it grows into a polyp and sprouts short, upward-facing tentacles to snatch food from the water above it.

3 Strobila
When the polyp has grown to its maximum height, it is called a strobila. It divides into a stack of small discs. Each disc will eventually pulsate off the end of the stack to become a new jellyfish.

Tentacles

Fixed foundation
The polyp is attached to the seabed.

Tiny budding jellyfish

Tiny tower
The full-grown polyp, or strobila, is no more than 3/16 in (5 mm) tall.

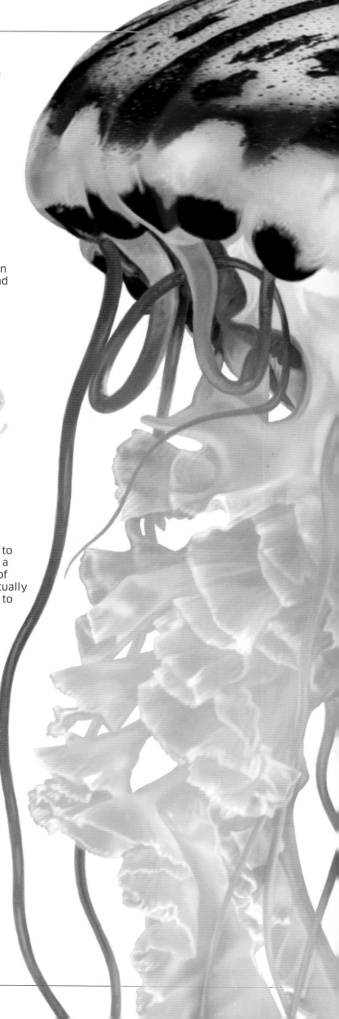

3 years–the **maximum life span of a purple-striped jellyfish.**

One species of jellyfish–**Turritopsis dohrnii–can revert back to its polyp stage** when it becomes sick or old and is known as the **immortal jellyfish**.

41

Broad bell
The large bell propels the jellyfish around by drawing water in and squeezing it out.

Frilly arms
Four fleshy oral arms hang down from beneath the bell. They encircle the mouth and help transfer prey into the stomach in the center of the bell.

Mouth
Hidden beneath the bell, the mouth of the jellyfish is where food enters and waste is expelled.

Purple markings
Distinctive dark purple-lined patterns mark the clear bell of a full-grown purple-striped jellyfish. Younger jellyfish are more pinkish in color.

CNIDARIAN
PURPLE-STRIPED JELLYFISH

Chrysaora colorata

Location: Northeastern Pacific Ocean

Width: Up to 19¾ in (50 cm) across bell

Diet: Tiny planktonic animals

Stinging tentacles
Eight tentacles hang down from the rim of the bell, carrying stinging cells called nematocysts.

Bag
A gas-filled bag floating on the sea supports the colony of tiny animals below it.

PORTUGUESE MAN O' WAR
Physalia physalis
Location: Warm oceans worldwide
Tentacle length: Up to 98 ft (30 m)

This animal looks like a jellyfish but is really a floating colony of small soft-bodied animals that hang down from a gas-filled bag. These all work together: some use stinging tentacles to kill prey, while others have mouths for eating.

Pointy body
The body is packed with transparent jelly.

ROCKET HYDROZOAN
Pandea conica
Location: Tropical Atlantic, Mediterranean
Bell length: Up to 1¼ in (3 cm)

This small, carrot-shaped relative of jellyfish lives in warm seas. Like jellyfish, it swims by pulsating its umbrella-like bell up and down, while trailing stinging tentacles to trap tiny plankton.

IRIDESCENT COMB JELLY
Beroe ovata
Location: Atlantic, Mediterranean
Length: Up to 6¼ in (16 cm)

Comb jellies look like jellyfish but are not closely related to them. Instead of using muscles to swim, they propel themselves by beating microscopic hairs called cilia. They trap their planktonic prey with sticky cells.

FRIED EGG JELLYFISH
Phacellophora camtschatica
Location: Cool waters worldwide
Length: Tentacles up to 19⅔ ft (6 m)

This jellyfish is named for its yellow yolklike body. Its stinging cells catch small animals but are not very strong. This makes it safe for other animals, such as crabs, to hitch a ride and share the catch.

BLUE DRAGON SEA SLUG
Glaucus atlanticus
Location: Warm waters worldwide
Length: Up to 1¼ in (3 cm)

Most sea slugs crawl around on the seabed, but this one spends its life near the surface. It preys on the Portuguese man o' war, feeding on its tentacles and stealing the creature's stinging cells to use as its own defense against predators.

Ocean drifter
The blue dragon floats upside down, propelled by currents.

GLASS OCTOPUS
Vitreledonella richardi
Location: Deep oceans worldwide
Length: Up to 17¾ in (45 cm)

Many open-ocean soft-bodied animals like this small octopus have transparent and almost colorless body parts. This makes them harder for bigger predators to spot.

440 lb (200 kg)—**the weight of Nomura's jellyfish** of the Pacific Ocean, **one of the biggest jellies** in the world.

43

Buoyancy bag

GIANT SIPHONOPHORE
Praya dubia
Location: Worldwide
Length: Up to 164 ft (50 m)

Glowing blue
Each creature in the siphonophore can produce bioluminescent light.

Snaking through the oceans as a glowing chain, the giant siphonophore is a colony of tiny animals. It can grow longer than a blue whale, making it one of the longest creatures in the ocean. It lives close to the surface, adjusting the gas levels in its buoyancy bag to control its depth.

Glowing "bomb"

GREEN BOMBER WORM
Swima bombiviridis
Location: Pacific Ocean
Length: Up to 1¼ in (3 cm)

This colorful sea worm has feathery gills that glow with a greenish light in the darkness of the deep ocean. If a predator threatens, the worm distracts it by detaching tiny parts from its gills and dropping them like glowing "bombs."

Soft-bodied Animals

Many ocean animals have soft, flabby bodies that would be impossible to move around out of the water but are perfectly adapted for life beneath the waves.

A huge variety of sea animals have similar lightweight, squishy bodies, including jellyfish, comb jellies, and many other kinds of ocean animals. Instead of being supported by hard body parts such as bones, these invertebrates—creatures without a backbone—are supported by the water around them. Their bodies are jellylike because their tissues are full of water, which can move and flow but cannot be compressed. This means they keep their shape even under the high pressures of the deep ocean.

CHAIN SALP
Pegea confoederata
Location: Worldwide
Length: Chain up to 5⅛ in (13 cm)

Salps are a type of sea squirt, most of which are seabed animals with fleshy, baglike bodies. However, salps live in open seas, jet-propelling themselves along by squirting water and gathering together in long chainlike colonies that drift with the currents.

GIANT FIRE PYROSOME
Pyrostremma spinosum
Location: Worldwide
Length: Up to 98 ft (30 m)

Like some other soft-bodied creatures, pyrosomes are not just one animal but huge tube-shaped colonies of lots of tiny animals. Fire pyrosomes are bioluminescent: they produce a bright glowing light.

PINK SWIMMING SEA CUCUMBER
Enypniastes eximia
Location: Deep oceans worldwide
Length: Up to 8 in (20 cm)

Sea cucumbers are usually sausage-shaped animals that live on the seabed, but this one has a frilly web that it flaps to propel itself up into the water. Because of its unusual appearance, it has been nicknamed the "headless chicken monster."

Box Jellyfish

In the shallow seas off South Africa, a group of box jellyfish swim in the sunlit waters just above the seabed.

Unusual for jellyfish, box jellyfish have complex eyes that attract them to light and even help them navigate around obstacles. Despite their flimsy appearance, these are formidable predators, and the stingers on their tentacles are thought to be more potent than cobra venom. They paralyze fish—their natural prey—but can be dangerous to humans, too, causing severe pain and sometimes heart failure.

Great Barracuda

A barracuda is a fast-swimming ocean hunter. Slender and powerful, it has huge jutting jaws and fanglike teeth. The great barracuda is the biggest species of this family of fearsome predatory fish.

A great barracuda usually seeks prey alone, just below the ocean surface, but sometimes it hunts in small groups. Its sharp teeth, which are strongly rooted in the bone of its jaw, deliver a powerful bite. The fish's streamlined shape enables it to cut through the water like a torpedo, but it is not flexible enough to make sharp turns. So the great barracuda relies on taking prey by surprise rather than chasing it for long distances. It selects a target, gets close, and then shoots forward with a sudden burst of speed.

Dorsal fins
Upright dorsal fins—one at the front and one further back—help stop the fish from rolling from side to side.

Eyes for hunting
Large eyes gather lots of light so the fish can spot prey underwater.

Pectoral fins
The pectoral fins control the fish's position in the water and help it steer.

Pelvic fins
These fins work with the pectoral fins to keep the fish horizontal in the water.

Two rows of teeth
An extra set of smaller razorlike teeth surround the inner daggers, to help slice through flesh.

Stacks of gill filaments

Water flows into mouth

Blood-filled gills absorb oxygen

Pointed jaws
The lower jaw juts further forward than the upper jaw, so the fish can grip heavy prey.

Blood-filled gills
Like other fish, a barracuda breathes through thin, blood-filled filaments called gills. Water entering its mouth supplies oxygen to the blood in the gills before carrying carbon dioxide waste—produced by muscles and organs—away through gill slits in the sides of the fish's head.

36 mph (58 km/h)—the estimated **top speed** of a great barracuda.

110 lb (50 kg)—the **maximum** recorded **weight** of a great barracuda.

47

Rear dorsal fin

Streamlined shape
The fish's body gets narrower toward the back, making it streamlined in the water.

Caudal fin
As the rear of the body waves from side to side, the tail fin pushes against the water, moving the fish forward.

Scaly skin
Tough, overlapping scales cover the skin of the fish.

Anal fin
This single fin works with the dorsal fins to stop the fish from rolling sideways.

Toothy killer

The great barracuda is a bony fish—it has a skeleton made mostly of bone (as opposed to cartilage). It spends much of its life in the open ocean. Young barracudas grow up in the shelter of coastal estuaries, mangroves, and reefs. As they get older and bigger, they venture further out to sea. Here, they have to cope with stronger currents—but can find large prey to satisfy their appetites.

FISH
GREAT BARRACUDA

Sphyraena barracuda

Location: Tropical and subtropical oceans

Length: Up to 6½ ft (2 m)

Diet: Fish, squid, octopus, and shrimp

Swimming movements

Many fish swim by moving their bodies in an S-shape, similar to the way in which snakes move by twisting from side to side. Fish such as eels swim this way using their whole bodies. However, the fastest swimmers, including barracudas, concentrate movements toward the rear of their bodies. While the tail flicks back and forth, the front of the body is held straight, so the fish can cut through the water quickly.

Swim bladder

Like most bony fish, barracudas have a gas-filled swim bladder to help them stay level in the water. When the fish swims downward, the higher water pressure shrinks the gas bladder. Gas from the blood is then added to the bladder to keep it expanded so the fish stays buoyant. When the fish swims up, lower pressure makes the bladder expand, so some gas moves out of it into the blood.

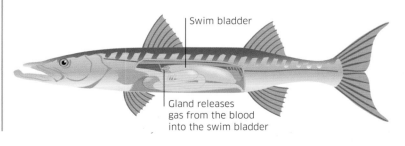

Swim bladder

Gland releases gas from the blood into the swim bladder

48 open ocean ○ **FISH OF THE OPEN OCEAN**

4 billion—the estimated **number of fish** in the **largest-recorded school of Atlantic herring**.

ATLANTIC FLYING FISH
Cheilopogon melanurus
Location: Tropical Atlantic Ocean
Length: Up to 12⅝in (32cm)

Flying fish escape ocean predators by leaving the water altogether. By rapidly flicking their tail, they generate enough thrust to launch themselves into the air and then are able to glide long distances—around 164ft (50m)—by using their fins as wings.

Fish of the Open Ocean

Far away from the shelter of rocks or reefs, fish in the open ocean live in an exposed environment. Although fewer species of fish live here than near the shore, this blue expanse is the single biggest habitat on Earth.

To survive, open-ocean fish must be big or fast, or have some other tactic to keep danger at bay. As a result, the wide expanse of the ocean is home to some of the fastest swimmers on the planet, who use speed to catch prey or to avoid being eaten. Other fish are protected by their camouflaged coloring—either blue to blend in with the ocean, or darker on the upper side and lighter underneath in order to match both the bright sky and the dark of deep waters.

Flying fins
Wide shoulder fins extend to act like wings, helping the flying fish to glide through the air.

Motorlike tail
The tail can be dipped back into the water and flicked again to provide an extra acceleration boost when the fish is being chased.

SEA LAMPREY
Petromyzon marinus
Location: North Atlantic Ocean
Length: Up to 4ft (1.2m)

The terrifying-looking lamprey is a jawless fish. It spends its early life as a filter-feeding larva in freshwater rivers, before migrating out to sea when it grows older. Here, it uses its suckerlike mouth to clamp onto other fish and feed on their blood.

Sharp teeth
The lamprey's mouth carries rings of sharp horny teeth for cutting into the flesh of its victim.

AUSTRALIAN GHOSTSHARK
Callorhinchus milii
Location: Southwestern Pacific Ocean
Length: Up to 4¼ft (1.3m)

Like related sharks and rays, ghostsharks have a skeleton made from rubbery cartilage, rather than hard bone. The Australian ghostshark uses its unique-shaped snout to search the ocean bottom for food. Then it crushes its prey with the hard grinding plates it has instead of teeth.

BLUE SKATE
Dipturus batis
Location: Northwest Atlantic Ocean
Length: Up to 4⅔ft (1.4m)

Like other skates, the blue skate has broad shoulder fins that stretch from head to tail. It flaps these like wings to move through the water but also spends a lot of time resting on the bottom of the ocean.

Brown coloring
The skate's dark brown back helps conceal it when it settles on the ocean floor.

62 ft (18.8m)—the **length of a whale shark,** the **biggest fish** of the open ocean.

300 million—the number of **eggs released by an ocean sunfish,** the **largest number** produced by any open-ocean fish.

49

WEST INDIAN OCEAN COELACANTH
Latimeria chalumnae
Location: Western Indian Ocean
Length: Up to 6½ ft (2 m)

This strange fish with thick fleshy fins is a living relative of ancient prehistoric fish, whose fins later evolved into limbs to allow them to walk on land. The modern-day coelacanth sticks to deep waters, where it lives among caves and rocky overhangs at the base of tropical islands.

GIANT OARFISH
Regalecus glesne
Location: Oceans worldwide
Length: Up to 26¼ ft (8 m)

The giant oarfish is the longest bony fish (fish that have a skeleton of hard bone) in the ocean. It has a ribbon-shaped body that can wind through the water like a snake—possibly inspiring stories of mythical sea serpents—but is rarely seen.

COMMON DOLPHINFISH
Coryphaena hippurus
Location: Tropical oceans worldwide
Length: Up to 7 ft (2.1 m)

Named for its broad dolphinlike head, this fast-swimming open-ocean fish swims in schools near the surface, where it preys on other fish and plankton. Sunshine illuminates its spectacular gold and blue coloring.

SLENDER SHARKSUCKER
Echeneis naucrates
Location: Tropical waters worldwide
Length: Up to 3⅔ ft (1.1 m)

The dorsal fin of the sharksucker is modified to work like a long sucker. It can grip to the underside of larger fish, such as sharks, and even the occasional whale or ship—allowing the fish to hitchhike from place to place.

Sucking disc

MAN O' WAR FISH
Nomeus gronovii
Location: Tropical eastern Atlantic Ocean, Indian and Pacific oceans
Length: Up to 4¼ ft (1.3 m)

This fish spends its life living among the stinging tentacles of the Portuguese man o' war—a relative of jellyfish that floats on the ocean surface. It eats the tentacles and has sting-resistant skin to protect it as it swims through them.

Blue skin
The fish's coloring helps hide it among the blue tentacles of a Portuguese man o' war.

YELLOWFIN TUNA
Thunnus albacares
Location: Tropical oceans worldwide
Length: Up to 5 ft (1.5 m)

One of the fastest fish in the ocean, the tuna uses a combination of powerful muscles and a streamlined body to cut through the water and hunt down smaller fish. This species can reach speeds of 47 mph (75 km/h).

OPAH
Lampris guttatus
Location: Oceans worldwide
Length: Up to 6½ ft (2 m)

The huge disc-shaped opah feeds on squid, octopus, and shrimp. Unlike most fish, it can keep its body temperature slightly warmer than its surroundings, helping it swim faster when hunting down prey.

Colorful fins
The fins are usually a bright red color.

ATLANTIC HERRING
Clupea harengus
Location: North Atlantic Ocean
Length: Up to 17¾ in (45 cm)

Shimmering scales
A silvery body helps make this fish hard to see.

As a herring swims through the ocean, special structures in its gills strain tiny plankton from the water into its mouth. This species lives in huge schools, which helps reduce the chance of any individual being picked off by predators.

Sweeping tail
The tail flicks rapidly back and forth to give the tuna speed.

50   open ocean • **SHORT-BEAKED COMMON DOLPHIN**

30 The **number of years** the average short-beaked common dolphin lives.

Powerful tail
The wide horizontal tail fluke flaps up and down to propel the dolphin forward in the water.

Folded fin
The baby's dorsal fin is initially bent from its time in the womb but will soon stand upright.

MAMMAL

SHORT-BEAKED COMMON DOLPHIN

Delphinus delphis

Location: Atlantic, Pacific, Indian, Mediterranean

Length: Up to 7½ft (2.3m)

Diet: Small fish

Breathing air

Dolphins must supply their lungs with air, but they do not have nostrils that connect to the back of the throat like humans do. Instead, their windpipe connects directly to an opening—the blowhole—at the top of the head. The blowhole opens to let in air when they surface and closes when they dive.

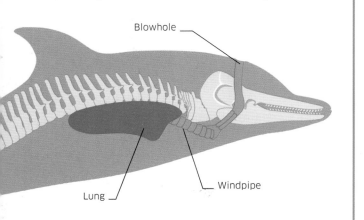

Blowhole

Lung

Windpipe

Birth creases
Newborn dolphins have creases in the skin and blubber from when the baby was curled up inside the womb. They disappear soon after birth.

Communication

Dolphins are social creatures, living together in groups called pods. They use a series of whistles and clicks to communicate with each another. Dolphins can identify one another from patterns of sounds and whistle more when excited or stressed.

Short-beaked Common Dolphin

A life in the ocean poses special challenges for an air-breathing mammal—especially for a dolphin that hunts, socializes, and even gives birth there.

The short-beaked common dolphin lives in open water, where nutrients rise upward to support shoals of tasty fish prey. Groups of this highly intelligent species come together so sometimes thousands of dolphins ride the waves, often leaping into the air. Like other mammals, dolphins breathe air and give birth to live young. After a pregnancy lasting nearly a year, females deliver their calves, sometimes with the help of other members of their social group.

First breath

A newborn dolphin can swim as soon as it breaks free of the umbilical cord that binds it to its mother. Its priority is to reach the surface and take a gasp of air through its blowhole. Its mother—or even another adult female—helps the newborn rise upward, gently nudging it with her beak.

Paler side
Adult common dolphins have a sandy-colored patch on the side of their body.

36 in (90 cm)—the **length of a newborn** short-beaked common dolphin.

10,000 The largest **number of short-beaked common dolphins recorded in a gathering**.

853 ft (260 m)—the **deepest dive** of a short-beaked common dolphin.

51

Breathing apparatus
The blowhole in the top of the head opens to suck in air whenever the dolphin surfaces.

Slippery skin
A dolphin has completely hairless skin so that it can slide seamlessly through the water.

A dolphin baby can suckle its mother's milk for
three years
or sometimes even longer.

Pointed beak
More than 250 small pointed teeth fill the mouth, or beak—perfect for grabbing fish.

Balancing fin
The dorsal fin helps stop the dolphin from rolling sideways in the water.

Shortened arm bones

Modified finger bones

Flipper bones
A dolphin's skeleton reveals how it is distantly related to humans. Its flippers are made up of recognizable arm and hand bones—modified by evolution into a paddlelike shape for swimming.

Cetaceans

The biggest, fastest, and most intelligent marine animals are a group of mammals called cetaceans. They include whales, dolphins, and porpoises, and most species live in the open ocean.

Like all mammals, cetaceans breathe air and nourish their babies with milk. Evolving from four-legged land animals, they developed flippers instead of feet, smooth skins for easy swimming, and a horizontal tail fluke to flap up and down for propulsion. Most have teeth and eat fish, but the largest whales have filters in their mouths called baleen plates, which trap microscopic food from the water.

HOURGLASS DOLPHIN
Lagenorhynchus cruciger
Location: Southern Ocean
Length: Up to 6¼ ft (1.9 m)

Swimming in the cold waters around Antarctica, this ocean acrobat surfs the waves, jumping and spinning in the air. Hourglass dolphins usually travel in groups of a dozen individuals and often follow ships, keeping in their wake for up to half an hour.

Flippers
These help control body position and assist with slowing down when swimming.

Spongy tool
The sponge protects the beak as the dolphin digs for food on the seabed.

Male fin shape

COMMON BOTTLENOSE DOLPHIN
Tursiops truncatus
Location: Tropical and temperate oceans
Length: Up to 12½ ft (3.8 m)

One of the best known of all cetaceans, the common bottlenose dolphin is intelligent and sociable. In Australia, females have learned to use a sponge to dig up prey from the seabed–a skill they pass on to their daughters.

SPECTACLED PORPOISE
Phocoena dioptrica
Location: South Atlantic, Indian, and Pacific oceans
Length: Up to 7¼ ft (2.2 m)

Despite its striking body pattern, this secretive, cold-water-loving cetacean is seldom seen because it rarely leaps above the surface. Females have a pointed dorsal (back) fin, while in males this is large and oval-shaped.

DALL'S PORPOISE
Phocoenoides dalli
Location: Northern Pacific
Length: Up to 8 ft (2.4 m)

This restless porpoise could be the fastest cetacean of all. At times, it reaches a speed of 34 mph (55 km/h) in quick bursts. Dall's porpoise rarely jumps from the water but can be recognized by the conspicuous V-shaped spray it sends from its blowhole as it surfaces.

490 The number of North Atlantic right whales, one of the **most endangered whale species**.

9,816 ft (2,992 m)—the **deepest dive** of any cetacean, achieved by a **Cuvier's beaked whale**.

53

LONG-FINNED PILOT WHALE
Globicephala melas
Location: Atlantic, southern Indian, and southern Pacific oceans
Length: Up to 22 ft (6.7 m)

A type of giant dolphin, this cetacean hunts at night for deep-water squid, sometimes diving down to more than 3,300 ft (1,000 m). At sunrise, pilot whales often gather in groups nearer the surface to socialize while resting.

Large domed head

Long flippers bend backward with a distinct "elbow"

CUVIER'S BEAKED WHALE
Ziphius cavirostris
Location: Tropical and temperate oceans
Length: Up to 23 ft (7 m)

Beaked whales lack baleen plates and have very few teeth. The males of this species have a single pair at the tip of their lower jaw, which protrude as mini-tusks. In females, teeth are not visible. Both sexes feed by sucking squid into their mouths.

NORTH ATLANTIC RIGHT WHALE
Eubalaena glacialis
Location: Northern Atlantic
Length: Up to 54 ft (16.5 m)

Swimming through swarms of plankton, mouth open, this whale traps its prey with its baleen plates. Closing the mouth to flush out water, it then swallows its meal. The whale usually moves slowly, resting near the surface for long periods.

PYGMY RIGHT WHALE
Caperea marginata
Location: Southern Atlantic, Indian, and Pacific oceans
Length: Up to 21⅓ ft (6.5 m)

This is the smallest of the toothless baleen whales. Though rarely seen, pygmy right whales may gather in numbers in the nutrient-rich waters over continental shelves and seamounts.

BELUGA
Delphinapterus leucas
Location: Arctic Ocean
Length: Up to 15 ft (4.5 m)

The white-skinned beluga has been nicknamed the "canary of the sea" because it produces one of the widest range of sounds of any ocean mammal. It uses more than 50 calls—including whistles, squeaks, and clicks.

Skin is gray colored in first year but turns whiter with age

PYGMY SPERM WHALE
Kogia breviceps
Location: Tropical and temperate oceans
Length: Up to 13¾ ft (4.2 m)

Like its better-known giant cousin, this small, toothed whale dives deep for squid prey. It may also hunt nearer the surface at night. Its pointed nose, underslung lower jaw, and long backward-pointing teeth make it look similar to a shark, which may help deter bigger predators.

HUMPBACK WHALE
Megaptera novaeangliae
Location: Worldwide
Length: Up to 55¾ ft (17 m)

One of the most widespread cetaceans, this baleen whale migrates long distances between its cold-water feeding grounds around the poles and its breeding waters closer to the equator. One family group was tracked for more than 5,160 miles (8,300 km) from Costa Rica in Central America to Antarctica.

Fishing for squid
Unusually for birds, albatrosses have a keen sense of smell—something they use to track shoals of squid or fish. Most prey is caught at the surface, but sometimes the bird must make a shallow plunge into the water to snatch it. Albatrosses also follow whales or fishing ships to pick up any leftovers.

Long, narrow wings
The vast wings use a lot of energy to flap, so the albatross avoids this when it can and relies on soaring to stay aloft.

Wandering Albatross

There are not many birds that spend as much time at sea as a wandering albatross. For months at a time, it soars over the waves—visiting land only to breed.

With a wingspan the length of a small car—one of the biggest of any bird—the albatross is perfectly equipped for riding the air currents. It rises and falls as it glides, swooping between giant ocean waves. Using this technique, it can cover long distances without ever flapping its wings, often traveling 600 miles (1,000 km) in a single day.

Snowy plumage
A full-grown albatross's feathers are a brilliant white. Juveniles are dark brown with a white face but become white as the bird matures.

Hooked bill
A large, strong bill is needed for grabbing slippery squid and fish. The tubular nostrils point forward to help pick up the scent.

Nostrils
Albatrosses and other ocean birds consume a lot of sea salt along with their prey. To prevent this from building up in their bodies, special glands in the head filter the excess salt from the bird's blood so that it can be expelled through their nostrils.

Giant warty squid
A favorite prey species of the albatross, this squid can grow to 3¼ ft (1 m) in length, but the bird targets smaller individuals.

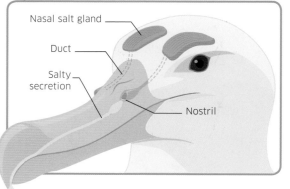

Nasal salt gland

Duct

Salty secretion

Nostril

34 mph (55 km/h)—the **top soaring speed** of a wandering albatross.

55

Black-tipped wings
Adult male albatrosses have dark areas on their wings and tail. Females have these patches, too, but also have more brown on the rest of their bodies.

Massive wingspan
When both wings are fully extended, the bird's wingspan can stretch up to 11½ ft (3.5 m) wide.

BIRD

WANDERING ALBATROSS

Diomedea exulans

Location: Southern Ocean

Body length: Up to 4½ ft (1.35 m)

Diet: Mainly squid, cuttlefish, and icefish

Soaring over the ocean

Lots of birds save energy by gliding—staying in the air without flapping their wings. Gliders eventually lose height, but albatrosses and some other birds can use the winds to prevent this from happening, or even to rise higher. This is called soaring flight. As albatrosses fly over the ocean, they face into the wind, which helps them gain height. Once they reach a certain height, they turn and glide downward with the wind, before repeating the action over again.

Short legs
The legs of an albatross are strong enough to support the weight of this big bird on land, but their short length makes the bird sway from side to side as it walks.

The wandering albatross
mates for life,
flying across the ocean to breed with the same bird every two years.

Wind direction

3. Rising back up
As wind blows over the albatross's wings once more, it provides the bird with lift, helping it rise to 50 ft (15 m) above the ocean.

1. Gaining height
Flying close to the ocean surface, the albatross turns into the path of the wind, which pushes it upward.

2. Drifting down
When the bird turns away from the wind, it drifts downward. Before it reaches the ocean surface, it turns to catch the wind again.

Webbed feet
When settled on the ocean surface, the albatross kicks back with its webbed feet, which push through the water to propel it forward.

Sargasso Sea

In the North Atlantic Ocean, 620 miles (1,000 km) from the coast of the United States, is a vast patch of ocean called the Sargasso Sea, where the waters are strangely calm.

The Sargasso Sea is at the peaceful center of a swirl of currents called a gyre. This sea within an ocean—the size of the Caribbean—is bordered by choppy waves instead of land. Much of it is covered with a floating seaweed called sargassum, which provides shelter, food, or even breeding grounds for many ocean animals—from fish and baby turtles to humpback whales and seabirds.

58 open ocean ○ **TWILIGHT ZONE**

1 percent of **sunlight reaches the top of the twilight zone,** 660 ft (200 m) below the surface.

Mighty movements
A flick of the viperfish's long tapering body propels it forward so it can quickly grab prey in the dim light.

Luring prey
A long ray stretching from the dorsal (back) fin of a viperfish ends in a luminous lure to attract prey.

Twilight Zone

At a certain depth in the ocean, it gets too dark for algae to grow, but if the water is clear, just enough light reaches down for animals to see.

This is the twilight zone, a huge area that reaches from about 660 ft (200 m) to 3,300 ft (1,000 m) deep. Without algae to make nutrients by photosynthesis, animals rely on food that comes down from above. Many of the creatures that live here have special adaptations that allow them to thrive in this low-light environment.

Viperfish
This lethal fish uses a luminescent (light-emitting) lure to draw in unsuspecting prey. But predators hunting in the gloom need to be sure that any prey caught can't escape. When the viperfish closes its wide jaws around a target, its long fangs trap the prey in its mouth like a cage, so it cannot reverse.

Gaping jaw
The viperfish can open its jaws more than 120 degrees, helping it swallow prey more than half of its body length.

Terrifying teeth
The fangike teeth of the viperfish are the longest in proportion to body size of any fish. They sit outside the fish's mouth when closed and reach up to its eyes.

Using bioluminescence
When living things generate light, this is called bioluminescence. The light is produced by a chemical reaction that is often controlled by bacteria that live in the animal's skin or in special capsules, such as the lure of an anglerfish. Some animals use light to signal to their own kind, but many also use it when they hunt for prey or to defend themselves from predators.

ATTACK

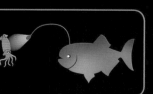

Lure
The light-producing reaction of some deep-sea fish is contained in a special bulb that acts as a lure to attract prey.

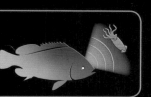

Shock
A flash of bright light in the gloomy twilight zone can stun prey, leaving it confused and more vulnerable to attack.

DEFENSE

Smoke screen
Some animals release a cloud of light-producing chemicals, which conceals them as they escape from predators.

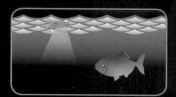

Counterillumination
By concentrating the glowing light along their underside, animals can obscure their shadow so they are harder to see.

Barreleye fish

The eyes of many twilight zone animals are big to collect the light. The barreleye fish has large tubular eyes that can move upward, but it also has a transparent head so even more light reaches the extra sensitive cells on the retina at the back of its eyes.

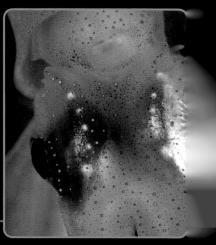

Illuminating organs
Light production in the skin of bioluminescent animals is concentrated in spotlike organs called photophores. The photophores are under the control of the nervous system, which flashes them on and off.

Letting in light
The skin of the barreleye fish and the top of its skull are made of transparent tissue.

Movable eyes
The eyes can point forward or upward to look for prey or predators.

Flashing camouflage
Sometimes the squid will flash brighter underneath to conceal itself from bigger predators below that look upward into the sunlight.

Blue luminescence
Each photophore shines with a blue light. Unlike many animals, which rely on bacteria to produce this light, the firefly squid produces the light inside its own cells.

Firefly squid

Some animals make their own light using special organs in their skin called photophores. The firefly squid can flash its lights on and off, which sends a visual signal to attract prey or a potential mate.

Giants of the Deep

The world's biggest toothed predator is a giant whale that plunges far down into the depths of the ocean to hunt for squid that can grow to the length of a bus.

By holding its breath for an hour or more, a sperm whale descends into the darkness. When vision becomes impossible, it starts using sound to home in on prey, sometimes coming across a formidable target: the colossal squid. This massive mollusk is the biggest animal without a backbone and fights back with tentacles armed with vicious hooks and suckers.

MAMMAL

SPERM WHALE

Physeter macrocephalus

Location: Oceans worldwide

Length: Up to 63 ft (19.2 m)

Diet: Mainly squid, sometimes fish

Muscle layers   Spermaceti organ

Junk

Lower jaw

Sound generator
The whale's nose carries parts that help it both communicate with other whales and detect prey by echolocation (see pp.148–149). In the spermaceti organ, clicking sounds the whale produces are bounced around, and the junk then focuses them as a beam out into the ocean.

Bulky snout
The gigantic nose makes up about a third of the animal's entire length.

Battle scars
Long marks on the head of the whale come from clashes with other territorial males in the deep ocean.

Skin scratches
Circular scars and tears may be left by the suckers and hooks of the colossal squid.

Sperm whale
Many whales use their huge mouths to strain small animals from the water, but sperm whales have a massive toothy bite instead. Squid are their favorite prey—they catch more than 30 in a single dive and around 750 each day. Males—which are bigger than females—catch the bigger species, such as this colossal squid.

Powerful tail
The sperm whale lifts its tough triangular tail fluke high into the air before making a dive.

Tiny eyes
Small eyes on the side of the head are set so far back that the whale cannot see directly ahead of its huge nose.

Deadly hooks
One pair of long tentacles is tipped with clubs armed with swiveling hooks.

Attacking arms
Four pairs of arms inflict damage using suckers and hooks but are shorter than the two long tentacles.

Colossal squid

Living in the perpetual darkness of the deep ocean and snatching up fish with its long tentacles, the colossal squid is a fearsome predator. But this giant cephalopod is elusive and rarely seen. Much of what we know about it comes from the hard remains found in the stomachs of sperm whales.

Sharp beak
The hard beak can effortlessly bite through the flesh of prey.

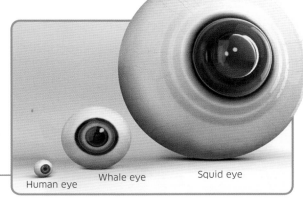

Human eye　　　Whale eye　　　Squid eye

Squid eye
Each of the colossal squid's eyes is about the size of a soccer ball—the biggest eyes of any animal. They contain special glowing organs that act like flashlights to scan the water for fish.

Cone-shaped teeth
The whale's narrow lower jaw carries up to 26 pairs of conical teeth. There are no properly developed teeth in the wider upper jaw.

MOLLUSK
COLOSSAL SQUID

Mesonychoteuthis hamiltoni

Location: Southern Ocean

Length: Up to 29½ ft (9 m)

Diet: Fish and smaller squid

Midnight Zone

Sunlight cannot penetrate more than half a mile below the surface of the ocean, so it is as dark as midnight at the greatest sea depths. In this alien world live some of the strangest ocean animals of all.

Life is a challenge in the deep. Water pressure near the seabed is high enough to crush a car, and temperatures can plummet to near freezing. In this cold, black habitat, food can be scarce, so animals make the most of what they can find and may go for long periods without eating.

GULPER EEL

Eurypharynx pelecanoides
Location: Deep oceans worldwide
Length: Up to 29½ in (75 cm)

The gulper eel swims with its huge, hinged mouth wide open in order to trap lots of small animals at once. It releases excess water through gill slits on the sides of its head.

Flexible jaw
The loose hinge of the jaw allows it to open very wide to trap as many small animals as possible.

Expandable stomach
Stretchy skin and stomach lining help the digestive cavity to consume prey twice its length.

Jagged teeth
Sharp, backward-pointing teeth ensure that prey cannot escape when the mouth is closed.

BLACK SWALLOWER

Chiasmodon niger
Location: North Atlantic
Length: Up to 13 in (33 cm)

Living up to its name, this slender fish has a stomach that can expand dramatically to accommodate fish prey much bigger than the swallower itself.

GIANT ISOPOD

Bathynomus giganteus
Location: W. Atlantic and Caribbean
Length: Up to 19¾ in (50 cm)

The giant isopod is a relative of the wood louse but the size of a small dog. Despite its fierce appearance, it is a harmless scavenger that grubs around on the ocean floor to look for food.

BEARDED SEA DEVIL

Linophryne densiramus
Location: Atlantic and Pacific oceans
Length: Up to 3½ in (9 cm)

This fish uses a luminous lure to attract inquisitive prey, which it then grabs with its big mouth. The light in the lure is produced by bacteria that live in the fish's flesh and can also be found in its glowing beard.

Luminous lure
A fleshy bulb, called an esca, contains a capsule with light-producing bacteria.

90 percent of the ocean's water lies in the **midnight zone**.

167 The number of species of **deep-sea anglers**, the **biggest** group of deep-sea fish.

26,250 ft (8,000 m)—the depth of the **deepest** recorded fish, the **Mariana snailfish**.

63

TAN BRISTLEMOUTH
Cyclothone pallida
Location: Deep oceans worldwide
Length: Up to 2¾ in (7 cm)

These fish have light-producing organs along their sides to help them communicate with other fish in the dark water. They also produce chemical scents called pheromones to attract mates.

DUMBO OCTOPUS
Grimpoteuthis sp.
Location: N. Atlantic and Pacific
Length: Up to 19 in (48 cm)

Like other octopus species, the dumbo octopus squirts water from a siphon to keep moving. But it also has a pair of earlike fins to control its position as it hovers over the ocean floor to search for prey, such as worms and shrimp.

Fleshy fins
Fins move up and down to help the octopus control its position in the water.

HELMET JELLYFISH
Periphylla periphylla
Location: Deep oceans worldwide
Diameter (of bell): Up to 6 in (15 cm)

This jellyfish can switch on light-producing organs in its glassy bell when it senses a disturbance. It is thought it does this to scare off predatory fish and shrimp.

VAMPIRE SQUID
Vampyroteuthis infernalis
Location: Deep oceans worldwide
Length: Up to 12 in (30 cm)

The umbrella-like vampire squid is named for its blood-red color rather than its behavior. It drifts in the dark ocean depths eating other invertebrates and the remains of dead animals and plants. It uses the suckered tips of its arms to transfer food into its mouth.

SEA PIG
Scotoplanes globosa
Location: Deep oceans worldwide
Length: Up to 4 in (10 cm)

The scavenging sea pig is a distant relative of the sea star. It belongs to a group of soft-bodied animals called sea cucumbers and uses suckerlike feet to crawl on the seabed, sometimes in huge herds.

ZOMBIE WORM
Osedax priapus
Location: Pacific
Length: Up to ⅝ in (1.5 cm)

This tiny worm burrows into the bones of dead whales and feeds on the fat locked inside. It has rootlike structures instead of a stomach, which contain special bacteria that help with digestion.

Whale bone

Three-legged tripod
Bony, stiltlike fin rays support the weight of the fish at rest.

TRIPOD FISH
Bathypterois grallator
Location: E. Pacific, Atlantic, and W. Indian oceans
Length: Up to 15¾ in (40 cm)

The tripod fish uses two long fin rays and a tail ray to rest on the ocean bottom. In this way, it can save energy while it waits for tiny planktonic prey to come along.

64 open ocean ○ **HYDROTHERMAL VENTS**

500 The number of **hydrothermal vent fields known to exist** in the oceans.

Hydrothermal Vents

Deep at the bottom of the ocean are cracks where hot water shoots upward through the ocean floor. Called hydrothermal vents, they form rocky chimneys that are home to some of the most unusual food chains on Earth.

Rising from the seabed, hot water spews from chimneys in clouds of either white or black smoke. This water comes from under the ocean crust where it is heated to temperatures of 750°F (400°C). Both the water and the chimneys contain a host of chemicals and minerals from deep inside Earth, which provide an important source of energy for the creatures that live without sunlight at these great depths.

Volcanic food chain

Growing on the walls of the chimneys, bacteria can turn carbon dioxide into food—like plants do—but instead of using energy from light to do this, they get energy from chemical reactions. In this unique habitat, these bacteria form the bottom of extensive food chains of animals that live entirely independently of sunlight—mussels, worms, crabs, and even the occasional fish.

How hydrothermal vents form

Cold ocean water can seep down through cracks in the rock of the ocean floor. As it gets deeper, it is heated by magma (molten rock), and minerals from the rocky crust dissolve into the hot water. Eventually, pressure builds up, forcing the water back upward. As it hits the ice-cold water above the ocean floor, the minerals it carries turn solid, building up over time to create chimneys. The water erupts from these in what looks like plumes of smoke.

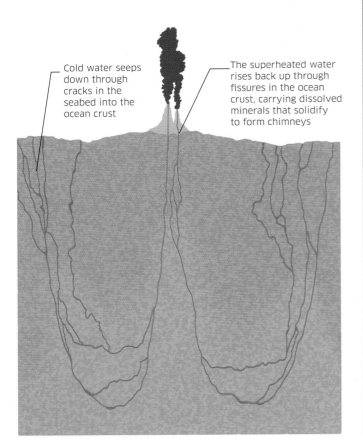

Cold water seeps down through cracks in the seabed into the ocean crust

The superheated water rises back up through fissures in the ocean crust, carrying dissolved minerals that solidify to form chimneys

Dandelion siphonophore
This relative of the Portuguese man o' war has a flowerlike body and swims around the vents, catching tiny animals.

Pompeii worms
Short tube worms called Pompeii worms, with a starlike fan of tentacles, can tolerate the extreme heat and live on the chimneys.

Chimney
Chimneys are made up of minerals such as iron sulfide that solidify from hot seawater as it rises, over time building up into tall towers.

Nutrient-rich water
Water spewing up through the vent contains hydrogen sulfide—a gas that smells like rotten eggs—which is used by bacteria as a source of energy to make food.

Hot water
The water that emerges through the vent in the ocean floor is at least 140°F (60°C) and usually much hotter.

16,400 ft (5,000 m)—the depth of **the Cayman Trough** in the Caribbean Sea, the site of **the deepest-known hydrothermal vents**.

200 ft (60 m)—**the height** a chimney can grow.

65

Black smoker
The chimney's distinctive dark smoke is formed from water and tiny black particles of iron sulfide.

Signs of bacteria
As bacteria use up chemicals spewing from the chimneys, their food-making chemical reactions leave waste products, such as yellow sulfur, that accumulate in patches on the chimney walls.

Cusk eel
This species is one of the deepest-known living fish and may be an occasional visitor to hydrothermal vent habitats.

Tube worms
Giant tube worms are one of the main animals found around Pacific Ocean vents. They can grow to 10 ft (3 m) in length.

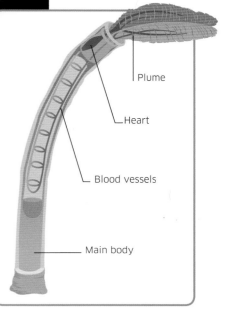

Plume

Heart

Blood vessels

Main body

Giant white clams
Each growing up to 10¼ in (26 cm) long, these live in dense colonies around the base of the vents. They are nourished by food-making bacteria that live in their gills.

Giant tube worms
Many animals living around the vent carry their own food-making bacteria. Giant tube worms lack a gut and instead use their plumes to collect chemicals, which blood vessels transport to the bacteria living inside cells within the worm's main body.

White vent crabs
These small crustaceans feed on bacteria and other tiny organisms living around the vents.

66 open ocean ○ EXPLORING THE OCEAN

68 The **number of new species identified** due to *Deepsea Challenger*'s research.

Exploring the Ocean

The deepest parts of the ocean—with their bone-crushing pressures and their cold, dark water—are inhospitable. But humans have explored this strange world in tough underwater vehicles called submersibles.

The deepest that humans can dive without any special equipment is little more than 330 ft (100 m). Armorlike suits allow divers to go a little deeper, but to travel any further, they need to ride in an underwater vehicle. Submarines, which are stocked with enough food, fuel, and oxygen, can carry their crew for months at a time. Smaller submersibles rely on a boat at the surface for support but are designed to go much deeper—right into the trenches that make up the deepest parts of the ocean.

Deepest dives

Deepsea Challenger is one of many submersibles built to explore the ocean. Crafts specifically designed to reach the deepest depths have to survive greater pressures and carry a source of oxygen with them. The *Trieste* was the first to travel down the deepest ocean trench back in 1960, but in May 2019, American explorer Victor Vescovo in DSV *Limiting Factor* broke all records by reaching a depth of 35,853 ft (10,928 m).

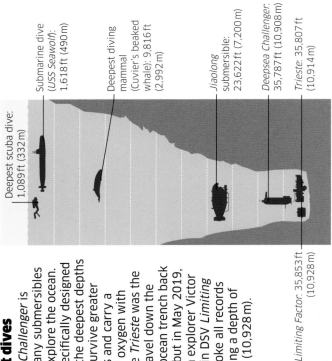

Deepest scuba dive: 1,089 ft (332 m)

Submarine dive (*USS Seawolf*): 1,618 ft (490 m)

Deepest diving mammal (Cuvier's beaked whale): 9,816 ft (2,992 m)

Jiaolong submersible: 23,622 ft (7,200 m)

Deepsea Challenger: 35,787 ft (10,908 m)

Trieste: 35,807 ft (10,914 m)

Limiting Factor: 35,853 ft (10,928 m)

Deepsea Challenger

This bullet-shaped submersible was designed to travel to the deepest part of the ocean—Challenger Deep, right at the bottom of the Mariana Trench in the Pacific Ocean. In March 2012, Canadian filmmaker James Cameron piloted the submersible on its voyage and became Challenger Deep's first solo explorer. The craft spent three hours on the ocean floor and collected samples of rocks and animals for scientists to analyze.

Floodlights
A panel of floodlights illuminates the dark deep ocean. Their light can penetrate up to 98 ft (30 m) if the water is clear.

Submersible body
The main body of the submersible is made of a foam consisting of glass beads embedded in a resin. This specially designed material can resist the high pressures of the deep ocean.

Batteries
An array of 70 batteries arranged in three packs powers the submersible. It can keep running on just one pack in an emergency.

Spotlight
One long metal pole carries a spotlight that the pilot can position to illuminate creatures on the seafloor.

Thrusters
Two types of thrusters sit on the sides of the submersible. Some propel the submersible sideways. Others propel it upward and downward.

24 ft (7.3 m)—the **full height of the** *Deepsea Challenger* submersible.

56 hours—**how long the pilot can breathe** using *Deepsea Challenger*'s two oxygen tanks.

67

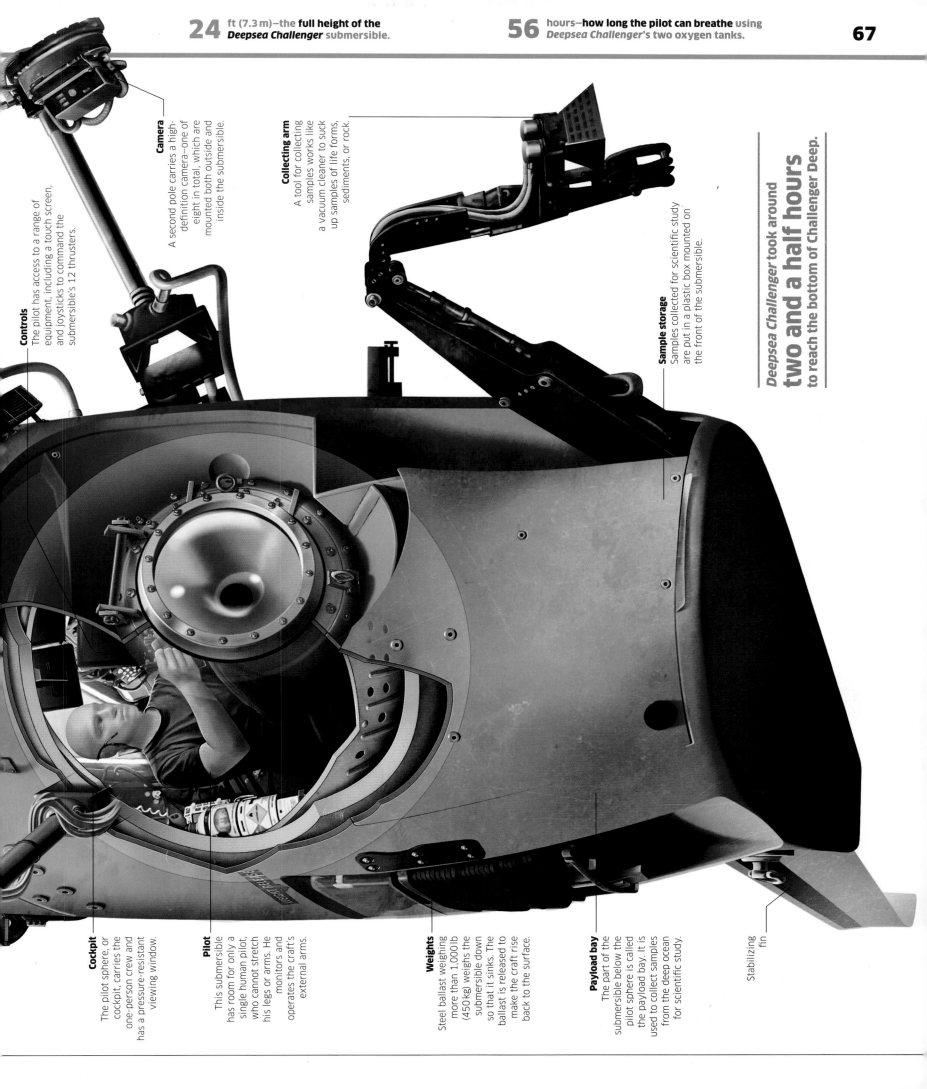

Controls
The pilot has access to a range of equipment, including a touch screen, and joysticks to command the submersible's 12 thrusters.

Camera
A second pole carries a high-definition camera—one of eight in total, which are mounted both outside and inside the submersible.

Collecting arm
A tool for collecting samples works like a vacuum cleaner to suck up samples of life forms, sediments, or rock.

Sample storage
Samples collected for scientific study are put in a plastic box mounted on the front of the submersible.

Deepsea Challenger took around
two and a half hours
to reach the bottom of Challenger Deep.

Cockpit
The pilot sphere, or cockpit, carries the one-person crew and has a pressure-resistant viewing window.

Pilot
This submersible has room for only a single human pilot, who cannot stretch his legs or arms. He monitors and operates the craft's external arms.

Weights
Steel ballast weighing more than 1,000 lb (450 kg) weighs the submersible down so that it sinks. The ballast is released to make the craft rise back to the surface.

Payload bay
The part of the submersible below the pilot sphere is called the payload bay. It is used to collect samples from the deep ocean for scientific study.

Stabilizing fin

Camouflage
White plumage helps camouflage the Arctic tern against the snow of polar habitats.

In flight
Long, narrow wings are good for hovering in the air before diving for fish, as well as for gliding on ocean breezes.

Flight control
The Arctic tern's wide tail, with long streaming side feathers, is used to control the position of the wings, as well as help with braking when landing.

Migration

Some of the longest journeys in the animal kingdom are made by animals that migrate around the oceans—either swimming below the surface or flying high above it.

Migrations happen when large groups of animals travel together at the same time and move from one place to another, then back again in a predictable routine. Some animals have migrations that are short and frequent, such as plankton that migrate daily between shallower and deeper waters, or invertebrates that move with the tides. But many oceangoing animals undertake yearly trips across vast distances between different feeding and breeding grounds.

The total distance an Arctic tern will typically fly during its lifetime equals three or four trips to the moon and back.

Champion migrator

No animal migrates as far as the Arctic tern. After breeding in the Arctic, this bird travels to the opposite side of the world to feed in the Antarctic. It times its trips to coincide with the two polar summers, which means it probably sees more daylight hours than any other species.

12,740 miles (20,500 km)—the **distance** covered by **leatherback turtles** as they travel between **foraging grounds** in the Pacific.

59,650 miles (96,000 km)—the **total yearly distance the Arctic tern travels** during its migration.

69

1 Breeding grounds
Between May and July, the Arctic summer, Arctic terns breed in colonies of up to 300 birds. It takes 6 weeks for the terns to incubate eggs and raise their young so they are old enough to fly and ready to join the migration.

2 Flying to the Antarctic
The Arctic terns flying south over the Atlantic follow two possible routes—one along the coastline of Africa and another along the coastline of South America.

3 Feeding grounds
November brings winter to the Arctic and summer to the Antarctic. The terns are arriving in Antarctica, where they rest and feed. At the height of the polar summers, the sun doesn't set—so for much of the year, these birds do not experience dark nights.

4 Flying to the Arctic
When the birds fly northward, they take a route that is further out to sea and away from the coastlines.

End-of-life migration
At the end of their lifetimes, European eels travel from fresh water to the Sargasso Sea in the Atlantic Ocean to spawn and then die. The young eels (pictured) migrate back to Europe and grow to maturity in rivers.

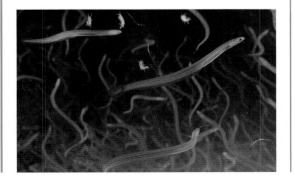

Tidal migration
As a rising tide covers the shore, underwater animals follow the water to feed over the flooded seabed. When the tide ebbs, shorebirds move further down the shore to prey on invertebrates burrowed in the mud.

Vertical migration
Tiny planktonic animals rise to feed near the surface at night but sink during the day to avoid predators. There are so many plankton that their total weight could make this daily migration the biggest on the planet.

SHALLOW SEAS

The areas of the ocean that lie between the shore and deeper water are known as shallow seas. They cover only 8 percent of Earth's surface, but because light and food are so plentiful here, these fertile shallow waters are home to an incredible number of animal and plant species.

SUNLIT SEAS

Every continent is edged by a shelf of land that lies submerged beneath the ocean and is known as the continental shelf. These shelves create shallow seas, no more than 660 ft (200 m) deep, which often can be warmer than the open ocean and rich in oxygen and nutrients. Sunlight penetrates all the way to the seafloor of these coastal waters unless they are very muddy, and as a result, they are usually teeming with life.

SUNLIT ZONE

The top layer of the ocean, where sunlight reaches, is known as the sunlit zone. All water above the continental shelf is within this zone. Organisms that get energy from the sun, through a process known as photosynthesis, thrive here. In shallow seas, these organisms include seagrass, the algae that live inside coral polyps, and other algae and microscopic phytoplankton that together form an abundant and important first link in the food chain as they become food for animals further up (see pp.34–35).

Nurseries
In the shallowest parts, seagrass and coral reefs provide sheltered nurseries for many species.

Light
In clear water, sunlight reaches all the way down to the seafloor, even at 660 ft (200 m).

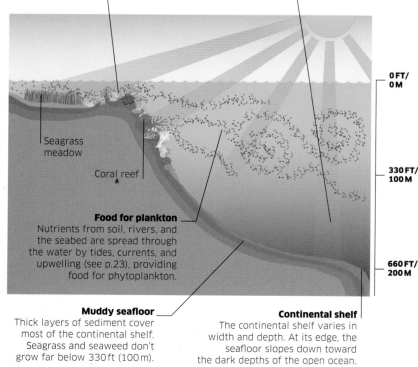

0 FT/
0 M

Seagrass meadow

Coral reef

330 FT/
100 M

Food for plankton
Nutrients from soil, rivers, and the seabed are spread through the water by tides, currents, and upwelling (see p.23), providing food for phytoplankton.

660 FT/
200 M

Muddy seafloor
Thick layers of sediment cover most of the continental shelf. Seagrass and seaweed don't grow far below 330 ft (100 m).

Continental shelf
The continental shelf varies in width and depth. At its edge, the seafloor slopes down toward the dark depths of the open ocean.

TROPICAL AND TEMPERATE SEAS

There are shallow seas in the polar regions, but most are in temperate or tropical zones (see p.9). Tropical shallow seas feature warm clear water, corals, colorful fish, and white sand, while colder murky water, with kelp forests and silvery or brown fish, is typical of temperate seas.

Temperate waters

Between the icy polar regions and the hot tropics lie the temperate ocean zones of the Northern and Southern hemispheres. Water temperatures here fluctuate with the seasons, ranging from 50°F (10°C) to 68°F (20°C). Many species make seasonal migrations as temperatures change.

Fine catch
Most commercially important fish species, such as cod and mackerel, are found in temperate seas.

Murky water
Cold water is often full of phytoplankton, which make it look less clear.

Large shoals
Fish thrive due to the high density of plankton.

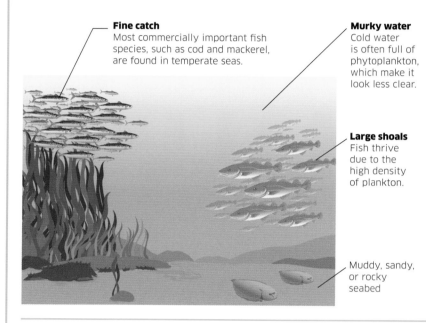

Muddy, sandy, or rocky seabed

Tropical waters

The regions of the Atlantic, Pacific, and Indian oceans bordering the equator are tropical seas. Water temperatures remain relatively constant at 68–77°F (20–25°C). Since there are fewer and less pronounced seasons here, tropical species follow other signs, such as lunar cycles, for mating and spawning. The diversity and number of species in tropical waters is stunning.

Crystal clear water
Waters are clear due to low levels of nutrients and plankton.

Bold colors
Tropical fish are often colorful, matching the vibrant coral reefs.

Crowded reefs
Many species have developed behaviors or body forms that help them live closely together on the reef.

SHALLOW SEAS HABITAT

Shallow seas are often characterized by what the seafloor is like—hard and rocky, soft and muddy, or covered in living structures such as corals. The seafloor is where most species feed, hide, and mate, so the environment determines what organisms live there.

Rocky seabed
Rocky habitats have lots of nooks and crannies for marine species to live in, especially those that can attach themselves to hard surfaces.

Coral reef
Mostly found in tropical waters, coral reefs create a stable and protective habitat for thousands of tropical fish and invertebrate species.

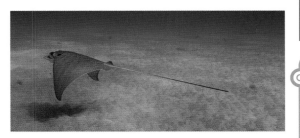

Sandy plain
This environment, constantly being reshaped by currents and waves, offers an ideal hiding place for species who can burrow in the sand.

Seagrass meadow
Seagrasses provide food for grazing sea creatures and serve as a nursery and a shelter from predators for many smaller species.

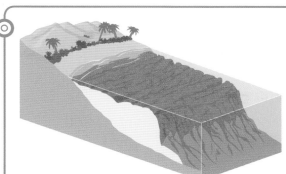

Fringing reef
These reefs form around the edges of islands and continents, extending from the shore.

Barrier reef
Barrier reefs also form parallel to the coast, but much farther out, with deep water in between.

SOUNDS OF THE REEF

Coral reefs aren't just colorful—they are also full of noise. Reef species make many different sounds, when eating, mating, showing aggression, or communicating with each other. With the latest recording equipment, divers can collect these noises so that scientists can study how important sounds are for a thriving reef.

SOFT AND HARD CORAL

Corals are grouped into two main types—hard and soft. The polyps of hard corals secrete a hard calcium-based skeleton that builds up reefs (see p.99), while soft corals contain spiny, pinlike structures within their bendy tissues that give them support and deter predators.

Hard coral
Hard coral species are reef-building, with living polyps adding new, expanding layers to the dead skeletons of older corals.

Soft coral
Soft corals contribute less to reef structure. Many species look like colorful plants or delicate fans or grasses.

CORAL REEF TYPES

Coral reefs are divided into three main types based on how they form. The most common type of reef is a fringing reef, lining the shore. Some of the most iconic reefs are those that form a barrier further offshore, such as the Great Barrier Reef and the Belize Barrier Reef. The third type of reef is an atoll. Circular or oval, atolls are all that remain of a submerged volcanic island (see p.18).

Sandy coral cay
(see pp.118–119)

Atoll
Fringing reefs surrounding volcanic islands become atolls if the island itself submerges.

Kelp Forest

In cool, clear coastal waters around the world, spectacular underwater forests of giant kelp support a rich variety of animals, including sea otters, seals, and even whales.

Large seaweeds known as kelp grow in the shallow coastal seas of all cool oceans. Many form dense, low-lying kelp beds that extend far offshore, hidden beneath the waves. But on some coasts, incredibly long fronds of giant kelp grow all the way to the surface through the clear water, creating submerged forests that provide food and shelter for a specialized community of marine life.

Kelp harvest

Kelp is harvested around the world for special chemicals called alginates that are used in producing food, clothing, and paper. It is part of Japanese and Korean cuisine and there is growing interest in using kelp as a biofuel. Each year, more than 660,000 tons (600,000 metric tons) of kelp are harvested.

Types of seaweeds

There are three main types of seaweeds in the ocean, classified by their color. They all live by absorbing the energy of sunlight and using it to make food by photosynthesis.

Green seaweed
These seaweeds are often delicate and have green fronds that look like the leaves of land plants such as lettuce.

Red seaweed
Usually found in dimmer waters and shady tide pools, the red seaweeds include coraline seaweeds that help build coral reefs.

Brown seaweed
The brown seaweeds include all the largest species, such as kelp and wracks, and often have broader fronds.

Monterey Bay

Just south of San Francisco, the sheltered waters of Monterey Bay conceal an underwater jungle of giant kelp. Anchored to the seabed by their clawlike holdfasts, the kelp form a forest of vertical stems that grow 164 ft (50 m) or more through the water to trail their leaflike blades on the sunlit surface.

Harbor seal
Diving harbor seals hunt the many types of fish that feed and shelter among the kelp fronds.

Olive rockfish
Spiny-finned rockfish hang beneath the kelp canopy, preying on tiny shrimplike animals and small fish.

Growing tall
Giant kelp can grow at the astonishing rate of 24 in (60 cm) a day, in order to reach the sunlit surface as soon as possible.

Sea urchin
Spiny sea urchins eat the kelp and may completely destroy it if there are no otters to keep their numbers under control.

Sleeping support
Resting otters wrap themselves
in kelp to avoid floating away.

Sea otter
Sea otters live and sleep on the surface of
the sea above the kelp forests. They are an
important part of the ecosystem, because
they prey on sea urchins—one of the main
consumers of kelp.

Balloonlike sacs
The air inside the bladders is a mixture
of oxygen, nitrogen, and carbon dioxide.

Bladders
Gas-filled bladders at the base of the leaflike
blades make the tip of each strand float near
the surface. This enables the kelp to soak up
the vital sunlight it needs.

Prickly prey
The needlelike spines of sea urchins are
no defense against sea otters, which
use stones to crack open their shells.

Holdfasts
At the base of each stem, a rootlike
holdfast grips a rock or other solid
object to prevent the kelp from being
swept away by the current.

76   shallow seas ○ **SEAGRASS MEADOW**

352 oz (10 liters)—the **amount of oxygen** that 11 sq ft (1 sq m) of **seagrass** can produce in **one day**.

Seagrass Meadow

Seagrasses are flowering plants that have, over millions of years, adapted to living in the ocean. They form large seagrass meadows, which are very important habitats that are now under threat.

Seagrass provides shelter for small animals in what would otherwise be a barren sandy-bottomed seascape. The sediment and decaying matter trapped by the roots of the seagrass provide nutrients for invertebrates. Juvenile fish hide behind the green blades while picking off invertebrates and, in turn, attract bigger fish, and so a large community builds up around the meadow. Once common in shallow waters across the world, many meadows have been lost due to coastal development and pollution.

Light
Like all plants, seagrass needs light and can grow only in shallow, clear waters where light is abundant.

Green sea turtle
Seagrass is a major part of the green sea turtle's diet. An adult will eat 4¹⁄₂ lb (2 kg) every day.

Turtle grass
A favorite grass of green sea turtles, turtle grass has a flat, broad ribbonlike blade that can reach 14 in (35.5 cm) in length and has an extensive root system.

Queen conch
About 12 in (30 cm) long, these giant sea snails are the cleaners of the seagrass meadow, eating up dead grass.

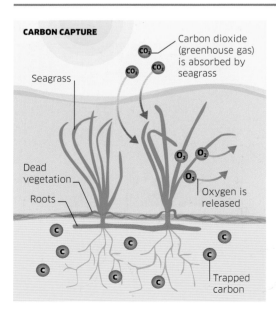

CARBON CAPTURE

Carbon dioxide (greenhouse gas) is absorbed by seagrass

Seagrass

Dead vegetation

Roots

O₂

O₂

O₂

Oxygen is released

C

Trapped carbon

Seagrass against climate change

Seagrasses harness the sun's light to make food through photosynthesis. In this process, the seagrass absorbs carbon dioxide and releases oxygen. The carbon is locked into the plant tissue. When a plant dies, it is buried in the seabed, trapping the carbon. This makes the seagrass meadow an efficient processor of carbon dioxide, one of the gases that cause climate change.

Sharptail eel
Often mistaken for sea snakes due to their lack of fins, these fish use their pointy snouts to burrow in the sand.

Seahorse
Seahorses cannot swim against strong currents so anchor themselves by wrapping their tail around seagrass.

2 football fields—the area of seagrass meadow lost every hour due to human impact.

1,737 sq miles (4,500 sq km)—the area of the world's largest-recorded seagrass meadow, in Australia.

77

Spotted sea trout
This is one of many species of fish that spends its life as a juvenile in seagrass meadows where food and shelter are both plentiful.

Manatee
Known as the cows of the seas, manatees are large marine mammals. They spend up to a quarter of their time feeding, grazing both day and night at depths of about 6½ ft (2 m).

Sunlit underwater meadow

There are many different species of seagrass, but all of them are green plants that need sunlight to grow. In this seagrass meadow on the coast of Florida, two species provide nutritious grazing for manatees and green sea turtles. They are joined by a number of other animals coming here to feed, shelter, or hunt.

Setting root
Part of the seagrass stem spreads underground, forming a network that holds sediment in place. Known as a rhizome, it produces both new shoots and anchoring roots.

Suckling calf
A manatee calf suckles from teats on the underside of its mother's flippers. Weaned at about one year old, it remains close to its mother for up to two years after birth.

Red cushion sea star
Moving across the seabed, red cushion sea stars graze on algae, sponges, and small invertebrates. Seagrass meadows provide perfect shelter while the sea stars develop from larvae to their adult, five-limbed shape.

Manatee grass
This species of seagrass takes its name from the manatees that love to eat it. The cylindrical blades can grow to 20 in (50 cm) long.

Clingfish shelter
The pelvic fins of this tiny emerald clingfish form a sucking disc that enables it to cling to blades of seagrass, out of sight of most predators.

Three hearts pump blue-green blood around a cuttlefish's body and gills.

Fin
The muscular fin ripples like a skirt, moving the cuttlefish in any direction.

Head

Mantle
Everything behind the head of a cuttlefish is known as the mantle. It contains the cuttlebone, the water-filled mantle cavity, and all organs except the brain.

Eye
Cuttlefish eyes are very large in proportion to their body. They have a very distinct W-shaped pupil. Cuttlefish can see aspects of light that are invisible to human eyes.

Beak
The parrotlike beak can crunch through the shells of prey and is a good defense against predators, too.

Siphon
Cuttlefish expel water through their siphon to quickly escape predators. Ink produced in an internal ink sac is also squirted out through the siphon to help confuse attackers.

Color-changing skin

Three types of color-changing cells in the surface layers of cuttlefish skin—yellow, red, and brown—combine to produce multiple color changes. A cuttlefish can quickly stretch certain cells out, much like blowing up a balloon, to make certain colors brighter, enabling it to change skin color in a flash.

Common Cuttlefish

Cuttlefish belong to the same group of mollusks as squid and octopus. All have multiple arms and a mantle, but cuttlefish have a broad, stout body, containing a cuttlebone, and move more slowly.

Common cuttlefish are mostly active at night, usually spending their days partly buried in the sandy seabed. Like all cuttlefish, this species is well known for its camouflage abilities, changing not only the color of its skin but also the texture in order to match its surroundings.

2 years—the maximum **expected life span** of a common cuttlefish.

4,000 The maximum number of **eggs laid** by the female common cuttlefish before she **dies**.

79

Crab catcher

A common cuttlefish puts on colorful skin displays and waves its arms to confuse a crab. Once the crab is within reach, the cuttlefish shoots out its tentacles. Suckers on the end of the tentacles lock onto the crab's shell just long enough for the eight arms to grasp it and bring it toward the cuttlefish's shell-crushing beak.

Arm
Once the cuttlefish captures its prey with its tentacles, it uses its eight sucker-lined arms to grasp it and bring it toward its beak.

Tentacle
Cuttlefish have two tentacles that they fire out from a pocket at the base of their arms to capture prey.

Suckers
Tentacles only have suckers on the end, where there are clusters of differently sized suckers to help snare prey.

Moving in all directions

Cuttlefish move their fins to travel backward or forward slowly. For quick escapes, they use jet propulsion—they suck water into their mantle cavity and quickly shoot it out through their siphon. To make movements up or down, they increase or decrease the amount of gas in their cuttlebone.

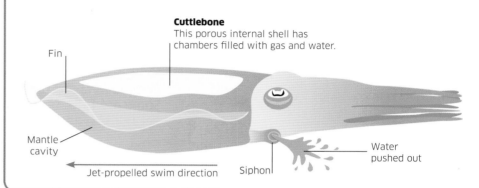

Cuttlebone
This porous internal shell has chambers filled with gas and water.

Fin

Mantle cavity

Jet-propelled swim direction

Siphon

Water pushed out

MOLLUSK

COMMON CUTTLEFISH

Sepia officinalis

Location: N.E. Atlantic, Baltic Sea, Mediterranean

Length: Mantle up to 19¼ in (49 cm)

Diet: Mollusks, crabs, shrimp, worms, fish

Prey
Crustaceans, such as this European spider crab, are a favorite prey, though the largest cuttlefish prefer fish.

A scallop can have more than **100 eyes**.

1,100 lb (500 kg)—weight of the **heaviest mollusk**, a colossal squid, **ever caught**.

GIANT PACIFIC OCTOPUS
Enteroctopus dofleini
Location: North Pacific
Total length: Over 10 ft (3 m)

The largest and longest-lived species of octopus in the world, the giant Pacific octopus feeds mainly on crabs, snails, shrimp, scallops, clams, and lobsters. It takes its food back to its den to eat and tosses any shells outside the entrance.

Mantle
The mantle is a sleeve of skin that surrounds the body, which contains the internal organs.

Mollusks

Mollusks are the most species-rich group in the ocean, making up about a quarter of all known marine animals. From colossal squid to tiny sea slugs, mollusks are very diverse in size as well as habitat and habit.

All mollusks are soft-bodied, with a muscular foot, a head, and a fleshy mantle. Many have shells, while some species have lost their shell through evolution, enabling them to grow larger and move faster than their shelled relatives. Some are filter feeders, others graze on algae or sponges, and many are predators.

No match
A giant Pacific octopus can trap small sharks such as this North Pacific spiny dogfish.

Head

Suckers
About 280 suckers line each long arm.

Octopus arms
All octopus have eight strong arms. Unlike squid and cuttlefish, they do not have a separate pair of longer tentacles (see p.79).

NEW ZEALAND GREEN-LIPPED MUSSEL
Perna canaliculus
Location: New Zealand
Shell length: Up to 10¼ in (26 cm)

These mussels filter microscopic algae and other plankton out of the water for food. Before they settle permanently in place as adults, they are called spats and move about on a muscular foot.

QUEEN SCALLOP
Aequipecten opercularis
Location: Northeast Atlantic
Shell length: Up to 3½ in (9 cm)

The shell of the queen scallop can vary in color. They live attached to the seabed until they have grown to about ¾ in (2 cm) in diameter, but from then on they become free-swimming.

Many eyes set around shell rim

SEA SLUG
Hypselodoris infucata
Location: Indo-Pacific
Length: Up to 2 in (5 cm)

These sea slugs eat sponges but are not harmed by the sponges' chemical defenses. Instead, they incorporate the toxic chemicals into their own body, making themselves distasteful to predators.

Gills for breathing

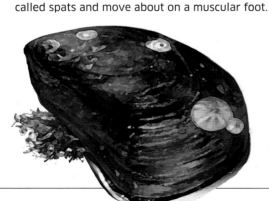

85,000 The **estimated number of mollusk species**, two-thirds of which live in the ocean.

1,180 The maximum **number of eggs** a female bigfin reef squid has been recorded laying **in one spawning**.

81

FLAMBOYANT CUTTLEFISH
Metasepia pfefferi
Location: Indo-Pacific
Mantle length: Up to 2³⁄₈ in (6 cm)

Small and colorful, these cuttlefish are highly toxic. Perhaps because of this, it is one of the few species of cuttlefish that is active during the day, hunting its prey of fish, crabs, and shrimp.

Mantle

Females are bigger than males

MALE

FEMALE

PALAU NAUTILUS
Nautilus belauensis
Location: Palau in the northwest Pacific
Shell diameter: Up to 9 in (23 cm)

Like most nautilus, this species migrates to shallower water at night and feeds on shrimp, fish, and crabs. During daylight hours, they sink deeper to avoid becoming food themselves.

MIMIC OCTOPUS
Thaumoctopus mimicus
Location: Indo-Pacific
Total length: Over 19 in (48 cm)

Earning its name for its ability to mimic other species, this octopus shapes itself to look like lionfish, sea snakes, jellyfish, flatfish (shown here), and many other marine animals.

Arms drawn together

BIGFIN REEF SQUID
Sepioteuthis lessoniana
Location: Indo-Pacific
Mantle length: Up to 13 in (33 cm)

Bigfin reef squid have a large fin that runs most of the length of the mantle. They grow very fast but live for less than a year, spending their early days in big shoals. Like all squid, cuttlefish, and octopus, they squirt ink in self-defense.

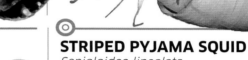

Ink jet

STRIPED PYJAMA SQUID
Sepioloidea lineolata
Location: Australia
Mantle length: Up to 2 in (5 cm)

A species of bobtail squid, the striped pyjama squid is small and chubby. It spends a lot of its time buried up to its eyes in sand at the bottom of shallow seas, with arms tucked in, waiting to pounce on its favorite prey of shrimp and fish.

TIGER COWRIE
Cypraea tigris
Location: Indo-Pacific
Shell length: Up to 6 in (15 cm)

This large omnivorous sea snail can extend the fleshy part of its body (the mantle) to cover its shell. It hides the mantle within its shell when it is threatened by predators.

Mantle

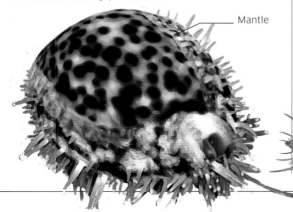

VENUS COMB
Murex pecten
Location: Indo-Pacific
Shell length: Up to 6 in (15 cm)

Many spines protect this snail from predators but also keep it from sinking down in the mud where it hunts for clams and other mollusks. To move, the snail uses its strong foot to raise its shell off the ground and slide away.

Snail moves with its slender tip pointing forward

Foot

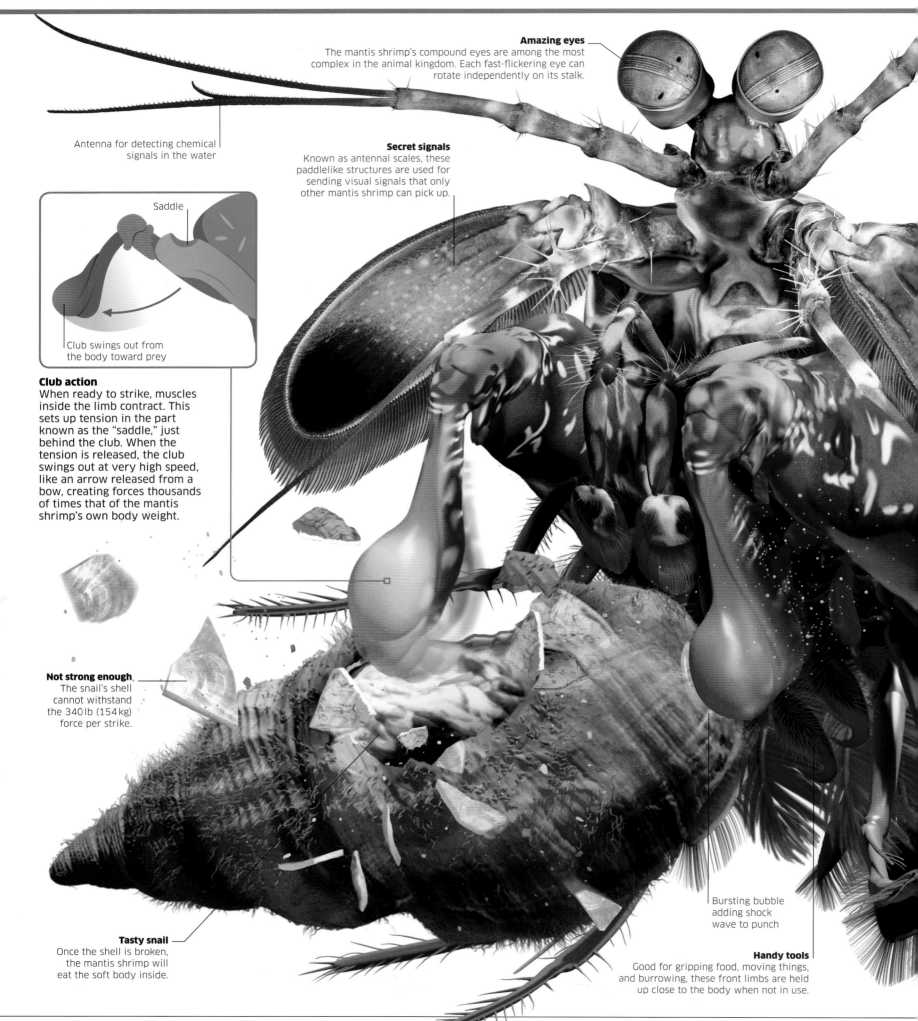

Amazing eyes
The mantis shrimp's compound eyes are among the most complex in the animal kingdom. Each fast-flickering eye can rotate independently on its stalk.

Antenna for detecting chemical signals in the water

Secret signals
Known as antennal scales, these paddlelike structures are used for sending visual signals that only other mantis shrimp can pick up.

Saddle

Club swings out from the body toward prey

Club action
When ready to strike, muscles inside the limb contract. This sets up tension in the part known as the "saddle," just behind the club. When the tension is released, the club swings out at very high speed, like an arrow released from a bow, creating forces thousands of times that of the mantis shrimp's own body weight.

Not strong enough
The snail's shell cannot withstand the 340 lb (154 kg) force per strike.

Tasty snail
Once the shell is broken, the mantis shrimp will eat the soft body inside.

Bursting bubble
adding shock wave to punch

Handy tools
Good for gripping food, moving things, and burrowing, these front limbs are held up close to the body when not in use.

50 mph (80km/h)—the **speed** at which the shrimp's **clubs shoot out** from the body.

16 The number of **different photoreceptors in** a mantis shrimp eye—**humans** have **three**.

83

Peacock Mantis Shrimp

Living in tropical waters, these colorful marine crustaceans may look a bit comical with their swiveling eyes and sudden darting movements, but they can throw a deadly punch.

There are many different species of mantis shrimp, grouped into two types based on the shape of their "weapons"—a set of limbs at the front of their body used for killing prey. The peacock mantis shrimp belongs to the smashers, which have two clublike limbs that strike through the tough shells and exoskeletons of their favorite foods. The other type of mantis shrimp are the spearers, who spear fish and worms for their meal. Peacock mantis shrimp live in burrows or in rock crevices, keeping their home tidy and sometimes disguising the entrance with bits of loose corals and stones. They may live for more than 20 years.

CRUSTACEAN
PEACOCK MANTIS SHRIMP
Odontodactylus scyllarus

Location: Indo-Pacific
Length: 6¾in (17cm)
Diet: Shrimp, crabs, clams, mussels, snails

Smash-up dinner
The peacock mantis shrimp uses the clublike heels of its large second pair of limbs like hammers to break shells. When it strikes, the club moves so quickly through the water that some of the water vaporizes (turns into a gas), creating a bubble that then quickly bursts. This sends a shock wave through the shell in addition to the impact of the punch itself.

Mantis vision
Mantis shrimp have compound eyes. These consist of thousands of small units, each made up of a cornea, a lens, pigment cells, and photoreceptors. The units work together, building a very wide-angled view of their surroundings. The range of light wavelengths the mantis shrimp eye can detect, from ultraviolet to near-infrared, far exceeds that of a human eye.

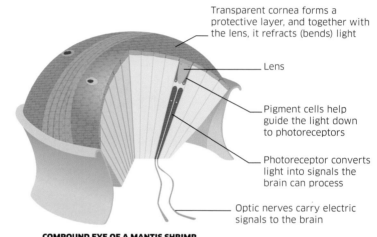

Transparent cornea forms a protective layer, and together with the lens, it refracts (bends) light

Lens

Pigment cells help guide the light down to photoreceptors

Photoreceptor converts light into signals the brain can process

Optic nerves carry electric signals to the brain

COMPOUND EYE OF A MANTIS SHRIMP

Clubs, tucked in when not used for defense or killing prey

Limbs for cleaning eyes and body

Swimming limbs also beat to keep water passing over the gills

Front limbs

A female mantis shrimp uses her front limbs to hold her many pink eggs

Walking limbs

Limbs used to swim backward

Legs for all occasions
Mantis shrimp have a lot of different limbs, known as appendages. Apart from their two clubs, they have one pair for cleaning themselves, three pairs for holding and burrowing, three pairs for walking, five pairs for swimming, and one paddlelike pair for swimming backward.

Spiny antenna
Like other crustaceans, the spiny lobster has four antennae that act as sensors. Two are longer than its body and covered in spines.

Carapace
Covering the head and front part of the body, the shieldlike carapace is the largest plate of a crustacean's external skeleton.

Protective spines

Smaller antennae

Lots of legs
All lobsters are decapods, meaning they have 10 legs.

PORCELAIN CRAB
Neopetrolisthes maculatus
Location: Indo-Pacific
Carapace width: Up to ⅜ in (1 cm)

Tiny and flat-bodied, porcelain crabs hide among sea anemones. The anemone's stinging tentacles protect the crab from predators, and in return the crab nips at anything threatening the anemone.

Crustaceans

Crabs, lobsters, crayfish, shrimp, prawns, krill, and barnacles are among the 67,000 species of crustaceans discovered so far, probably only a tiny fraction of the total number that exist. Most crustaceans live in water, the majority in salty seas.

Crustaceans belong to the same group of animals as insects—they are invertebrates (animals without a backbone), but their bodies are supported by an external skeleton. This gives them a hard protective casing but means that they have to shed their skeleton as their body grows. Some marine crustaceans can swim, but many mostly walk on the seabed.

HARLEQUIN SHRIMP
Hymenocera picta
Location: Indo-Pacific
Length: Up to 2 in (5 cm)

These beautiful shrimp feed almost exclusively on sea stars. Usually found living in pairs, the shrimp work together to turn over a sea star to get at its soft, edible underparts.

GIANT TIGER PRAWN
Penaeus monodon
Location: Indo-Pacific
Length: Up to 12 in (30 cm)

When they are young, these prawns live in sandy estuaries and mangroves, moving into deeper waters only as adults. They feed on debris on the seafloor, occasionally taking a worm or another crustacean.

ANEMONE SHRIMP
Periclimenes sagittifer
Location: N. E. Atlantic, E. Mediterranean
Length: Up to 1 in (2.5 cm)

By making its home among the long, stinging tentacles of the snakelocks anemone, this little shrimp is sheltered from predators. It is not known whether the shrimp offers benefits to the anemone in return.

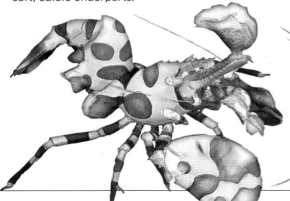

CARIBBEAN SPINY LOBSTER
Panulirus argus
Location: Atlantic, Caribbean, Gulf of Mexico
Length: Up to 23⅝ in (60 cm)

Unlike some lobsters, spiny lobsters lack large claws. They feed on snails and small mollusks called chitons and will also eat dead animals they find on the ocean floor. Females carry their eggs on the underside of their abdomen. When the larvae hatch, they swim freely for about a year before settling in seagrass beds. As adults, each year they march in a single line toward deeper waters to spawn.

Made for walking
The jointed legs are used for walking on the seabed.

SALMON LOUSE
Lepeophtheirus salmonis
Location: Pacific, Atlantic
Length: Up to ⅜ in (1 cm)

This parasite is usually found on salmon. The salmon louse attaches itself to the fish, feeding on its mucus, skin, and blood. Salmon lice are found in natural conditions, but they breed faster in salmon farms, where they can rapidly spread out of control.

| Body

Future generation
This female salmon louse is carrying eggs in two long strings.

ACORN BARNACLE
Balanus glandula
Location: Pacific coast of N. America
Diameter: Up to ¾ in (2 cm)

This species is found in large numbers in the upper and middle shore level. Like other barnacles, when covered by water it filter feeds using its hairlike cirri. At low tide, the cirri retract inside the shell.

Closed in
Layers of chalky shell protect the soft body inside.

Cirri

SHAMEFACED CRAB
Calappa calappa
Location: Indo-Pacific
Carapace width: Up to 6 in (15 cm)

Named for the way its claws fold up to cover its face, this crab can burrow quickly to avoid predators. It specializes in feeding on mollusks such as clams, using the pincers at the end of its claws to prise open or break their shells.

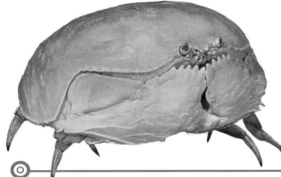

BRISTLED SPONGE CRAB
Austrodromidia octodentata
Location: Southern Australasia
Carapace width: Up to 3⅛ in (8 cm)

Like all its sponge crab relatives, this bristly species uses sponges as protective camouflage. It carries the sponge on its back, holding it in place with its rearmost pair of legs.

COMMON LOBSTER
Homarus gammarus
Location: East Atlantic, Mediterranean, Black Sea
Length: Up to 25⅝ in (65 cm)

These large lobsters prefer to live on rocky seafloors, spending their days hiding in little caves or crevices. They emerge at night to feed on invertebrates such as crabs, mollusks, sea urchins, and sea stars.

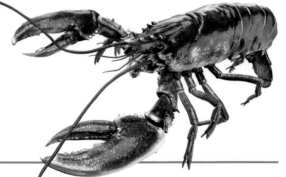

JAPANESE SPIDER CRAB
Macrocheira kaempferi
Location: Coasts of Japan and Taiwan
Carapace width: Up to 15¾ in (40 cm)

If its long legs are added to its carapace width, this crab can reach an impressive total width of 12 ft (3.7 m). Japanese spider crabs are rarely found at depths of less than 165 ft (50 m).

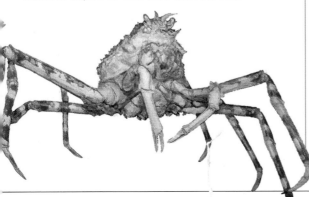

DECORATOR CRAB
Camposcia retusa
Location: Indo-Pacific
Carapace width: Up to 1¼ in (3 cm)

Decorator crabs fool their enemies by camouflaging themselves with items from their surrounding environment. They snip off tiny scraps of algae, sponges, and even anemones and attach them to their shell and limbs. The small bristles on a decorator crab's body hold the disguise in place.

All dressed up
Even the legs are covered as part of this crab's disguise.

Horseshoe Crab

Having changed little in more than 400 million years, horseshoe crabs are like "living fossils." They are more related to spiders than true crabs.

Horseshoe crabs spend most of their life walking along the sandy ocean floor, eating worms and mollusks. But during the breeding season, they head for beaches where the females lay their eggs. They have a unique swimming style, moving upside down and at an angle using their long tail as a rudder, like this horseshoe crab in the Pacific Ocean. This reveals body parts normally hidden beneath its helmetlike shell, such as the waving jointed legs and the gill flaps that help it swim.

88   shallow seas ○ **FLOWERY FLOUNDER**

Colorful **pigment spots** appear on only one
side—the side **facing the seabed** is plain **white**.

1 **Young flounder larva**
Only about ³/₁₆ in (5 mm) long, this young
flowery flounder larva has an eye on each side
of its head and swims upright. Long fin rays
help make it appear larger to predators, but
these will soon fall off.

2 **Transformation**
Soon the right eye starts to
migrate. The larva has now begun
swimming at a tilt, with more of its
left side angled up to the sky. The
tilt angle increases steadily.

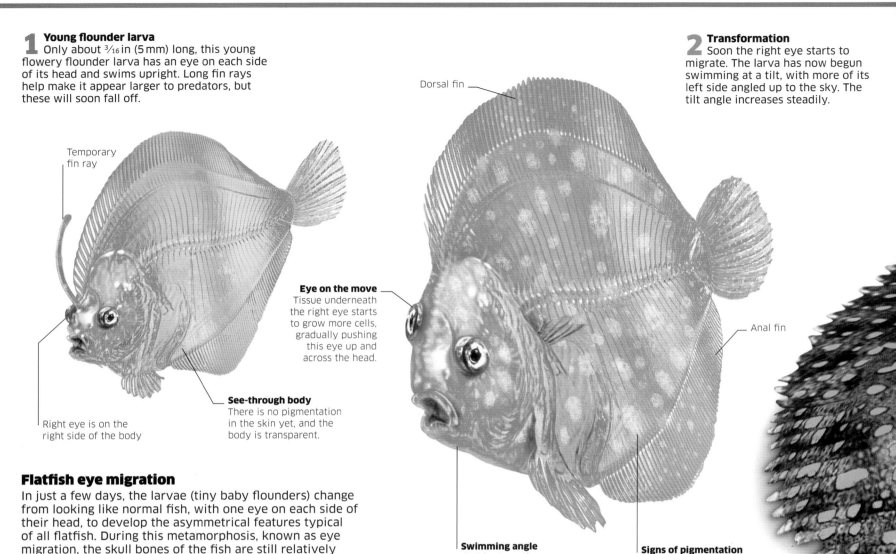

Temporary
fin ray

Dorsal fin

Eye on the move
Tissue underneath
the right eye starts
to grow more cells,
gradually pushing
this eye up and
across the head.

Anal fin

Right eye is on the
right side of the body

See-through body
There is no pigmentation
in the skin yet, and the
body is transparent.

Flatfish eye migration

In just a few days, the larvae (tiny baby flounders) change
from looking like normal fish, with one eye on each side of
their head, to develop the asymmetrical features typical
of all flatfish. During this metamorphosis, known as eye
migration, the skull bones of the fish are still relatively
soft and pliable and shift to let one eye migrate from
one side of the skull to the other.

Swimming angle
At this stage, the
flounder swims at an
angle of around 20°.

Signs of pigmentation
The skin on the left side
of the body begins to get
some color.

Swimming style

Although flowery flounders typically "crawl" along the
bottom using the dorsal and anal fins that line their body,
they also swim when needed. They undulate their body
and use their dorsal, anal, and tail fins for propulsion.
They never stray far from the bottom while swimming.

Spot the flounder

Like all flounders, flowery flounders can quickly change
color to match their background. This helps them hide from
predators, as well as approach prey of their own without being
seen. They also bury themselves in sand for extra camouflage,
totally blending in with the seabed.

2–8 seconds—**the time** it takes for a flounder to **change color**.

If a flounder gets **sand in one eye**, it briefly **loses its ability** to **camouflage** itself since it **needs to see** its surroundings to **color match** them.

89

Pectoral fin
Often raised for a sudden take-off, the long pectoral fin is folded flat down when not needed.

Tail, or caudal fin

3 Adult flounder
Once eye migration is complete, juvenile flowery flounders settle flat on the bottom, but they are still only about 1⅜ in (35 mm) long. They don't become mature adults, like the one shown here, for around one year. By then they will have grown to 10 times the size and still continue to grow.

Dorsal fin
The dorsal (back) fin ends up on one side, flat on the seabed.

Anal fin
Opposite the dorsal fin, the anal fin now also sits along one side of the body.

Multitasking fins
Propelling the flounder when it swims, these fins can also be used for "walking" on the seafloor.

Eyes on stalks
Positioned on short, thick stalks, the flounder's eyes can each rotate 180° independently of one another. This gives the fish a very large field of vision.

Spots of color
The adult flowery flounder can make its blue spots look very bright.

Flowery Flounder

Part of the large flatfish family, flowery flounders belong to a group known as left-eyed flounders. This is because, as adults, both their eyes sit on what looks like their back but actually is the left side of their flat body.

These fish are not born this way but transform in an astonishing process known as eye migration. At the same time, they also become bottom-dwelling as they settle sideways on the seabed. Flounders spend most of their time partially hidden in the sand, with only their swiveling eyes sticking out and scanning for prey.

FISH
FLOWERY FLOUNDER
Bothus mancus

Location: Tropical Indo-Pacific, east Pacific

Length: Up to 20 in (51 cm)

Diet: Small fish, crabs, shrimp

Seabed Fish

Fish that live near or on the seabed are known as demersal fish. They are divided into two groups—those that spend most of their time lying right on the bottom and those that swim just above it.

Bottom dwellers come in all different shapes and sizes and can be found anywhere from shallow waters to deep-sea shelves. Many have flat bodies that allow them to lie on the bottom, while others bury themselves deep in the sand, with only their eyes uncovered to watch for passing predators and prey. Those with upturned mouths can grab prey as it swims by, while a downturned mouth is useful for digging things out of the seabed.

Camouflage
Semitransparent lobes of skin look like seaweed.

LEAFY SEADRAGON
Phycodurus eques
Location: Southern Australia
Length: Up to 8⅝ in (22 cm)

The leafy seadragon belongs to the same family as the seahorse. It has a slender, pipelike mouth that it uses to suck up tiny organisms. The seadragon's brownish-green, leaflike body parts make it hard to spot among seaweed and kelp. Females lay their eggs on the tail of the males, who carry them until they hatch.

Spines for defense

Toothless snout

SPOTTED GARDEN EEL
Heteroconger hassi
Location: Tropical and subtropical Indo-Pacific
Length: Up to 15¾ in (40 cm)

Living in big groups, the spotted garden eel sits in its burrow with a third of its body poking out, facing the current and catching food as it drifts by. When threatened, it quickly withdraws inside.

ANGLER FISH
Lophius piscatorius
Location: Northeast Atlantic, Mediterranean Sea
Length: Up to 40 in (100 cm)

The spines on the angler fish's head have evolved into "lures." The angler fish lies on the seabed, half buried in mud or sand, waving its lures about to make it look like small wiggling fish. Any fish coming in to investigate becomes a meal itself.

Lure

MANYTOOTH CONGER EEL
Conger triporiceps
Location: Western Atlantic
Length: Up to 31½ in (80 cm)

The manytooth conger eel is commonly found searching out prey around rocky seafloors or coral reefs near islands. After hatching, it can spend up to a year as a tiny, transparent, flat larva that looks nothing like an adult conger.

Fins are merged together, forming one continuous fin

50 years—the **maximum recorded age** of an Atlantic halibut.

73 miles (117 km)—the **distance** that a **thornback** skate can **migrate in a month**.

91

ALLIGATOR PIPEFISH
Syngnathoides biaculeatus
Location: Indo-Pacific
Length: Up to 8 in (20 cm)

The body is covered with bony plates instead of scales

Found in colors from yellowish green to brown, the thin, grass-shaped alligator pipefish blends in among seagrass or seaweed. To look even more grasslike, it spends a lot of time in a near vertical position with its head pointing down. A poor swimmer, it uses its flexible tail to anchor itself to the vegetation so as not to get swept away by strong currents.

STRIATED FROGFISH
Antennarius striatus
Location: Tropical and subtropical oceans
Length: Up to 4 in (10 cm)

Specially evolved leglike fins allow this bottom dweller to "walk" along the ocean floor. Snatching prey in ferociously fast movements, the frogfish stretches its mouth so much that it can swallow fish the same size as itself.

Fins used for walking

ATLANTIC COD
Gadus morhua
Location: North Atlantic, Arctic
Length: Up to 3¼ ft (1 m)

The Atlantic cod spends its days in schools swimming about 98–262 ft (30–80 m) above the sea bottom. However, as it gets dark, these groups break up, and individuals swim down to feed on invertebrates and smaller fish that live on the seabed—including juveniles of their own species.

SPLENDID TOADFISH
Sanopus splendidus
Location: Cozumel Island, Mexico
Length: Up to 9½ in (24 cm)

This brightly colored member of the toadfish family feeds on fish, snails, and marine worms. It is often found lurking beneath coral outcrops or near rocky caves, with only its mouth sticking out.

ATLANTIC STARGAZER
Uranoscopus scaber
Location: Eastern Atlantic, Mediterranean Sea
Length: Up to 8⅝ in (22 cm)

Like other fish in the stargazer family, the Atlantic stargazer has eyes on the top of its head that are pointed skyward. It is well adapted for lying buried on the seafloor with only its eyes exposed. It has a special organ that can generate sound and electric pulses, used for communication and defense.

ATLANTIC HALIBUT
Hippoglossus hippoglossus
Location: North Atlantic
Length: Up to 15½ ft (4.7 m)

Endangered due to overfishing, the Atlantic halibut is the largest flatfish in the world. The maximum reported weight is 705 lb (320 kg). When it is small, it eats mostly invertebrates, switching to a more fish-based diet as it grows.

THORNBACK SKATE
Raja clavata
Location: Eastern Atlantic, southwest Indian Ocean, Mediterranean Sea
Length: Up to 33½ in (85 cm)

A ridge of enamel-covered, thorn-shaped denticles (see p.92) runs along the back of the thornback skate. Females even have a thorny underside. Young skates stick near shore while adults head to deeper waters, coming into shallow water only in spring and summer.

ROCKSUCKER CLINGFISH
Chorisochismus dentex
Location: Southeast Atlantic
Length: Up to 12 in (30 cm)

The rocksucker lives in very shallow waters, even within the intertidal zone. It can cling to rocks with fins that work like sucker pads and uses its large canine teeth to pick off the limpets that are also sticking to the rocks.

Great Hammerhead

Largest of the nine different species of hammerhead sharks, the great hammerhead has a wide, straight "hammer" and a tall dorsal fin. Formidable hunters and swimmers, these sharks make long seasonal migrations, moving from warm waters to cooler ones during the summer months.

The great hammerhead shark is an endangered species, having long been targeted for its dorsal fin, which is used for shark fin soup and as medicine in some countries. Because hammerheads are slow to reproduce—females carry their young for 11 months, and breed only once every two years—it is hard for the species to recover from overfishing.

Dorsal fin
This large fin stabilizes the shark when moving forward but also helps the shark make sharp turns.

Shark skin
A close-up of shark skin reveals tough, V-shaped scales. Called dermal denticles, these are structured in the same way as teeth and covered by a layer of enamel. This helps reduce drag and turbulence.

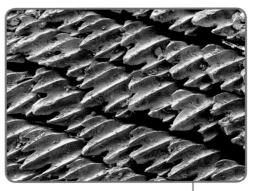

Superb swimmer
A hammerhead is always on the move—if it stops swimming, it suffocates, since water does not flow over its gills if it stays still. Its light skeleton and body shape make it a very efficient and fast swimmer. To turn, it changes the angles of its fins to alter the flow of water over its body.

A second dorsal fin stabilizes the back end of the shark

Tailfin
This is the shark's propeller, moving side to side to push the shark forward. Hammerhead tailfins have two unevenly sized lobes, the upper one always larger than the lower one.

Locating prey
When hunting, great hammerheads swim near the seabed, making broad back and forth movements with their head, as though they are scanning the ocean floor. This is because in addition to sight and smell, they have tiny electrical sensors on their cephalofoil. These detect the electric impulses of their prey, helping the shark to find food hiding in the sand.

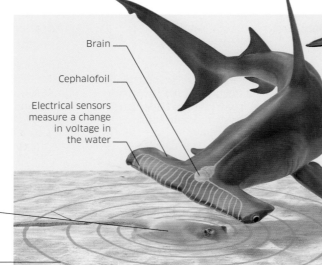

Brain

Cephalofoil

Electrical sensors measure a change in voltage in the water

Stingray hidden in the sand

Electric field formed by pulses produced by the stingray's muscles

Pelvic fin
A pair of pelvic fins help the shark turn, roll, and move up and down.

Countershading
The shark's pale underside makes it less visible against the sunlit surface and hard for fish or other prey to spot when it approaches from above.

1,864 miles (3,000 km)—the **distance** great hammerheads **migrate** in a year.

30,000 The number of **teeth** a shark can get through **in a lifetime**.

93

Eye

Nostril
Water flows in through the nostrils, where sensory cells detect chemicals in the water, such as those associated with blood.

Electrical sensors
A network of jelly-filled pores, called ampullae of Lorenzini, lies along the hammer. The pores help sharks detect electric fields, such as those generated by fish moving in the water.

Handy hammer
The broad, flattened hammer-shaped head is known as a cephalofoil. Supported by a wide cartilaginous skull, it contains key sensory organs.

Smell detector
Behind each nostril is a large sac full of sensory cells that pick up different smells. This gives hammerheads an extremely good sense of smell.

Skull

Nostril

Optic nerve
The optic nerve connects the eye to the brain. In hammerheads, it may be up to 12 in (30 cm) long.

Eye
The position of the eye at the end of the head enables the hammerhead to see 360° in all directions—above, below, behind, and in front.

Cartilaginous skeleton
Cartilage is a rubbery tissue that is lighter and more flexible than bone, making sharks more efficient swimmers than their bony fish relatives.

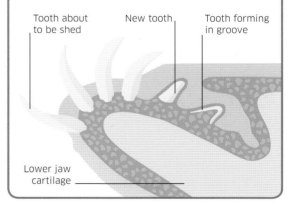

LOWER JAW OF GREAT HAMMERHEAD SHARK

Tooth about to be shed

New tooth

Tooth forming in groove

Lower jaw cartilage

Gill slits
To breathe, hammerheads take in water through their mouth as they swim. This water flows over the gills in their mouth and then out again through the gill slits in the skin.

Bright new teeth
Unlike human teeth, shark teeth don't have roots and are not embedded in the jaw but sit in soft tissue and are replaced constantly. Old teeth fall out as new teeth form inside a groove in the gum and are pushed out, similar to a conveyor belt.

Pectoral fin
These large fins act like the wings of a plane. When angled up, they generate lift as the shark swims forward.

FISH

GREAT HAMMERHEAD

Sphyrna mokarran

Location: Warm temperate and tropical waters

Length: Up to 19⅔ ft (6 m)

Diet: Invertebrates, fish, sharks, rays

100 million sharks are **killed each year** by humans, while only about **six humans** are **killed by sharks**.

Sharks

There are more than 500 shark species–the smallest is as long as a pencil; the largest is longer than a city bus. They all have a skeleton made of a springy material called cartilage, rather than hard bone, and all have an acute sense of smell.

Sharks are as varied in their habits as they are in size and appearance. Many spend nearly all of their time in shallow waters, cruising coastlines or coral reefs. Others live in deeper waters, visiting warmer shallow seas only in winter or to take advantage of seasonal food sources such as seal pups or migrating fish. Some sharks are swift and skilled predators, while others feed on microscopic organisms that they filter from the water or munch on hard-shelled mollusks that live on the seafloor.

TIGER SHARK
Galeocerdo cuvier
Location: Warm waters worldwide
Length: Over 18 ft (5.5 m)

The distinctive dark stripes that give the tiger shark its name are far more prominent in younger animals and fade with age. Tiger sharks eat a huge variety of food, from sea snakes and squid to seals and dolphins.

BASKING SHARK
Cetorhinus maximus
Location: Worldwide
Length: Over 33 ft (10 m)

With its gigantic mouth gaping wide, the filter-feeding basking shark swims slowly at the surface, taking in water and trapping plankton, including fish larvae and other tiny prey. These minute organisms are caught by bristles called gill rakers.

BLACKTIP REEF SHARK
Carcharhinus melanopterus
Location: Indo-Pacific
Length: Up to 6½ ft (2 m)

This is one of the most common shark species to be found around shallow coral reefs. Blacktips tend not to roam far, preferring to stay in the same area for several years. They typically eat mollusks such as squid and octopus, fish, and crustaceans.

BULL SHARK
Carcharhinus leucas
Location: Warm coastal waters
Length: Up to 11⅙ ft (3.4 m)

Found in shallow coastal areas, bull sharks are unique in being able to thrive in both salt and fresh water and have been known to swim far up rivers. They eat a wide variety of animals.

TAWNY NURSE SHARK
Nebrius ferrugineus
Location: Indo-Pacific
Length: Up to 10½ ft (3.2 m)

Tawny nurse sharks spend their days piled on top of each other inside sea caves or under rocky ledges. At night, they emerge to feed by sucking out octopus, sea snakes, fish, and invertebrates from their burrows and crevices.

Spines sit at the front of each dorsal fin

HORN SHARK
Heterodontus francisci
Location: Pacific coast of N. America
Length: Up to 3¼ ft (1 m)

This nocturnal hunter feeds on mollusks, sea stars and urchins, and crustaceans. The horn shark has a powerful bite that cracks through the shells of its prey. Relatively small and slow moving for a shark, this species has large spines on its dorsal (back) fins for defense.

70 years—the possible **life span** of a male **great white** shark.

513 The approximate **number** of **shark species** discovered so far.

500 tons (450 metric tons)—the amount of **water** a basking shark **filters** through its gills every hour.

95

COOKIECUTTER SHARK
Isistius brasiliensis
Location: Warm waters worldwide
Length: Up to 22 in (56 cm)

This little shark is a parasite. It uses its uniquely shaped mouth like a pastry cutter to bite out pieces of flesh from other fish and marine mammals without intending to kill them. It feeds at dusk, moving up from the deeper ocean to near the surface.

ANGEL SHARK
Squatina dumeril
Location: Eastern US, Caribbean
Length: Up to 5 ft (1.5 m)

Sometimes mistaken for a ray or skate because of its flattened body, the angel shark often lies buried on the seafloor, waiting to snatch passing fish or squid. It lives in shallow seas in summer and fall, moving to deeper water for winter and spring.

COMMON SAWSHARK
Pristiophorus cirratus
Location: Southern Australia
Length: Up to 5 ft (1.5 m)

Also known as the longnose sawshark, this species has a long snout ringed with sharp teeth and often swims in large groups. It feeds on small fish and crustaceans, using the whiskerlike barbels on its snout to detect prey and its sharp teeth to slash at its victims.

Barbels contain taste buds for sensing prey

Seal prey

GREAT WHITE SHARK
Carcharodon carcharias
Location: Worldwide
Length: Up to 19²⁄₃ ft (6 m)

Great whites live in coastal and offshore waters all around the world and can tolerate a range of temperatures from 41–77°F (5°C–25°C). Females are usually larger than males. Unlike many sharks, great whites regularly lift their head above water and have been seen taking birds from the surface.

CHAIN CATSHARK
Scyliorhinus retifer
Location: Northeast Atlantic Ocean, Gulf of Mexico, Caribbean Sea
Length: Up to 23¼ in (59 cm)

The beautifully marked chain catshark spends its days resting on the seabed but becomes active at night to feed on squid, fish, and crustaceans. This species is biofluorescent—it absorbs the blue light of the ocean, making its skin glow green.

WHITESPOTTED BAMBOO SHARK
Chiloscyllium plagiosum
Location: Japan, Southeast Asia
Length: Up to 37³⁄₈ in (95 cm)

This nocturnal shark feeds on fish, small crabs, and shrimp around shallow coral reefs. Preyed on by larger sharks, it has a narrow enough body to take refuge in small crevices. Bamboo sharks are often captured as aquarium pets, which may eventually threaten their numbers.

96   shallow seas ○ SARDINE RUN

4 miles (7 km)—the **estimated length** of some of the **larger shoals** off South Africa's coast.

Sardine Run

Most winters, a spectacular event takes place off the coast of South Africa. This is the sardine run, when millions of migrating sardines attract lots of hungry predators in a frenzied feast.

Fish often form groups, called shoals. Sometimes, a shoal swims in close formation, synchronizing every move. This behavior, known as schooling, is used when fish migrate or to deter predators. Sardine runs occur in many places across the world, but the South African shoals are among the largest, although the number and sizes vary from year to year.

Bait ball breakup

Large shoals of migrating sardines quickly attract the attention of predators. When the sardines sense predators nearby, their response is to confuse them by swimming closer together, packing themselves into tight spheres called bait balls. Common dolphins are usually the first at the scene, working to push the sardines closer together and up toward the surface, leaving them no place to go. Soon other predators come to take part, both from the surrounding sea and the air above. As they attack, the bait ball breaks up.

Going with the cold flow

Sardines prefer lower temperatures, and in summer they are restricted to cool waters off South Africa and in the chilly Benguela current to the west. In winter, coastal seas up the eastern coast get cold enough for the sardines to migrate farther north to spawn—something they do in their millions. Afterward, they probably return south in the deeper, cooler waters beneath the warm Agulhas current.

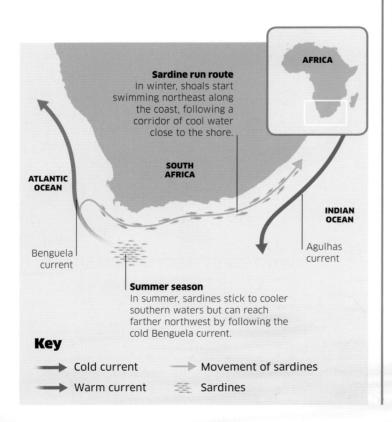

Sardine run route
In winter, shoals start swimming northeast along the coast, following a corridor of cool water close to the shore.

AFRICA

ATLANTIC OCEAN

SOUTH AFRICA

INDIAN OCEAN

Benguela current

Agulhas current

Summer season
In summer, sardines stick to cooler southern waters but can reach farther northwest by following the cold Benguela current.

Key

→ Cold current

→ Warm current

→ Movement of sardines

≈ Sardines

Jackass penguin
Penguins are fast, agile swimmers but must beware of becoming prey themselves for fur seals and sharks.

Cape fur seal
Hunting in small groups, fur seals swim straight through the bait ball, snatching at prey.

Bait ball
This formation confuses predators' senses and makes it harder for them to single out individual prey.

Bronze whaler shark
These sharks work with each other to herd prey fish closely together and then take turns swimming through the bait ball to grab any fish they can.

Long-beaked common dolphin
Pods of dolphins follow the shoals, cleverly herding sardines together in an ever tighter group before snatching their share.

Cape gannet
Hitting the water at speeds approaching 75 mph (120 km/h), this large seabird dives straight into the bait ball then swims back up toward the surface, swallowing its catch on the way.

Breaking up the ball
Predators such as sharks have their best chance of seizing prey when they can break up a bait ball into smaller groups.

Lateral line

Sardine
There are many species of fish commonly referred to as sardines or pilchards. The Southern African pilchard can be up to 12 in (30 cm) long.

The lateral line
Fish have good vision, but they need additional senses to help them keep very close without crashing into each other when they move in a school. All fish have a lateral line, which is a system of sensory channels running around the head and along the body. The channels have highly sensitive hair cells that detect tiny changes in water currents to help the fish coordinate their movements.

98 shallow seas ○ **CORAL REEFS**

Coral reefs make up only around **1 percent** of the ocean floor but are **home** to **25 percent** of ocean **species**.

Coral Reefs

So large they are visible from space, coral reefs are built up over thousands of years by living, growing corals. Hot spots of marine life, reefs also protect coastlines from tropical storm waves.

Corals, consisting of many connected tiny coral polyps, are invertebrate animals, and most need sunlight to stay healthy. Together with sponges and other reef-forming organisms, they provide a habitat for other living things. Their structure creates perfect habitats for algae and tiny invertebrates. These attract an abundance of different species coming here to feed, each adding its own colors, shapes, sounds, and visual displays to the vibrant scene.

Day and night on the reef

During the day, the reef is busy with many kinds of colorful fish. They spend their time grazing and protecting their territory. Beneath ledges and in crevices, nocturnal fish can be found resting. At night, most herbivores seek shelter and more carnivorous fish come out to hunt. Nighttime is also when most corals open their polyps to feed.

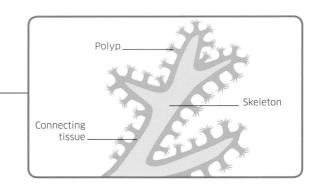

Polyp

Skeleton

Connecting tissue

Coral colony
Corals are large groups of tiny animals called polyps living together, connected by living tissue. The polyps secrete a mineral called calcium carbonate, forming the hard skeleton that gives the colony its shape.

Longnose butterflyfish
These fish chase away any intruders from their patch of coral.

DAYTIME REEF

Parrotfish
This parrotfish feeds on corals and the algae living inside them.

Regal angelfish
This angelfish likes to feed on sponges—simple animals that look like plants and are attached to the reef bed.

Chromis
These small fish school above the coral to feed on plankton.

Sea fan
Sea fans are soft corals. They don't produce a hard calcium carbonate skeleton.

Brain coral
The round shape and curly grooves of this sturdy coral make it look a bit like a brain. It doesn't feed during the day so keeps its tentacles retracted until nighttime.

Shark hideout
Whitetip reef sharks spend their days resting in caves and under reef ledges.

Sea slug
Often poisonous, sea slugs cruise the reef munching on sponges.

Yellow tang
The bright yellow is a daytime color—at night, it fades while a prominent white stripe develops.

Tube sponge

33 percent of the world's **coral reefs** are in **Australia** and **Indonesia**.

1,000 The approximate number of **hard coral species** around the **world**, supporting more than **4,000** species of **fish**.

99

NIGHTTIME REEF

Whitetip reef sharks on the hunt
These nocturnal predators hunt in groups, seeking out fish hiding in coral crevices.

Squirrelfish
Hidden during the day, squirrelfish come out at night to feed on crabs and shrimp.

Soldierfish
Large eyes help these fish see in low light as they cruise above the reef to catch tiny crustaceans in the plankton floating by.

Filter-feeding brain coral with open polyps

Moray eel
Moray eels hunt at night, smelling out their prey.

Sea urchin
With venomous spines as defense, sea urchins crawl out across the reef to graze on algae.

Sleeping parrotfish
The parrotfish covers itself in a protective bubble of mucus that helps mask its scent.

Coral feeding time
Like most corals, the black sun coral feeds at night. Its polyps open to extend their delicate stinging tentacles to capture plankton that floats by.

Coral polyp

Each polyp on a coral is an individual organism. Its tentacles, visible only when the polyp is open, contain special stinging cells to immobilize its prey—plankton and small fish. The tentacles transfer the food to the central mouth. Each soft polyp sits within its own casing, a tiny part of the skeleton called corallite. As polyps grow, they add more minerals to the coral's skeleton, making it grow thicker.

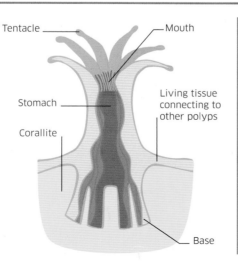

Tentacle

Mouth

Stomach

Living tissue connecting to other polyps

Corallite

Base

Coral bleaching

Microscopic algae called zooxanthellae live within the coral's tissues, helping feed the coral by using sunlight's energy to make food. If water temperatures rise as little as 1.8°F (1°C) above average, the coral may expel the algae. This leads to bleaching. Unless more algae move in within a short period of time, the coral may die, leaving only a pale skeleton.

Cleaning stations

Cleaning stations are areas, often on reefs, where aquatic animals know they can come to get cleaned of parasites, algae, and dead tissue by other animals. Animals that come to these stations are known as "clients."

Lining up
Clients will line up at cleaning stations. While they do, they watch the cleaners at work. If the cleaner-fish cheats and takes a nip of the client, those in the line might decide to go elsewhere. Here, a green sea turtle waits for yellow tang to finish off the client in front.

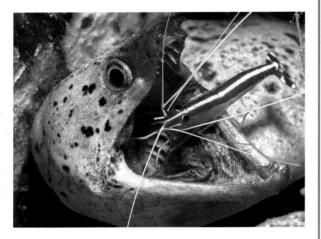

Cleaner shrimp
Fish aren't the only group of cleaners in the ocean. There are also species of shrimp that specialize in removing parasites from clients such as this moray eel. Cleaner shrimp are often found at coral reef cleaner stations, sometimes even alongside cleaner wrasse.

Useful relationship

This tomato grouper benefits from having parasites and dead tissue picked from its body. In return, the wrasse get a good meal. Once the grouper has gained the attention of this cleaning crew, it assumes a relaxed position that shows the cleaners that it is safe to start work. Each client species has its own relaxed pose.

FISH

BLUESTREAK CLEANER WRASSE

Labroides dimidiatus

Location: Indian and Pacific oceans

Length: Up to 5½ in (14 cm)

Diet: Crustacean parasites, dead skin, mucus

Cleaner Wrasse

Cleaner wrasse earn their name from their unusual feeding behavior. Working together in groups called "units," these fish are specialists in picking off and eating parasites, dead skin, and mucus from other fish.

A unit can consist of one male accompanied by several females, of one male and one female, or of juveniles only. All cleaner wrasse are born female. When a male dies, the largest female will turn into a male and take his place. If a male loses all the females in his unit, he will pair with the first cleaner wrasse he finds, including another male. If this happens, the less dominant male of the pair will turn back into a female. Cleaner wrasse spend their whole life on coral reef cleaning stations in shallow tropical coastal waters.

Greeting
Cleaner wrasse greet their potential clients with dancelike behavior that involves bouncing their tail up and down, especially when the client is new, or the cleaner wrasse is a juvenile and so more likely to be eaten.

Protractile jaws
The mouths of cleaner wrasse extend out letting them grab parasites, as if with a pair of tweezers, then drawing them into the mouth.

Recognizable uniform
At a distance, clients recognize adult cleaner wrasse by the prominent black stripe down each side.

Clean eyes
Dead skin and parasites are even removed from around the client's eyes.

Joining the crew
This young female has begun changing into adult colors.

Risky business
The client fish opens its mouth wide to let the cleaners get right inside. It doesn't eat the wrasse because it prefers a clean-up to a quick snack.

On the menu
The cleaners eat parasites called gnathids. These tiny crustaceans spend part of their juvenlie stage feeding on blood by attaching themselves to the skin or gills of a fish.

102 shallow seas ◦ **REEF LIFE**

42 The number of **different species** of **triggerfish** living in coral reefs across the world.

Reef Life

Often called the tropical forests of the sea, coral reefs shelter a huge variety of species. Their complex structures make homes, and feeding and hunting grounds, for many colorful invertebrates and fish.

Growing in warm waters around the globe, vibrant reefs support a large number of life forms. Microscopic marine algae, which create their own food from sunlight, grow in abundance. Countless small invertebrates and fish feed on these tiny organisms and, in turn, attract larger fish to the reef and are eaten themselves.

CHINESE TRUMPETFISH
Aulostomus chinensis
Location: Indo-Pacific, excluding the Red Sea
Length: Up to 31½ in (80 cm)

Trumpetfish are lie-in-wait predators. They hide behind a coral or a sea fan until a small, unsuspecting fish comes within range. Then, using their paddlelike caudal (tail) fins to propel their long bodies, they burst out of cover and snatch their prey.

Mouth opens wide to suck in prey

CROWN-OF-THORNS STARFISH
Acanthaster planci
Location: Indo-Pacific
Diameter: More than 27½ in (70 cm)

With up to 23 arms covered in toxin-filled spines, the crown-of-thorns starfish is a formidable sea star that feeds on coral. An increase in its population, combined with the rise in ocean temperatures due to climate change, has destroyed some coral reefs.

YELLOW-LIPPED SEA KRAIT
Laticauda colubrina
Location: Indo-Pacific
Length: Up to 5 ft (1.5 m)

Hunting eels in shallow reefs, this venomous sea snake returns to land to digest its meal. As it grows, it also sheds its skin on land. Females like to eat large congers, while males prefer a diet of small moray eels.

CARPENTER'S FLASHER WRASSE
Paracheilinus carpenteri
Location: Western Pacific
Length: Up to 3⅛ in (8 cm)

This fish gets its name from the way the males of the species use speed and displays of color to try to impress the females. Their courtship ritual involves dashing from a reef into open water, "flashing" their fins while briefly making their color patterns stronger and brighter.

CHRISTMAS TREE WORM
Spirobranchus giganteus
Location: Tropical oceans worldwide
Length: Up to 1½ in (3.8 cm)

This worm builds a chalky tube, buried in the coral, to live in. It extends a twin spiral "Christmas tree" of tentacles above the coral surface for breathing and to capture plankton for food as it floats by. If threatened, the worm retreats rapidly into its tube.

ATLANTIC GOLIATH GROUPER
Epinephelus itajara
Location: Tropical coastal Atlantic
Length: Up to 8¼ ft (2.5 m)

Looking for prey, this large fish cruises slowly around the reef. It searches for crustaceans, particularly spiny lobsters, but also turtles, octopuses, and fish, and often rests in caves or shipwrecks.

Large mouth makes it easy to swallow prey whole

1,003 lb (455 kg)—the weight of the **heaviest Atlantic goliath grouper** ever caught.

Snapping shrimp **snap their claws** shut very fast to **create bubbles of water vapor** that explode loudly enough to **stun prey.**

103

MANDARINFISH
Synchiropus splendidus
Location: West Pacific
Length: Up to 2¾ in (7 cm)

These fantastically colored fish live in small groups in the rubble around coral reefs. They are very rare among vertebrates in producing their blue color with skin pigment rather than by reflecting blue light. A coating of foul-smelling mucus deters predators.

STRIPED BURRFISH
Chilomycterus schoepfi
Location: Western Atlantic
Length: Up to 11 in (28 cm)

This fish belongs to the porcupine fish family, which are named for their spiny skins. It lives in reefs and seagrass beds, feeding on snails, bivalves, and crustaceans. Like other porcupine fish, it can inflate its body when threatened.

PICASSO TRIGGERFISH
Rhinecanthus assasi
Location: Indo-Pacific
Length: Up to 12 in (30 cm)

Like all triggerfish, this species has a spine that can be locked in the upright position by a smaller spine just behind it, known as the "trigger." The fish uses the upright spine to lock itself into crevices to prevent being dragged out of its hiding place by predators. Once danger has passed, the fish unlocks itself.

Upright spine

HARLEQUIN FILEFISH
Oxymonacanthus longirostris
Location: Indo-Pacific
Length: Up to 4¾ in (12 cm)

Often found in pairs or small groups, the harlequin filefish nests on algae growing at the base of dead corals. It is very particular in its diet, eating the polyps of only one type of stony coral. The fish smells like the coral it eats, which helps mask it from predators.

BASKET STAR
Astrocladus euryale
Location: South Africa
Diameter: More than 3 ft (1 m)

Related to sea stars, the basket star has 10 arms that branch out into ever finer limbs. It uses its long, twisty arms to catch food, usually tiny crustaceans, and carry the meal to its mouth, located at the center of its disc-shaped underside.

SNAPPING SHRIMP
Alpheus randalli
Location: Indian Ocean
Length: Up to 1¼ in (3 cm)

Using its large claw, this candy-striped snapping shrimp digs a burrow in the rubble around reefs. Here it lives alongside a fish called a goby. The goby is the same size, or bigger, than the shrimp and has better eyesight, so if it dives for shelter in the burrow, the shrimp follows its lead.

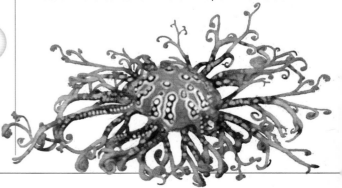

Close Neighbors

Coral reefs are vibrant worlds teeming with life, where lots of different species live at close quarters, with neighbors above, below, and on each side.

Some reef inhabitants have found ways of living together that are beneficial for them both. This Clark's anemonefish, living in a bubble-tip anemone in the Indo-Pacific, resists the stings of the anemone's tentacles. It helps clear debris from the tentacles and in exchange gets both food and a safe place to live.

There are around **3 million** shipwrecks lying **on the bottom** of the oceans.

Salvage diver
Specialized salvage divers may recover useful or valuable parts and cargo from sunken ships.

Octopus alterations
Animals such as this common octopus may move or break parts of a wreck to make a home for themselves.

1 Sinking ship
Depending on how and why a ship sinks, it may fall to the ocean floor mostly intact, like this one, or in pieces. In an accidental sinking, spillage of a dangerous or toxic cargo, such as oil, can have a serious impact on the environment.

2 Breaking up
The iron hull has started to rust, which weakens the metal. Corroded parts break off, and visiting animals can cause damage. How fast a wreck breaks up depends on the hull material and age, depth, waves, water oxygen levels, and temperature—it goes faster in choppy and warmer waters.

Moving in
The nooks and crannies of the wreck will make perfect shelters for crabs like this, which might otherwise be exposed on the seabed.

Shipwreck

Storms, collisions, sea battles, and navigational hazards such as reefs or shifting sand banks may cause ships of all sizes to sink to the bottom of the sea. In time, many become part of the marine environment.

Wrecks are not always the result of accidents; today, old vessels about to be scrapped may be sunk on purpose to create artificial reefs. However they come about, shipwrecks can provide habitats for marine life, attract more fish and so increase fishing yields, and boost diving tourism.

From wreck to reef

This sunken ship, resting on the seabed off the Outer Banks, North Carolina, lies at a depth of about 98 ft (30 m). Coral and fish larvae carried on the currents soon settle down, and a new reef habitat appears. Gradually, its iron hull has been transformed from a recognizable man-made object to a seemingly natural habitat.

123 The **number of species** that had **colonized** the wreck of USNS General Hoyt S. Vandenberg after only **one year**.

It's not just ships that make great artificial reefs—**subway cars**, **tanks**, and **planes** have also been sunk for this purpose.

107

Fish diversity
The stripy sheepshead is just one of many different fish species that live in and around the wreck.

Graveyard of the Atlantic

Off the coast of North Carolina, moving sandbanks and frequent rough seas have led to the demise of more than 5,000 ships since the early 16th century, from pirate ships to modern cargo ships. During World War II, the area was known as Torpedo Alley as German U-boats sank many merchant ships here. Today, many of the wrecks are popular dive sites.

Cape Hatteras

Diamond shoals

Cape Lookout

Marine graveyard
Not all wrecks are under water—over the centuries, many ships have hit the shifting shores of the flat Outer Banks.

Cape Fear

Cape Lookout shoals

Frying Pan shoals

Key

○ Shipwreck

▢ Shoal (sandbank)

SHIPWRECKS OFF NORTH CAROLINA

3 Sea life sanctuary

Larvae of corals, sponges, and anemones, carried by the currents, settle and grow on the wreck. This in turn attracts more marine creatures who come here for shelter, food, or company.

Shark hangout
Predators, such as this sand tiger shark, visit wrecks for the bountiful food supply. Many wrecks also serve as nurseries for newborn sand tiger shark pups, or as gathering spots for juvenile sharks.

4 Artificial reef

In time, the hull of the ship becomes barely recognizable as it is covered and teeming with marine life. It has become a coral reef, built not over centuries of slow growth but, depending on location and depth, in as little as a few decades.

Icicle-shaped lumps

of rust, called rusticles, often grow on the iron parts of a shipwreck.

SEASHORES

The border between land and sea is known as the seashore—an ever-changing environment that is constantly affected by the tides. Waves crashing high up the shore carry salty spray onto the land, while low tides leave sea creatures exposed. Despite challenging conditions, seashores are overflowing with life.

SHORES

The seashore is where the ocean meets the land. The coming together of these two different worlds creates a unique environment where living things must cope with extremes—pounded by waves and by turns submerged or exposed by the changing tide. There are different types of seashores—some are rocky, while others are sandy or swampy. Tides, waves, and currents shape these shorelines and affect both the animals and people who live there.

DIFFERENT TYPES OF SHORES

Much of what a shore looks like depends on its geology—how the movement of tectonic plates shaped Earth's crust there and what rocks and minerals are present. But shores are also shaped by water, while the plants that grow there define them, too. Different shore types include rocky coasts, flat shores made of sand, and muddy shores lined by mangroves or salt marshes.

Rocky coast
Stable rocky coasts provide a solid surface for algae and animals to cling to, but they can be a brutal habitat in areas battered by waves.

Sandy beach
Sandy shorelines can change shape dramatically over short periods of time. Tiny animals live in the spaces between grains of sand.

Mangrove forest
Adapted to live on the fringes of salt water, mangrove trees protect the shoreline from erosion and provide shelter for many animals.

TIDES

Sea levels rise and fall with the tides (see pp.28–29). Most places have two high tides in every 24 hours, but the tidal range—how far tides rise and fall—can vary depending on factors such as the shape of the coastline and the continental shelf lining the shore.

High tide
These large fishing boats are moored in the Bay of Fundy, Canada, where the difference between high and low tide can be up to 52 ft (16 m).

Low tide
As the tide goes out, and the water level reaches its lowest point, the boats end up on the seabed. Areas usually under water are exposed to the air, along with the animals living there.

BREAKERS

Winds cause waves to build up at sea. As a wave approaches the shoreline and the water gets shallower, the wave height reaches a point when the wave becomes unstable. This is called "breaking." When and how the wave breaks depends on the energy of the wave as well as the slope of the beach.

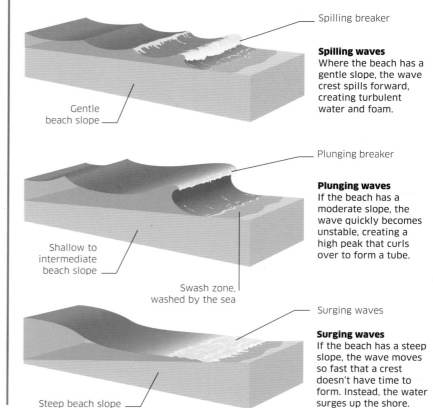

Spilling breaker

Gentle beach slope

Spilling waves
Where the beach has a gentle slope, the wave crest spills forward, creating turbulent water and foam.

Plunging breaker

Shallow to intermediate beach slope

Swash zone, washed by the sea

Plunging waves
If the beach has a moderate slope, the wave quickly becomes unstable, creating a high peak that curls over to form a tube.

Surging waves

Steep beach slope

Surging waves
If the beach has a steep slope, the wave moves so fast that a crest doesn't have time to form. Instead, the water surges up the shore.

CHANGING COASTLINES

Coastlines are continually shaped by the effects of wind, waves, tides, and currents. These forces erode the coastline in some places (see pp.114–115) while building it in others. Seasonal winds and wave action might reshape a shoreline from one season to another, while some changes take place over much longer periods of time.

How beaches form

Sediment, consisting of soil, sand, and stones, is carried by rivers, currents, and waves. As waves hit the shore at an angle, their swash brings sand onto the beach, while the backwash takes it back out again. This zigzag motion is necessary for longshore drift, a process in which sand and water move along the shore. Over time, in spots where the water moves with less energy, sand is deposited.

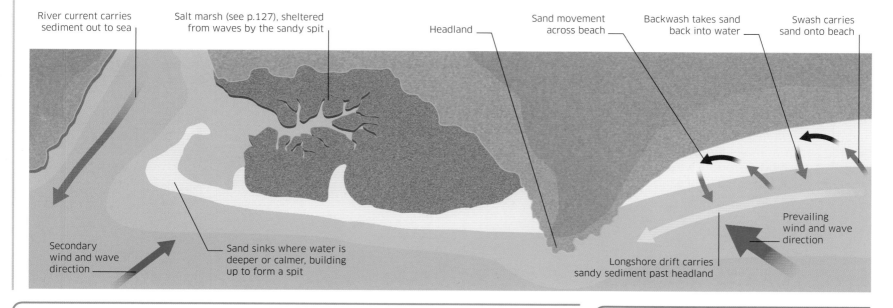

River current carries sediment out to sea

Salt marsh (see p.127), sheltered from waves by the sandy spit

Headland

Sand movement across beach

Backwash takes sand back into water

Swash carries sand onto beach

Secondary wind and wave direction

Sand sinks where water is deeper or calmer, building up to form a spit

Prevailing wind and wave direction

Longshore drift carries sandy sediment past headland

COASTAL DEFENSES

The energy of the ocean can be overwhelming in some coastal areas, with waves battering the shoreline, eroding land, and buffeting roads, railroads, and buildings. Natural and man-made defenses can help lessen the impact of waves on the shoreline, helping protect it from weathering and erosion.

Sea wall
Walls or embankments, commonly made of concrete, can help stop coastal erosion but are costly to build.

Dunes
Grasses can trap sand blown onshore by winds to create dunes that prevent beaches from being washed away.

Groynes
Structures built at right angles to the beach, usually of wood or rock, can reduce longshore drift and trap sand.

Storm-surge barrier
Protecting low coastal areas from flooding, these allow tidal flows but can close when seas are high or stormy.

DISAPPEARING COASTS

When solid rock is broken up into small fragments, this is known as weathering. It can happen in a variety of different ways (see p.115). When waves, currents, and tides move these fragments away from the shore, this is known as erosion. Some shores erode quicker than others, such as this one in Crimea on the Black Sea coast, where people's houses are at risk and one has already tumbled down the eroded cliff.

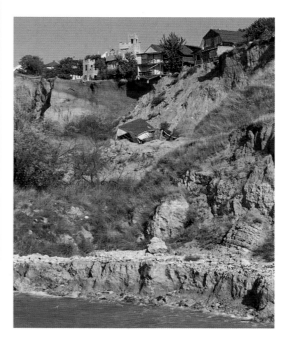

Rock Pool

Many rocky shores are shaped in such a way that the rocks trap pools of water when the tide goes out. These rock pools provide food and shelter for many species of sea life.

Although rock pools offer refuge, living in one comes with challenges. At low tide, as pools get exposed to the sun and lose the cooling effects of the ocean, the water in the pool can heat up quickly. Hotter water contains less oxygen and evaporates quicker, which increases the salt level, while heavy rain can reduce it. Some marine creatures get trapped as the tide recedes; others depend on the pool and try to avoid getting swept out by high tide or waves. The seaweeds and diverse set of animals living in rock pools have found different ways of coping with these extremes.

Sea palm
The sea palm's strong, trunklike stalk lets it sway without being torn from the rocks, whether it is under water or pounded by waves as the tide changes.

Sea sacs
Also known as dead man's fingers, this seaweed has water-filled sacs that protect it from drying out at low tide.

California mussels
Firmly glued to the rocks, these large mussels grow all over the shore, both in and out of pools. During a heat wave, however, those outside of pools risk boiling in their shells at low tide.

Rockweed
Rockweed can bear drying out at low tide and so thrives throughout the intertidal zone. Many creatures hide from predators beneath this brown seaweed.

Botanical Beach pool

On the west coast of Canada lies Botanical Beach, full of rock pools just like this one, rich in intertidal life. High tide and waves bring fresh nutrients, from plankton to small fish, but waves can sweep away any resident that isn't firmly attached to the rock. To stay put, mussels and barnacles use a gluelike substance, seaweeds are secured by their holdfasts, while others cling on to the rocks as best they can.

Purple shore crab
These small crabs scavenge any food but mainly eat green algae and also juvenile shrimp, bivalves, and snail eggs.

Black turban snail
Black turban snails graze on algae. Once the snail dies, their shell often makes a home for a hermit crab.

Purple starfish
This top predator uses its arms to widen the tiny gap in a mussel's shell then squeezes part of its own stomach through the gap to eat the soft body.

12 ft (3.7 m)—the **maximum difference** between **high and low tide** measured at Botanical Beach.

18°F (10°C)—the number of degrees the **water temperature** can **fluctuate** in a Canadian rock pool **between tides.**

113

Great blue heron
While rock pools provide sanctuary for small marine animals in a receding tide, predators such as this heron come here for an easy meal.

Life in the tidal zone

Rock pools lower on the shore are often home to more species than those higher up. This is because the farther up the shore a pool sits, the less often it gets topped up by new seawater that can regulate temperature or salt levels.

Rock pool

Rock pool

Spray zone

Highest tide

Mean sea level

Lowest tide

Gooseneck barnacles
The body of a gooseneck barnacle is encased inside a shell that is fixed to the rock with a strong, flexible stalk. Instead of using its feathery legs for swimming, it flicks them out into the water to catch food.

Corallina seaweed
This species of red seaweed has a rough, gritty, coral-like texture. The seaweed produces chemicals that attract herbivores, such as sea urchins, who graze off the green algae growing on it.

Tidepool sculpin
These small fish can tolerate living in water of relatively high temperature and with low oxygen levels. When oxygen levels get very low, they will gulp air at the surface.

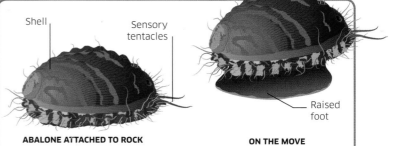

Shell

Sensory tentacles

Raised foot

ABALONE ATTACHED TO ROCK

ON THE MOVE

Purple sea urchins
Purple sea urchins can live for more than 50 years. While inhabiting this rock pool, they feed on algae and sponges growing on the rock.

Giant green anemone
These anemones have algae sheltering in their tissues, which provide them with nourishment and contribute to their bright green color.

Abalone
When threatened by a predatory sea star, abalone (a type of sea snail) stretch up on their strong muscular foot and spin their shell back and forth rapidly to shake it off.

Cliff consisting of limestone and sandstone

Headland
This part of the cliff is harder rock so it erodes slower than the area carved out into a bay.

Weak rock
A hollow has appeared where water has worn away weaker rock.

Retreating cliff
The shoreline retreats inland as chunks of cliff fall away into the ocean.

Cutting caves
Waves force their way into cracks in the rock. This causes pressure that starts to split the rock, forming a cave.

Bay
Bays form where soft rock has eroded away faster than the rest of the shore.

Wave action
Thousands of years of waves beating against the cliff cause damage to the stone.

1 Exposed headlands
Headlands form when softer rock sections erode faster than harder rock, leaving the harder parts jutting out into the ocean. They are exposed to extreme wave and wind action. The more exposed a headland gets, the more it erodes.

2 Visible signs of erosion
Waves start to chip away at the base of the cliff. Weak areas in the rock are opening up further to create large caves. Broken-off rocks are picked up by the waves, accelerating erosion as they bash against the rock.

Tumble-down rocks
Beneath the water are rocks that have tumbled into the ocean from the cliff, known as scree.

Coastal Erosion

Some parts of a coastline are made of the hardest rock, while others are made of softer rock types or sediments such as clay or sand. When waves beat against these coasts, the softer parts get worn away faster, and new coastal shapes form.

As the waves scour away the coastline at different rates, bits of land—from small chunks to large cliff sections—fall into the sea. The material is broken down into smaller and smaller pieces and washed away in a process called erosion. This eroded material is carried on the tide and currents until it sinks to the seabed or gets washed up on the shore. Extreme weather and sea-level rise associated with climate change are both predicted to accelerate coastal erosion.

Changing coastline

The shaping of headlands and bays, and fascinating rock formations such as those seen on this stretch of Portugal's Atlantic coast, are all caused by erosion. The changes occur slowly. It may take over hundreds of thousands of years between the first appearance of headlands and the early signs of an arch beginning to be carved out by the waves, and then another ten thousand years until the arch collapses—although the collapse itself is always sudden and dramatic.

86 percent of east coast **beaches in the US have experienced erosion** in the last 100 years.

2017 The year the **famous limestone arch** in Malta, known as the Azure Window, **collapsed**.

115

How a cliff is worn away

Waves break down rocks into smaller fragments—this is known as weathering. This can happen chemically, when the rock decomposes because of a chemical reaction, or mechanically (attrition, abrasion, and pressure). The type of rock, the shape of the shore, and the power of the waves all affect these processes.

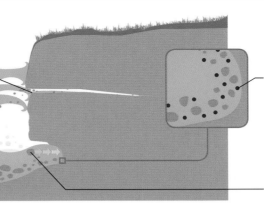

Pressure caused by water
Waves breaking on the cliff compress air in cracks in the rock. Known as hydraulic pressure, this creates further cracking.

From rock to pebble
Wave action causes rocks to hit against each other, getting smaller and smaller in a process called attrition.

Corrosion
Seawater chemically breaks down, or corrodes, rock such as limestone.

Abrasion
The cliff is broken down by waves breaking against it. Loose rocks in the waves hack and grate the cliff.

Eroding headland
As erosion continues to weaken areas of the headland, it becomes more exposed to waves and erodes at a faster rate.

Arch
Waves have broken through the cave from both sides to create an arch.

Collapsed arch
Waves carve out a bigger and bigger arch until it collapses under its own weight and falls into the sea.

Freestanding stack
The collapsed arch has left a tall stack. The stack base continues to erode and will eventually collapse to form a shorter stump then disappear altogether.

Sandy beach
Soft rock is broken down into ever smaller pieces. These eventually become sand, which is carried by the sea. Where it settles, a beach might form.

3 Changing shapes
Erosion has caused the cliff to retreat further inland. As weaker parts of the headland erode faster than the harder stone, unique coastal features begin to take shape, such as arches. In sheltered bays, where there is less wave action than around the headlands, sand is deposited and beaches form.

Wave-cut notch
Waves erode the rock at the base of the cliff, between the high and low tide marks, weakening the stability of the cliff above.

4 Eroded coast
Erosion processes have changed the shape of the cliff entirely. Even the hardest elements of rock, once left exposed, will be damaged by the action of the waves.

Wave-cut platform
The collapsed material of the cliff is gradually broken down, and eventually an underwater platform builds up.

All gone
The cliff overhang has collapsed into the sea.

Wave Power

Seawater is constantly eroding the coastline, but when strong winds combine with a high tide, the effects are dramatic.

When storms whip up a calm ocean surface into a heaving, roaring mass of water, the waves hitting the shores can reach incredible heights. The powerful waves shown here seem to dwarf the 33 ft (10 m) tall lighthouse on a pier in the estuary of the Douro River on the coast of Portugal, and the pier takes the full impact. Waves carry a huge amount of energy, and in some places across the world, this power can be captured and converted into electricity thanks to new technology.

Sandy Shore

Some sandy beaches are formed when sand is deposited on coasts and island shores. Others, known as cays, appear on top of coral atolls. Rising and falling tides play a part in providing food to the beach, as well as shaping it.

Beaches build up in areas where currents and waves are weak enough to allow sand and pebbles in the water to fall to the bottom (see p.111). Depending on how waves and winds move the sand, some beaches are eroding, others change shape, while some are relatively stable. Although not as rich in species as rocky shores, beaches attract invertebrates that live in or on the sand, as well as birds that feed on the invertebrates, catch fish from the sea, or come here to breed.

Green tree frog
The only amphibians living on this cay, green tree frogs spend the hot days hiding in shrubs. In the evening, they come out to hunt for insects.

Heliotropium
This flowering shrub, common on sandy cays, tolerates salty ocean water.

Black noddy
As part of their mating display, these birds constantly nod their heads as if bowing to each other.

Ruddy turnstone
Looking for food, this shorebird turns over small stones to reveal invertebrates beneath.

White-bellied sea eagle
Nesting and feeding near the shore, these birds of prey grab fish from the water with their talons.

Brown booby
This spectacular diver catches fish by plunging into the ocean at great speed.

Coral cay beach

Lady Elliot Island, a coral cay on Australia's Great Barrier Reef, has been established long enough to have shrubs and trees take root in the sand. Their roots help stabilize the upper beach, but waves and currents shift the sand and shape the edges of the cay. Only 0.3 miles (0.5 km) wide, the cay is full of birds, both permanent residents and seasonal visitors coming here to breed.

Living coral
Cays are surrounded by shallow coral reefs, rich in marine life.

Nesting noddy
On the cay, noddy birds nest in trees and bushes, in colonies of no fewer than 20 birds. In summer, resident noddies are joined by thousands of visiting ones who come here to breed and nest.

Pisonia tree
Sticky pisonia seeds glue to birds' feathers, so they spread to other cays and islands. Sometimes the birds get so covered with the sticky seeds that they can no longer fly and eventually die.

Coral cay formation
Currents can deposit sand on areas of shallow coral reef. Over time, as sand accumulates, the corals die, leaving a hard calcium carbonate base on which the sand builds up to form a small, flat island called a cay. As the cay grows, birds may start to visit, leaving nutrient-rich droppings that, with time, may enable plants to grow.

Buff-banded rail
These shorebirds prefer the dry sand close to vegetation, where they pick through leaf litter for insects and other invertebrates, with their black downy chicks in tow.

Reef base
The shallow, bowl-shaped coral reef base helps keep the cay's sand in place.

Coral sand
Coral that has been broken down into sand-sized particles gets carried on currents onto shallow reef flats. Here, it builds up but rarely rises higher than a few yards above sea level.

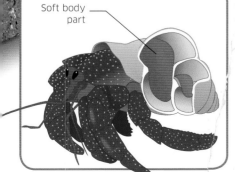

Soft body part

Hermit crab
Not fully covered by an exoskeleton, the hermit crab lives in empty sea shells that protect its soft body. As it grows, it frequently upgrades its shell for one that is bigger or stronger. Sometimes crabs gather for a group shell-swap, which may mean having to fight other hermit crabs for the best shell.

Parrotfish sand factory
Parrotfish use their powerful beaklike mouth to bite off chunks of coral. They digest the algae growing in the coral and the coral itself. What comes out of the other end of the fish is sand-sized grains of the coral's hard, rocky skeleton. This sand spreads in the water, much of it eventually getting washed up on beaches.

62 lb (28 kg)—the **weight** a coconut crab can **lift** with its **strong claws**.

Soldier crabs perform **an acrobatic somersault** to shed sand off their back.

SAND BUBBLER CRAB
Scopimera inflata
Location: Eastern Australia
Carapace width: Up to ½ in (1.2 cm)

Filtering sand through their mouth in search of food, these crabs create intriguing patterns on the beach as they move around in circles, discarding sifted balls of sand as they go.

Tiny sand ball

SAND FIDDLER CRAB
Uca pugilator
Location: Southeastern US
Carapace width: Up to 8¼ in (21 cm)

Sand fiddlers live on sandy or muddy shorelines in estuaries or sheltered coastal areas. Males wave their large single claw back and forth to attract females to their burrows and warn off other males.

CHRISTMAS ISLAND RED CRAB
Gecarcoidea natalis
Location: Christmas Island, Cocos Keeling Island
Carapace width: Up to 4⅜ in (11 cm)

Normally, these crabs hide in the shade of forests or in deep burrows in the sand, but in December and January around 30 million crabs migrate to the ocean to mate and spawn.

COCONUT CRAB
Birgus latro
Location: Indo-Pacific region
Carapace width: Up to 8 in (20 cm)

Coconut crabs are land dwelling, returning to the ocean only to lay their eggs. They are the largest land-based crab, with a leg span of up to 3¼ ft (1 m). They feed on nuts and fruit, including coconuts, and dead animals.

Specialized antennae
This crab uses its antennae to help it sniff out food.

Fresh coconut

Coastal Crabs

Crabs are nature's beach cleaners. Many play an important role in the intertidal zone, feeding on dead organic matter, such as fish or even other crabs, that is left behind by a receding tide.

Most kinds of crabs breathe underwater using gills, but many living along the shoreline can survive out of water as long as their gills stay wet. Some, such as fiddlers, stay in burrows in the sand during high tide and emerge when waters recede to scavenge for food. A few crabs, including coconut crabs, have lungs for breathing air. They only come down to the water to release their eggs and might drown if they fall in.

Come-back claw
If a male loses its claw in battle with another male, it will regrow.

Agile feet
Unlike most crabs, these nimble movers can use their eight walking legs to move in all four directions, not just sideways.

LIGHT-BLUE SOLDIER CRAB
Mictyris longicarpus
Location: Indo-Pacific region
Carapace width: Up to 1 in (2.5 cm)

Emerging from the sand at low tide, these tiny, forward-walking crabs march together—like an army of soldiers—toward the ocean, where they feed in the moist sand along its edge..

PAINTED GHOST CRAB
Ocypode gaudichaudii
Location: Southeastern Pacific Ocean
Carapace width: Up to 4 in (10 cm)

These shore crabs feed on algae, dead fish, insects, and other organisms they find in the intertidal zone. Both males and females have one slightly larger claw and both dig deep burrows.

Fighting males

5 mm (⁵⁄₁₆ in) – the diameter of the tiny **pea crab**, **which lives inside clams or oysters**.

On the **Galápagos islands**, Sally Lightfoot crabs crawl all over **marine iguanas** to feed on their **ticks**.

121

CRUSTACEAN

SALLY LIGHTFOOT CRAB

Grapsus grapsus

Location: Southeastern Pacific Ocean

Carapace width: Up to 3⅛ in (8 cm)

Diet: Algae, small animals, dead organic matter

Colorful carapace
Born with black carapaces (shells), these crabs get their striking red and blue colors only after several molts. Each new shell is brighter than the one just shed.

Dead baby sea turtle

Well watered

Most shore crabs have gills that they need to keep moist in order to breathe. They hold a water supply in their gill chambers, inside their exoskeleton. Sally Lightfoot crabs sometimes use this water to "spit." They are thought to use the spitting as a defense mechanism but probably also to get rid of excess salts in their body.

Opportunistic feeders

Sally lightfoot crabs scramble among the rocks and in the sea spray of the intertidal zone. They are excellent leapers, able to avoid rogue waves in a single bound. While they spend a lot of time grazing algae, they will take any opportunity for an easy meal, including baby sea turtles.

Green Sea Turtle

Green sea turtles are superbly adapted for life in the water, but they have to return to land to lay their eggs. Many swim vast distances to reach their breeding beaches.

Green sea turtles live in warm oceans all over the world. They spend most of their time in shallow seas, feeding in seagrass meadows and coral reefs. These feeding grounds can be as far away as 1,615 miles (2,600 km) from their nesting grounds. Females make this long trip to lay their eggs on the shore after mating at sea.

Beach nursery

Female green sea turtles come ashore to bury their eggs in warm sand. Each female excavates a hole, lays her clutch of eggs, and covers them up before returning to the water. When the baby turtles hatch, they must make a hazardous dash across the sand to reach the sea. When old enough to breed, females instinctively find their way back to the beaches where they were born, to lay their own eggs.

1 Leaving the sea
Each female may be up to 20 years old before she breeds for the first time. She usually arrives on the beach at night.

Distant water
The sea is far enough away from the nest that the eggs will remain dry.

2 Making the nest
The turtle drags herself above the high tide line and digs a hole with her back flippers. The hole can be more than 20 in (50 cm) deep.

GREEN SEA TURTLE

Chelonia mydas

Location: Tropical and subtropical oceans

Length: Up to 5 ft (1.5 m)

Diet: Seagrass (adults), jellyfish, fish eggs

3 Laying the eggs
When the hole is deep enough, the turtle lays up to 200 eggs. Each egg is perfectly round, with a leathery shell.

Less than **1 percent** of newly hatched green sea turtles will **survive** until breeding age.

25,000 The number of green sea turtle **nests** made each year on the beaches of **Ascension Island**—a popular nesting site in the middle of the Southern Atlantic.

123

Life at sea

Mature green sea turtles are excellent swimmers and divers, using their two strong front flippers to power through the water and their hind flippers as rudders. This skill is put to good use during their migrations between feeding and nesting grounds. Baby turtles start swimming as soon as they reach the sea.

Turtle anatomy

A green sea turtle's streamlined shell is made up of fused bones covered in hard plates, made from the same material as human fingernails—keratin. Unlike tortoises, sea turtles cannot pull their head or limbs into their protective shell.

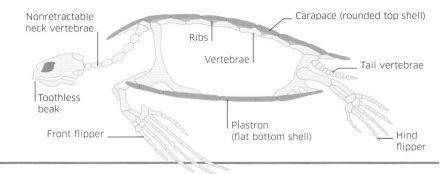

Nonretractable neck vertebrae

Ribs

Carapace (rounded top shell)

Vertebrae

Tail vertebrae

Toothless beak

Front flipper

Plastron (flat bottom shell)

Hind flipper

Returning to the sea
The female leaves as soon as her eggs are buried.

Picked off
Many baby turtles are seized by birds, crabs, and other hunters before they reach the sea.

Seeing the light
The baby turtles follow moonlight reflecting on the water to find their way to the sea. Artificial light sources, such as streetlights, can confuse them.

4 Eggs develop
Hidden from predators and incubated by the warm tropical sand, the baby turtles develop inside the eggs for 8 to 10 weeks.

5 Hatching
When the baby turtles hatch, they stay hidden until they are all ready to emerge at once. Then they scuttle down the beach to the sea as fast as they can.

124 seashores ○ **MANGROVE FOREST**

27 The number of mangrove tree species in the Sundarbans.

Mangrove Forest

Rooted in salty ocean water, trees called mangroves grow along tropical coastlines. The largest mangrove forest in the world is in the Sundarbans, a region that straddles India and Bangladesh.

Coastal life poses important challenges to mangroves. They must stay firmly upright in the soft mud, and they need to tolerate high levels of salt that would kill most other kinds of trees. But mangroves are well adapted to their aquatic life and grow into tangled thickets that provide important habitats for many seashore creatures.

White-bellied sea eagle
One of the habitat's top predators perches in the treetops to scan for potential prey.

Mudskipper
By using its fins like legs, this fish walks over mud at low tide and clings to mangrove roots. A mouthful of seawater keeps its gills supplied with oxygen when out of water.

Indian python
This heavyweight snake kills prey by constriction and is perfectly at home swimming in water.

Saltwater crocodile
The largest species of crocodile swims freely through the ocean water. It sometimes even swims far out to sea to reach distant islands.

Pencil-like roots
Some mangroves develop root tips that reach upward out of the mud to help collect oxygen.

Scat
This deep-bodied shoaling fish is a scavenger. It can tolerate changes in salt levels where fresh water from rivers flows into the coastal sea.

Needlefish
The long toothy jaws of a needlefish are perfect for grabbing small animals, such as shrimp.

The Sundarbans

Several kinds of mangroves thrive in the Sundarbans. Some have arching stiltlike roots, while others have roots that poke upward from the mud like stalagmites. A rich diversity of animals live in these surroundings—all the way from the treetops to the muddy shallows.

9 ft (2.8 m)—the **annual rainfall in the Sundarbans region**.
80 percent of this occurs during monsoon season.

108,000 sq ft (10,000 sq m)—the **total area**
of the **Sundarbans** mangrove forest.

125

Rhesus macaque
This monkey is mainly vegetarian,
but in the Sundarbans it regularly
comes down to the mudflats to
hunt for fish.

Bengal tiger
The mangroves provide good cover
for the largest predator in Asia. This
stealthy tiger ambushes pigs and
monkeys in the thickets.

Surviving high salt

Mangroves are exposed to large amounts of
salt. They deal with this by filtering it out,
and by expelling it through leaves as white
salty grains. Sometimes they will concentrate
all the salt into an old, yellowed leaf and
shed this part of the plant.

Coping with low oxygen

Not much oxygen penetrates soft sticky
mud, and what little there is is used
up by bacteria breaking down rotting
material. To get the amounts they need,
some mangroves have upward-pointing
roots that stick out from the mud. These
can absorb oxygen straight from the air
at low tide and then channel this to the
rest of the plant.

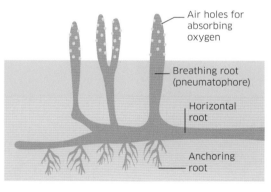

Air holes for
absorbing
oxygen

Breathing root
(pneumatophore)

Horizontal
root

Anchoring
root

Growing seedlings

Instead of scattering their seeds, mangroves
hold onto them so they grow into seedlings
attached to the parent tree. By the time they
drop, they are big enough to survive drifting
on the water and eventually settle on the
mud to complete their germination.

Sawfish
This relative of flat-bodied
rays has a long saw-edged
snout, which it uses to slash
through shoals of fish prey.

Fiddler crab
Emerging from his mud burrow, a male
fiddler crab waves his oversized colorful
claw as a signal to others—telling other
males to keep away or enticing females
to join him.

Stiltlike roots
Certain kinds of mangroves spread their
weight over a large area, which helps keep
them stable on the soft mud.

Mudflat

In some coastal areas, usually where rivers meet the ocean, low tides reveal banks of mud known as mudflats. Full of gooey, smelly muck, they are a treasure trove of life.

Mudflats develop when tiny particles, carried by a river or on the tide, separate from the water and fall to the bottom. If the area is sheltered from waves, these deposits build up, year upon year, creating a thick mud layer. When the tide is in, creatures emerge from the mud to feed on nutrients brought in by the tide. When the tide is out, these creatures may in turn become food for foraging birds, unless they hide deep in the mud.

Dinner in the mud

Mudflats exist across the world. In the UK, worms and bivalve mollusks are among the most common species in mudflats, though many groups of invertebrates are expert at finding food in the nutrient-rich sediments. The sheer number of invertebrates found here makes these habitats an important food source for shorebirds.

Cordgrass
This tough grass can tolerate salt and grows on mudflats. Its roots help stabilize the mud, preventing land erosion.

Common shore crab
These shore crabs match the color and patterns of the mud they live in for better camouflage. Their prey include worms, clams, and shrimp.

Mud shrimp
Tiny mud shrimp use their sturdy antennae to burrow in the mud and to "rake" microscopic organisms into their burrows to feed on them.

Capitella worm
This worm burrows through muddy sand, feeding on microscopic organisms and dead organic material.

Razor clam
Razor clams have a long, soft body encased in a hinged shell that is open at both ends. They bury themselves in the mud using their muscular foot. They feed by drawing muddy, nutritious water through a siphon down to their mouth, which sits deep within the shell.

Razor clam foot

Burrowing lugworm
Lugworms live in U-shaped burrows that they make by swallowing sand. As they feed on nutrients in the sand, they eject undigested waste sand into piles outside their burrows.

100,000 The number of **mud shrimps** found in **11 sq ft (1 sq m)** of a mudflat.

1 second—the **time** it takes a razor clam **to dig** ⅜ in (1 cm).

127

Salt marsh
These low-lying, sea-soaked marshes help prevent coastal erosion and provide a rich habitat for crabs, shorebirds, and plants.

Highest tide line
Salt marshes are flooded on the highest tides of the year.

Mudflat
No plants grow in the lowest parts of the intertidal zone.

Oystercatcher
These shorebirds use their long, strong orange bills to burrow after worms in the mud and force open shells.

Salt marshes

When enough mud builds up to keep a mudflat out of the water during all but the highest tides, salt-tolerant plants such as cordgrass can begin to grow. They help mud accumulate even faster. Eventually a salt marsh forms and other plants, such as sea lavender, take root.

Changing tides
Incoming tides regularly cover the mudflat.

Common mussel
Live mussels attach themselves to hard surfaces in the intertidal zone. This one has been picked up, prized open, and eaten by the oystercatcher.

Baltic clam
Like cockles and razor clams, this clam is a type of mollusk known as a bivalve; it has two shells held together by a strong muscle. Baltic clams vary in color from white to yellow, orange, and pink.

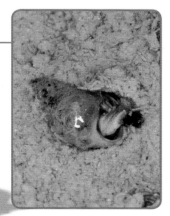

Laver spire shell
Often called mudsnails, these tiny mollusks rarely reach more than ³⁄₁₆ in (5 mm) in length. They thrive in salty, or partly salty, habitats.

Common cockle
A favorite food of oystercatchers and shore crabs, common cockles extend tubelike siphons to the surface of the mud to filter food when the tide is in.

Ragworm
Ragworms wriggle through the mud, feeding on both plant and animal matter, but often fall prey to mud-probing birds.

Estuary

Where rivers meet the ocean, partially enclosed areas may form where fresh water and salt water mix. These are known as estuaries.

This satellite photo shows the estuary of the Geba River, in Guinea-Bissau, West Africa, rich in mangroves, marine life, and large flocks of shorebirds. Tides bring salty Atlantic water, while the river carries sand and other sediments, showing up as streaks of white. The sediments that settle out at the mouth of the river have created vast sandbanks and low-lying wetlands as well as the 88 islands dotted across the estuary, home to manatees and sea turtles.

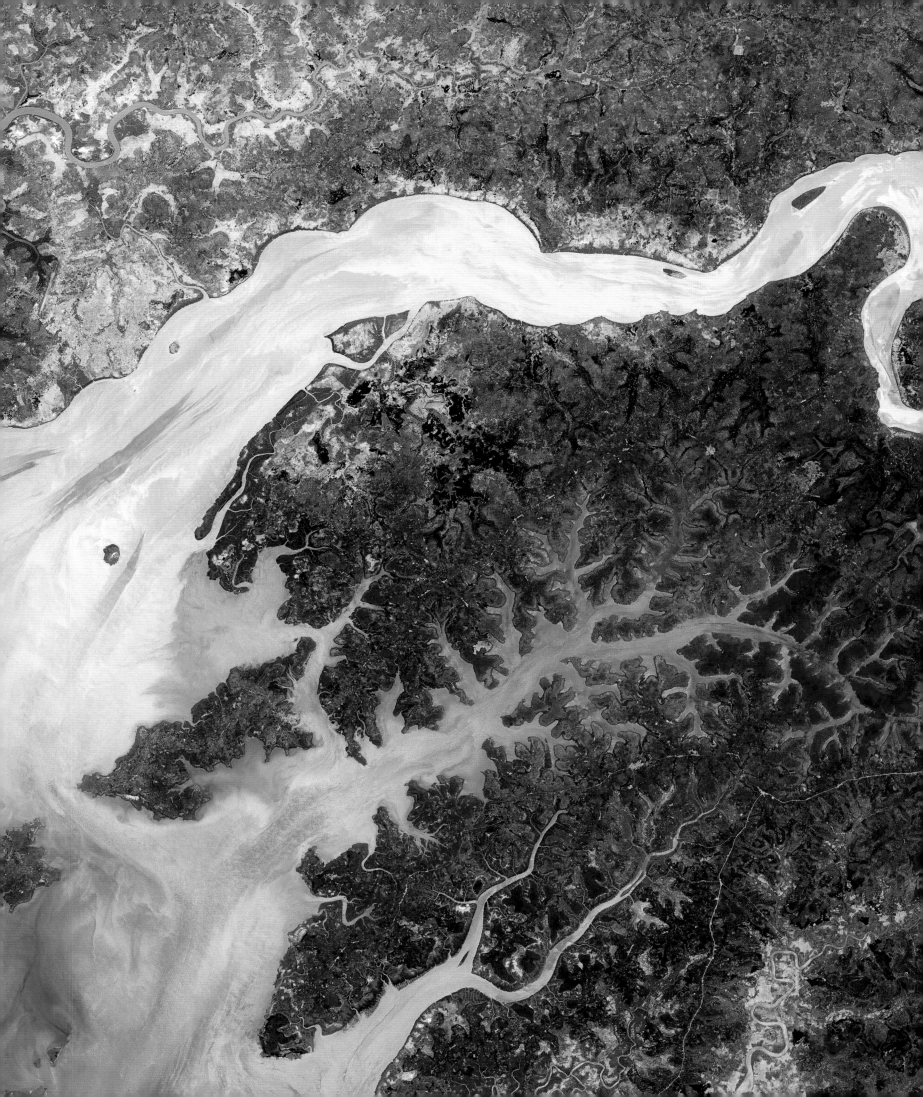

Puffin nest

Puffin pairs rear their young together. The male cuts a burrow out of the soil with its beak. Deep inside, the female lays a single egg. Once the chick has hatched, parents take turns feeding it until it is ready to leave.

Black guillemot

Black guillemots stay away from the crowds, nesting in pairs or small groups. They keep others away by calling out aggressively, showing their bright red mouths.

Crowded cliff

In summer, vast numbers of seabirds stake their claim to nesting sites on sheer cliffs like this one in Witless Bay Ecological Reserve in Newfoundland, Canada. This reserve is home to more than 260,000 breeding puffin pairs each summer and is thought to be North America's largest puffin colony. The puffins nest at the top, while black guillemots, black-legged kittiwakes, common murres, and other seabird species fill up all available space on the rest of the cliff.

Beak full of fish

Puffins have ridges on the top side of their beak, which can hold about 10 fish at a time.

Puffin pair

Male and female puffins tap their brightly colored bills together in a courtship ritual.

Not much space

Cliff-top space is at a premium. Every usable ledge is occupied and fiercely defended by its inhabitants.

2-3 years—the amount of **time** before a puffin chick **returns to land** for the first time.

Black-legged kittiwakes fight one another in the air by gripping their rivals' **beak** and **twisting** them.

131

Black guillemot chicks
Black guillemots lay their eggs in narrow crevices. About one month after hatching, chicks fly out to sea, independent of their parents.

Northern gannet
Circling around the edge of the colony, northern gannets make spectacular dives for mackerel and herring in the water deep below.

Kittiwake dinner
Black-legged kittiwakes pluck fish either by dipping their heads under the water as they sit on the surface or by making shallow dives from flying low over the water.

Nesting kittiwakes
Male and female black-legged kittiwakes work together to build a small nest made of mud, grass, and seaweed.

Common murre
Laying its single egg in cramped conditions, straight onto the hard rock ledge, the common murre needs to be an extra careful parent. The pointy eggs come in many colors, from cream to turquoise.

Gone fishing
Black-legged kittiwakes travel up to 30 miles (48 km) in a single fishing trip to find food for their chicks.

Seabird Colony

Seabirds return to land during the breeding season to find a mate and raise their young. Coastal cliffs are an ideal location—fish can be found nearby, but land predators can't get close.

Hundreds of thousands of birds may make up a single colony, with different species occupying slightly different areas of the cliff depending on their nesting requirements. Although safe from most predators except those that fly, cliff living can be risky. Balancing on ledges, these birds and their young are exposed to high winds and wave spray when storms roll in. Fights break out over space, and eggs and chicks may fall or get picked off. Despite this, noisy colonies thrive all over the world.

PELAGIC CORMORANT
Phalacrocorax pelagicus
Location: Northern Pacific
Length: Up to 30 in (76 cm)

The small, solitary pelagic cormorant dives down into the sea as deep as 120 ft (36.5 m) to find food, such as small fish, shrimp, and worms. It nests in small colonies or alone, building structures out of seaweed, grass, and moss. Sometimes these nests are lodged on steep cliffs.

SANDERLING
Calidris alba
Location: Worldwide
Length: Up to 8¼ in (21 cm)

Sanderlings are small wading birds that are often found in groups running up and down the beach as waves lap the shore. When the waves retreat, the birds search out crabs and other invertebrates in the sand or mud. After summertime breeding in the Arctic, they migrate to beaches around the world.

BELTED KINGFISHER
Megaceryle alcyon
Location: North America
Length: Up to 13 in (33 cm)

Belted kingfishers perch on branches overhanging rivers or streams to look for fish. They hover until just the right moment, then plunge into the water to catch their prey, which includes trout, crayfish, and frogs. On the coast, these shaggy-crested birds are often found near estuaries.

Females have a band of rust-colored feathers

Coastal Birds

Many different species of birds live along coasts, getting their food from the shore or the nearby ocean. Many have evolved to live in and around water, with special features such as waterproof feathers and body shapes suited to swimming and diving.

Several of these birds, including kingfishers and ospreys, are at home on the coast but also live near lakes and rivers. Others, such as cormorants, spend a lot of time at sea. True shorebirds walk along the seashore, probing the sand for food, and many have long legs, enabling them to wade through shallow water, and long beaks that are ideal for stabbing into sand or mud.

PERUVIAN PELICAN
Pelecanus thagus
Location: Chile, Peru
Length: Up to 5 ft (1.5 m)

With their 7¼ ft (2.2 m) wingspan, these large birds can glide for great distances. They usually search for prey while swimming, dipping their beak below the surface to catch fish, but sometimes they dive from a low height to make a catch. Often living in small groups, Peruvian pelicans nest on the ground.

Throat pouch
Flexible skin attached to the beak expands to hold fish scooped up from the water.

In proportion to their body, **only flamingos have longer legs** than the black-winged stilt.

3.5 gallons (13.5 liters)—the amount of **water** a **pelican** can hold in its **throat pouch.**

133

OSPREY
Pandion haliaetus

Location: All continents except Antarctica

Length: Up to 22¾ in (58 cm)

Unlike diving birds, which usually dive head first, the osprey plummets feetfirst into water to grasp prey. Its outer toes can be swung backward to help it grip slippery fish.

BLACK HERON
Egretta ardesiaca

Location: Sub-Saharan Africa, Madagascar

Length: Up to 26 in (66 cm)

These waders occasionally feed on mudflats, but have a unique method for fishing in ponds. Standing in water, they spread their wings to create shade, tricking any fish that is seeking cover from predators above. With the fish schooling below its wings, the heron has easy pickings.

Clever trick
The wings swing around to form a shading "umbrella" that attracts fish.

Bright feet
Adults have yellow feet at the end of their long dark-gray legs.

LAUGHING GULL
Larus atricilla

Location: North America, Caribbean, South America

Length: Up to 18 in (46 cm)

This gull gets its name from its loud call, which sounds like "ha ha ha." Its diet consists of crustaceans, insects, and fish. It sometimes steals food from brown pelicans, landing on a pelican's head to snatch food straight from its throat pouch.

Gray wings
Laughing gulls have much darker gray wings than most small gulls.

AMERICAN AVOCET
Recurvirostra americana

Location: US, Mexico, southern Canada

Length: Up to 20 in (51 cm)

The graceful, web-footed American avocet lives in inland lakes but may spend winters and breed in estuaries and tidal flats. It uses its long, upturned bill to gather up worms, crustaceans, and mollusks from the mud.

EURASIAN CURLEW
Numenius arquata

Location: Eurasia, Africa

Length: Up to 23⅝ in (60 cm)

One of the largest waders, the long-legged Eurasian curlew spends winters on coastal mudflats and estuaries. It uses its extremely long, curved bill to probe deep into the mud to pull out clams, crabs, and worms.

Probing tool
The highly sensitive bill tip detects hidden prey.

BLACK SKIMMER
Rynchops niger

Location: North and South America

Length: Up to 18 in (46 cm)

Black skimmers fly low over the surface of lagoons, lakes, and salt marshes as they look for food. Placing the lower part of their bill in water, they skim the water's surface for fish and insects. When the bills touch prey, they snap shut.

FUEGIAN STEAMER DUCK
Tachyeres pteneres

Location: South America

Length: Up to 33 in (84 cm)

This sturdy duck has too small a wingspan for it to lift off the ground and fly. Instead, it uses its wings to paddle across the water's surface when it wants to move quickly. It eats mollusks, crustaceans, and small fish and lives in pairs or family groups.

BLACK-WINGED STILT
Himantopus himantopus

Location: Worldwide

Length: Up to 15¾ in (40 cm)

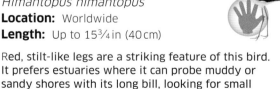

Red, stilt-like legs are a striking feature of this bird. It prefers estuaries where it can probe muddy or sandy shores with its long bill, looking for small invertebrates or fish. When it's time to breed, it moves inland.

POLAR OCEANS

Bitterly cold, windswept, and covered with floating ice in winter, polar oceans can seem like some of the most hostile regions on the planet. But in fact, their icy waters teem with life, ranging from clouds of microscopic algae to seals, penguins, and gigantic whales.

ICY WATERS

The polar oceans are the smallest and coldest of the world's oceans. In winter they freeze at the surface, turning open water into vast tracts of ice. Some polar waters are frozen throughout the year. Despite this, they are not as cold as some places on land. Even at the North Pole, the sea ice is only a few degrees below freezing because it is floating on relatively warm liquid water. This means that, in winter, polar oceans are far less hostile than windswept polar shores, and in fact they are rich habitats for life throughout the year.

SOLAR ENERGY

The regions around Earth's North and South poles have a cold climate throughout the year. This is because the sun's energy is dispersed over a wider area compared with regions nearer the equator, so its heating effect is less intense.

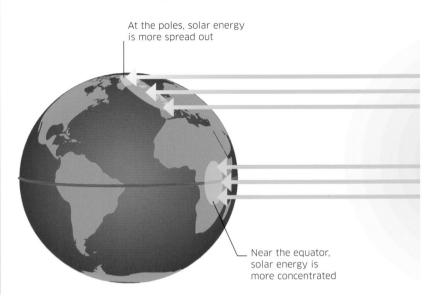

At the poles, solar energy is more spread out

Near the equator, solar energy is more concentrated

POLAR SEASONS

Earth spins on a tilted axis, which causes the North and South poles to tilt toward the sun at different times of year. In December, it is winter in the Arctic because the North Pole is tilted away from the sun, resulting in 24-hour darkness. With no solar heating, temperatures fall to extreme lows and Arctic seas freeze over. At the same time, the South Pole is tilted toward the sun, which means it is summer in the Antarctic. The region experiences 24-hour daylight, causing temperatures to rise and most of the sea ice to melt. Six months later, in June, it's winter in the Antarctic and summer in the Arctic.

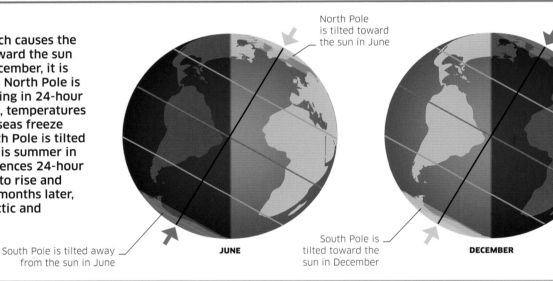

North Pole is tilted toward the sun in June

North Pole is tilted away from the sun in December

South Pole is tilted away from the sun in June

JUNE

South Pole is tilted toward the sun in December

DECEMBER

FROZEN SEAS

In winter, when the poles are in constant darkness, extremely low temperatures cause sea ice to form and spread, covering the majority of polar waters. In summer, much of the ice melts, but the weak sunshine in these regions ensures that some survives throughout the year. These two images show the extent of sea ice in the polar oceans in winter when the ice levels are at their greatest.

ANTARCTIC IN WINTER

Spreading ice
In the Antarctic, the cold Southern Ocean surrounds a frozen continent that is covered by permanent ice sheets up to 6,600 ft (2,000 m) thick. Antarctic sea ice spreads out from Antarctica to cover the Southern Ocean.

ARCTIC IN WINTER

Connecting continents
In the Arctic, the winter waters form a frozen polar ocean surrounded by land. Sea ice spreads out from the region around the North Pole to cover most of the Arctic Ocean, Baffin Bay, and Hudson Bay.

TEEMING SEAS

Despite their near-freezing temperatures, polar waters are full of life. In the warm summer months, massive clouds of phytoplankton—microscopic, single-celled algae such as diatoms—bloom in many polar oceans, such as the Barents Sea (pictured). Cold, saltier water sinks, forcing deeper nutrient-rich water to the surface, providing an essential food source for the phytoplankton.

ARCTIC FOOD WEB

At the bottom of the Arctic food web are phytoplankton, producers that make their own food through photosynthesis. The dense phytoplankton in the Arctic Ocean support swarms of zooplankton, including tiny copepods and larger, shrimplike krill. These are eaten by large shoals of filter-feeding fish. Krill and fish support seals and seabirds, such as Arctic terns. Many of these animals are preyed upon by hunters such as orcas and polar bears.

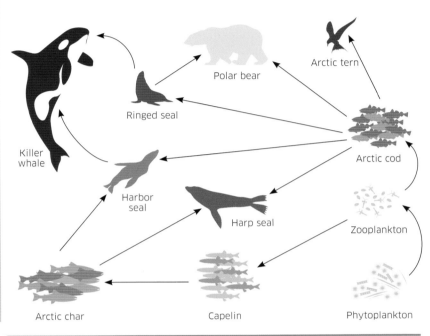

COASTAL COLONIES

The land surrounding—or surrounded by—polar oceans is much colder than the frozen seawater in winter. But when the sun rises above the horizon in spring, it melts some of the snow to reveal bare rock and sand and even some vegetation. This provides a vital habitat for animals that feed at sea but cannot breed there. These are mostly seals and seabirds such as penguins and albatrosses. In order to have easy access to food, these king penguins on South Georgia breed close to the shore in colonies of more than 100,000 penguins.

MELTING AWAY

The impacts of climate change are more extreme in the polar regions than anywhere else. Polar oceans are warming twice as fast as temperate and tropical waters. This is because while sea ice reflects heat from the sun like a mirror, the denser seawater absorbs it and warms up, melting the ice. As more sea ice melts to reveal more seawater, the rise in temperature increases. The warming water is already affecting polar marine ecosystems, and the melting ice will have catastrophic consequences for ice-breeding seals. It will also make survival very difficult for polar bears, which are adapted for hunting on sea ice.

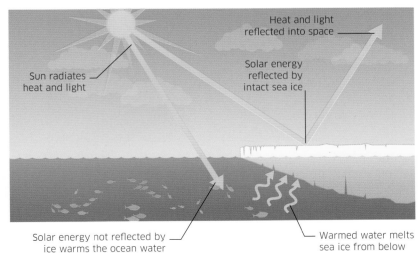

138 polar oceans ○ **SEA ICE**

13 percent—**the rate, per decade,** at which **multiyear sea ice in the Arctic is shrinking due to climate change.**

Ice shelves

All around Antarctica, parts of the continental ice sheet spill out over the sea as floating ice shelves. Some of these are colossal: the Ross Ice Shelf is the size of France and ends in an ice cliff more than 370 miles (600 km) long. An ice shelf behaves like a giant tidewater glacier, creeping downhill and out to sea where vast slabs of ice break off and drift away as huge, tabular (flat-topped) icebergs.

Sea Ice

As winter grips the polar regions, bitterly cold winds chill the ocean surface and make it freeze. Little by little, open water is transformed into a solid layer of sea ice.

At first, the ice is no more than a slush of separate crystals floating near the surface. As the temperature drops, the ice crystals are welded into solid sheets. Storm waves break them up, but they freeze together again, creating vast expanses of thick, floating pack ice that drifts with the currents. Some Arctic sea ice drifting over the North Pole can survive for several years (this is known as multiyear ice), but a lot of sea ice melts away each summer. However, as the planet gets warmer, the area of ocean that freezes over again each winter is shrinking.

Pressure ridge
Ocean currents can crush the pack ice together to form heaps of upended ice floes.

Thick ice
Pack ice can be more than 4 ft (1.2 m) thick, especially if it is more than a year old.

Fragile sheets
Sheets of nilas ice can be thick enough to stand on, but break up easily.

Frozen plates
Each plate of pancake ice has a raised lip around the edge. Pancake ice is created by waves. If conditions are calm, frazil ice can instead form a sheet known as nilas ice.

Crystal sea
Crystals of frazil ice form a soft surface layer, which is moved by wind and waves, and readily pushed aside by small boats.

Freezing over

Sea ice starts to form wherever the air temperature is lowest. In the far south, as shown here, icy winds blowing off Antarctica make the sea start freezing over nearest the shore, and the ice extends gradually out over the Southern Ocean. In the north, the ice expands from a core of multiyear sea ice near the North Pole.

1 Frazil ice
Plunging temperatures cool the sea below its freezing point of 28.4°F (−2°C). Tiny ice crystals form near the surface, giving the water a greasy look.

7 million sq miles (18 million sq km)—the **area of sea ice** around **Antarctica** in winter; **bigger than the continent** itself.

4,200 sq miles (11,000 sq km)—**the size** of the **biggest tabular iceberg** recorded.

139

Tidewater glacier
In polar regions, glaciers flow right down to the sea and out over the water.

Glacier ice
The ice that forms glaciers is made of compacted snow.

Birth of an iceberg
Big chunks of ice break off the floating ends of glaciers and drift out to sea as icebergs.

Iceberg
An iceberg floats with 90 percent of its mass below the surface.

5 Fast ice
Ice that freezes to the shore is called fast ice. As the tide rises and falls, the floating edge of this fast ice rises and falls, too, and pieces break off.

Shear zone
The rift between the fast ice and the drifting pack ice creates a zone of open water dotted with ice floes called the shear zone.

4 Pack ice
As more water freezes, the ice gets thicker and more rigid. Waves break it up into smaller slabs called ice floes, which freeze together again in tumbled masses of thick, drifting pack ice.

3 Thickening ice
The pancake ice rafts together and grows thicker as more frazil crystals grow, and longer crystals—known as columnar ice—form underneath.

Icebreaker
Ships with specially reinforced hulls, known as icebreakers, are able to force a passage through pack ice.

2 Pancake ice
The ice crystals group to form rounded, pancake-like plates. As they are bumped together by waves, their edges are crumpled.

Ice-powered currents

When sea ice is forming on freezing polar oceans, salt is expelled. This makes the water below the ice more salty. The water is also very cold, and the combination makes it denser and heavier, so it sinks. The sinking of this cold, salty water drives powerful deepwater currents that flow around the globe. Surface water is also drawn toward the sinking zone to replace the sinking water, helping drive surface currents.

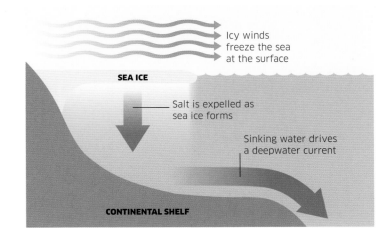

Icy winds freeze the sea at the surface

SEA ICE

Salt is expelled as sea ice forms

Sinking water drives a deepwater current

CONTINENTAL SHELF

140 polar oceans ○ **UNDER THE ICE**

80 minutes—**how long a Weddell seal can hunt beneath the ice** before returning to its **breathing hole**.

Under the Ice

Seas freeze over in the polar winter, but life goes on beneath the floating ice. There is even life within the ice itself, waiting to burst into action when it is flooded with sunlight in spring.

Sunlight in the Antarctic makes the ice glow blue and triggers the growth of microscopic algae—a vital food source for other sea creatures—that live on the underside of the ice. Meanwhile, cold, salty water seeping from the ice sinks through the water below and freezes it to form icy brinicles that often extend to the seabed. Bright spots lead hunting Weddell seals to gaps in the ice, which they enlarge with their teeth to make breathing holes.

An icy meal

Food is often scarce under the Antarctic sea ice, so the scent of a seal carcass attracts scavengers from far and wide. Creeping over the seabed, sea stars and long-legged sea spiders compete with giant isopods and squirming ribbon worms for the rich pickings. But some cannot move fast enough to avoid being frozen to death by the brinicles growing down through the water from the ice above.

Breathing hole
The floating pack ice is made up of ice floes that have frozen together, leaving small gaps.

Diving for dinner
Weddell seals hunt fish and squid beneath the Antarctic sea ice.

Speedy squid
Fast-swimming squid prey on small fish and are hunted in turn by seals.

All legs
Giant sea spiders have legs that span 10 in (25 cm) or more.

Starry swarm
Sea stars crawl over the seabed, searching for anything edible.

Giant isopods
These marine relatives of wood lice are common Antarctic scavengers.

Drifting jellies
Antarctic jellyfish swim slowly through the cold water, snaring small prey.

6½ ft (2 m)—the **depth** of the **thickest** drifting Antarctic sea ice.

Pouches of the sea spider's gut **reach into** the **base of its legs** to increase area for **digesting and absorbing food**.

141

Grazing krill

Living inside the sea ice are diatoms—single-celled algae that are a major food source for Antarctic krill. The krill use their front legs to scrape the algae off the ice. When the ice melts, the algae multiply in the water and trigger a population explosion of krill. The krill form huge swarms in the water, supporting penguins, seals, and filter-feeding whales.

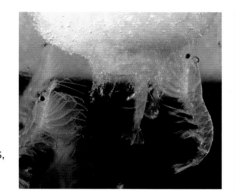

Ice anemone

The sea anemone *Edwardsiella andrillae* lives on the underside of Antarctic sea ice. It lodges its body in the ice, without freezing solid, and extends its long, delicate tentacles into the water to snare tiny drifting food particles. It was first seen beneath the immensely thick Ross Ice Shelf, where no one had expected to find any life at all.

Ice-dwelling algae
Tiny, salty channels within the sea ice house diatoms—microscopic algae—which are a vital source of food for Antarctic krill.

Antarctic toothfish
These big, perchlike fish are among the favorite prey of Weddell seals.

Icy fate
This unlucky Antarctic sea star has been frozen to the seabed by brinicles.

Creeping killer
Deadly ice extends over the seabed from the tip of a brinicle, freezing any creatures that get caught in its path.

Brinicles
Extra-salty water (brine) sinking from the freezing ice above is so cold that it freezes the water around it.

Slithering scavengers
Ribbon worms up to 40 in (100 cm) long converge on the remains of a dead Weddell seal.

BLACK-FINNED ICEFISH
Chaenocephalus aceratus
Location: Southern Ocean
Length: Up to 28⅜ in (72 cm)

Icefish blood is colorless. It has no red hemoglobin, which in other fish carries most of the oxygen that their gills absorb from the water. Because its blood contains a lower amount of oxygen, the icefish has a large heart that pumps a high volume of blood to provide it with enough oxygen.

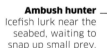

Ambush hunter
Icefish lurk near the seabed, waiting to snap up small prey.

GIANT ANTARCTIC ISOPOD
Glyptonotus antarcticus
Location: Southern Ocean
Length: Up to 3½ in (9 cm)

This crustacean, a relative of land-living woodlice, lives in shallow coastal seas around Antarctica. It is larger than most isopods and preys on bottom-living animals, often scavenging dead remains.

Bottom crawler
The isopod crawls on strong legs.

GIANT VOLCANO SPONGE
Anoxycalyx joubini
Location: Southern Ocean
Length: Up to 6½ ft (2 m)

Like all sponges, this simple animal lives by straining food particles from seawater drawn through the pores in its vaselike body. It grows very slowly in the cold water, and some scientists think it can live for 1,000 years or more.

Polar giant
This sponge can grow large enough to fit a fully grown human inside.

Life in the Cold

The cold polar seas contain far more oxygen and often more nutrients than warm seas. This allows fish and marine invertebrates to flourish in vast numbers, despite the near-freezing water.

These animals are cold-blooded, so they cannot generate heat of their own to combat the cold. Many survive because their body fluids contain antifreeze proteins, preventing the growth of ice crystals that would destroy their vital organs and kill them.

GIANT WARTY SQUID
Kondakovia longimana
Location: Southern Ocean
Length: Up to 7½ ft (2.3 m)

Armed with long feeding tentacles bristling with sharp hooks for seizing prey, this big, powerful squid hunts in the open ocean all around Antarctica.

EMERALD ROCKCOD
Trematomus bernacchii
Location: Southern Ocean
Length: Up to 13¾ in (35 cm)

Specialized for survival in the very cold water beneath the sea ice of the Southern Ocean, the emerald rockcod lives mainly on the seabed where it feeds on worms, snails, crustaceans, and some algae.

ANTARCTIC KRILL
Euphausia superba
Location: Southern Ocean
Length: Up to 2½ in (6.2 cm)

Shrimplike Antarctic krill feed on microscopic plantlike plankton and multiply to form vast swarms that drift with the currents. They are the main food of many much bigger Antarctic animals, including Adélie penguins, crabeater seals, and the colossal blue whale.

Filter feeder
Feathery front legs form a strainer that filters plankton from the water.

400 years—the possible **life span of a Greenland shark**, thanks to its **slowed-down lifestyle**.

98 ft (30 m)—the **length** of the stinging tentacles of **the biggest lion's mane jellyfish** ever found.

143

ARCTIC CHARR
Salvelinus alpinus
Location: Arctic waters
Length: Up to 24 in (61 cm)

Closely related to salmon, Arctic charr can live in Arctic rivers, lakes, or coastal seas. They breed in fresh water, so charr that live at sea must migrate upriver to spawn then return to the sea. They repeat the trip many times in their lives.

GREENLAND SHARK
Somniosus microcephalus
Location: Arctic waters
Length: Up to 21 ft (6.4 m)

This shark deals with the near-freezing water of its habitat by living in slow motion. It attacks fish, seals, and seabirds, creeping up on them so slowly that it catches them by surprise.

Huge shark grows only by ⅜ in (1 cm) a year

LION'S MANE JELLYFISH
Cyanea capillata
Location: Arctic waters
Bell length: Up to 8 ft (2.4 m)

This gigantic jellyfish lives in cold seas as far north as the Arctic Ocean. As it drifts with the ocean currents, its stinging tentacles trail behind it through the water to snare prey such as fish and other, smaller jellyfish.

Pulsing bell
The jellyfish pulsates its bell-shaped body to push itself through the water.

Venomous trap
Each tentacle is peppered with thousands of microscopic stinging cells.

SNOW CRAB
Chionoecetes opilio
Location: Subarctic waters
Carapace width: Up to 6 in (15 cm)

This big, leggy crab lives around the fringes of the Arctic in the cold seas off Alaska, Canada, Greenland, Russia, and Siberia. It preys on other seabed animals, including clams and sea stars, but also scavenges for edible scraps such as the bodies of dead fish.

ARCTIC COPEPOD
Calanus hyperboreus
Location: Arctic waters
Length: Up to ¼ in (7 mm)

Billions of these tiny crustaceans live in the oceans, forming part of the zooplankton that drift near the surface feeding on microscopic algae. This species is so numerous that it is a vital food for Arctic fish, seabirds, and even giant whales.

Mobile antennae
The copepod swims by using its strong antennae as oars.

Swimming "wing"
A pteropod "flies" through the water.

PTEROPOD
Clione limacina
Location: Arctic waters
Length: Up to 2 in (5 cm)

Pteropods are sea slugs that live in open water, swimming by beating short winglike extensions of their bodies. This pteropod preys on smaller species, seizing them with tentacles unfurled from its mouth.

144 polar oceans · **BLUE WHALE**

99 percent—the **reduction** in blue whale numbers caused by whaling since **1900**.

Blue Whale

Despite being the biggest animal that has ever lived, the blue whale is specialized for catching and eating some of the smallest animals in the sea.

The blue whale belongs to a group called the baleen whales, which feed by straining seawater through a filter of bristly plates called baleen. This whale targets the shrimplike krill found in oceans worldwide, especially the vast swarms of Antarctic krill in the plankton-rich Southern Ocean around Antarctica. Almost wiped out by hunting over the past 200 years, the blue whale has been very slowly recovering since commercial whaling was banned in 1986.

Lunge feeder

Like several other species of baleen whales, the blue whale uses a dynamic feeding technique. It lunges into a krill swarm with its mouth open, forcing a vast volume of water and food into its expandable, pleated throat cavity.

Swarming prey
Billions of tiny krill form a huge pink cloud, which the whale gulps in.

Upper jaw
The blue whale's broad, flat upper jaw carries the baleen plates.

Baleen filter
In place of teeth, the whale's mouth is lined with bristly plates of baleen. Made of keratin, the same material as human fingernails, the baleen plates fray at the edges to form a mesh of fibers.

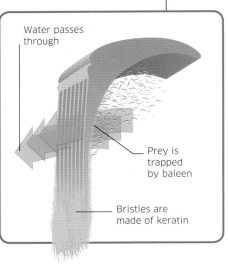

Water passes through

Prey is trapped by baleen

Bristles are made of keratin

Huge mouthful
In just one mouthful, the whale scoops up its own weight in water.

Powerful tongue
A blue whale's tongue weighs about 3.3 tons (3 metric tons)—as much as an elephant.

Inside a whale's mouth

A whale's throat, which extends far down its body, has amazing capacity, expanding like a balloon as food-rich water flows in through the mouth. As the whale closes its mouth, the tongue moves up and forward, forcing the water through the baleen. A baleen whale burns up a lot of energy capturing a meal in this way but is rewarded by each huge mouthful of food.

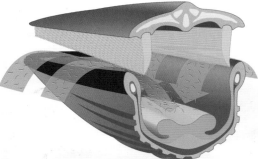

Sucked in
After drawing in a mouthful of water and krill, the whale starts to close its mouth. Its huge throat stretches to capacity, and the whale's normally streamlined shape expands.

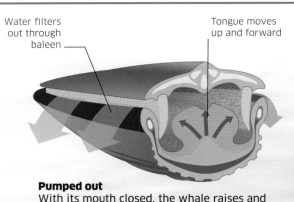

Water filters out through baleen

Tongue moves up and forward

Pumped out
With its mouth closed, the whale raises and pushes forward its tongue and the pleated throat contracts, forcing out water through the baleen and trapping the krill.

13,200 lb (6,000 kg)—the amount of **krill** a blue whale can **eat in one day**.

165 tons (150 metric tons)—the **max weight** of a mature blue whale.

Flippers
A pair of slender flippers near the whale's head help it maneuver in the water.

Pleated throat
The pleats allow the throat to stretch and hold a colossal volume of water.

MAMMAL

BLUE WHALE

Balaenoptera musculus

Location: All oceans except High Arctic

Length: Up to 107 ft (32.6 m)

Diet: Mainly krill

Migrating to breed

In summer, blue whales feed intensively in the cold Southern Ocean or in cold waters around the Arctic. As the sea freezes over, they migrate to warmer but less food-rich waters to breed. Each female has a single calf that lives on her milk for six months before it can feed itself.

Coming up for air

In winter, Narwhals hunt in family groups under the ice for fish such as Arctic cod. They keep in contact using a variety of chirps, whistles, and squeaks, and rely on finding gaps in the ice where they can surface to breathe. Sometimes this can be dangerous for narwhals as very cold winds can make the sea freeze over rapidly, trapping the narwhals below the ice where they run out of air.

Narwhal

Uniquely equipped with a long, spiral tusk rooted in its upper jaw, the spectacular narwhal is a marine predator specialized for hunting below the Arctic pack ice.

The narwhal is a species of whale and in general only the male has a tusk. Its main function is still not known, but since female narwhals manage perfectly well without one, the tusk cannot be vital for catching food. It is likely that males use them to display to females or rivals, with the most magnificently tusked male winning the contest. But the tusk is also highly sensitive, so it may be used to sense temperature or the saltiness of the water.

Sensitive tusk
The tusk is filled with highly sensitive nerves.

Melon
Many whales, including narwhals, use echolocation to sense prey (see p.149). The forehead contains a fatty "melon" that focuses the echolocation calls.

Small eye

Blowhole
Like other whales, the narwhal breathes through a blowhole in the top of its head.

Flippers
A narwhal drives itself through the water with its powerful tail and uses its front flippers for steering and maneuvering close to fish and other prey.

Tuskless female
Very rarely, a female may grow a tusk, but most females are tuskless.

MAMMAL
NARWHAL

Monodon monoceros

Location: Arctic seas

Body length: Up to 16⅓ft (5 m)

Diet: Fish and squid

In medieval times, the **tusks of narwhals were traded** for **vast sums** as the tusks of **mythical unicorns**.

147

Sparring males

Narwhals spend most of their time under thick Arctic ice, so little is known about their behavior, but males are often observed above the surface gently crossing tusks. This may be a way of communicating or to assess each other's strength.

Extended tooth
The male's tusk can be up to 10 ft (3 m) long but usually grows to about 6½ ft (2 m). It is a modified canine tooth, which nearly always projects from the left side of the narwhal's upper jaw through the upper lip.

Skull
The narwhal's tusk is rooted in the jaw. Some males have been found with two tusks—one on each side.

Toothless mouth
Apart from its tusk, the narwhal has no teeth. It probably feeds by creeping up on prey, sucking it into its mouth, and swallowing it whole.

White with age
As a narwhal ages, its skin gets whiter, especially on its underside. The oldest narwhals may be almost entirely white.

Warm streamlining
A thick blubber layer under the skin prevents the narwhal from losing body heat and gives it a streamlined shape.

Orcas often leap right out of the water, a behavior known as breaching. They may do this just for fun.

35 mph (56 km/h)—the top speed of an orca through the water.

1 Spy-hopping
The orcas check the location of a seal on the ice by "spy-hopping"—swimming vertically to raise their heads above the surface for a better view.

Ice floe
Small, isolated slabs of floating pack ice are known as ice floes.

2 Diving in formation
Swimming in perfect unison, the three orcas dive beneath the surface. Their combined forward thrust pushes up a wave that surges toward the ice.

Wave movement
The waves increase in size as the orcas build momentum.

Countershading
The orca's pale belly makes it less visible to fish swimming below, while the black skin on its back hides the orca from the seal.

Orca

The biggest of all the dolphins, the orca is the most powerful, deadly hunter in the polar seas. It is also the most intelligent, often using pack tactics to outwit its prey.

Also known as killer whales, orcas are armed with stout, pointed teeth ideal for seizing large animals such as sharks, seals, and even other whales. They live in small family groups that hunt together, ranging widely through the world's oceans from the Antarctic pack ice to the fringes of the Arctic. Each local population has developed specialized techniques for catching different types of prey.

MAMMAL
ORCA

Orcinus orca

Location: All oceans

Length: Up to 32 ft (9.8 m)

Diet: Fish, marine mammals, birds

Wave hunting
Antarctic orcas hunting in the pack ice often join forces to capture seals resting on ice floes. After pinpointing their target, they swim in formation beneath the ice to push up a wave; this sweeps over the ice floe, washing the seal into the water where the orcas can seize it.

Orcas have been known to **attack and eat great white sharks—** the **biggest and most dangerous** of all predatory sharks.

On the shores of Patagonia, orcas swim right up onto the beach to seize young sea lions.

149

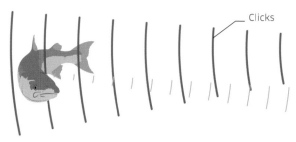

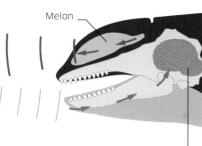

Clicks

Melon

Echolocation
An orca targets some prey—especially fish— by echolocation. It sends out a stream of clicks, focused into a beam by the "melon" in its forehead, and listens for any echoes.

Click echoes
Echoes bouncing off the prey travel through the orca's lower jaw to its ears.

Decoding
The ear sends nerve signals to the brain to form a "sound image" of the prey.

Communication
Orca family groups often travel with related families in larger groups called pods. Each pod has its own distinctive language of clicks, whistles, and other calls.

3 Swept away
The wave hits the ice floe catching this unlucky crabeater seal by surprise. The seal cannot stop the wave picking it up and sweeping it off the ice, straight into the jaws of the orcas waiting below.

Local variations
Each local population of orcas has its own distinctive pattern of black and white markings.

No escape
Strong, sharp-pointed teeth and muscular jaws allow the orca to grip struggling, often slippery prey.

Walrus

Renowned for its magnificent tusks, the walrus is a big, thick-skinned relative of seals and sea lions. It hunts in shallow seas around the Arctic Ocean, diving to the seabed beneath the pack ice to find its prey.

Walruses feed mainly on clams and similar shellfish, which they locate in the cloudy, often dark water by feeling for them with their luxuriant, highly sensitive whiskers. A walrus often uses its mouth to blast jets of water into soft sand to expose any hidden animals. When it finds a clam, it seals its lips to the shell and pulls back its tongue to suck out the soft meat.

Powerful swimmer

Although it has strong front flippers, the walrus swims using the same technique as a true seal, flexing its body and hind flippers to propel itself through the water like a fish. If it needs to, a walrus can swim at speeds of up to 22 mph (35 km/h), but it usually moves at a far more leisurely pace.

MAMMAL	
WALRUS	
Odobenus rosmarus	
Location:	Arctic Ocean
Length:	Up to 11½ ft (3.5 m)
Diet:	Seabed animals

Clambering onto ice

Adult males use their tusks to show off to rivals or fight, but both male and female walruses also employ their tusks in more peaceful ways. When swimming below pack ice, they use their tusks to stop ice from forming over vital breathing holes. And by jabbing the strong tusks into the ice, they can use them like grappling hooks to haul their bulky bodies out of the water.

Thick skin
Tough, wrinkled skin covers a thick layer of insulating fat. Adult males have extra-thick skin to protect them from serious injury during fights with rival males.

Sturdy flippers
Strong forelimbs help the walrus steer in the water and also support the walrus's great weight on the ice.

Singing males

A walrus has a big air sac in its throat that it can inflate to keep its head above water; the walrus may even sleep like this. Males also use the air sac to add resonance to their calls when competing with rivals or displaying to females. They call with clicks, whistles, and haunting bell-like tones.

Skull and tusks

Tusks are massively enlarged canine teeth that grow from the upper jaw. Since the walrus does not chew its food, its other teeth are quite small, and there are not many of them. These teeth are sometimes used to crush food.

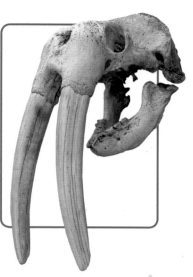

Mobile eyes

A walrus's eyes protrude from its skull in such a way that it can look straight up as well as forward, giving the walrus a good all-around view of its surroundings.

Self-sealing nostrils

As with all seals, the walrus's nostrils close automatically to keep water out when the walrus is submerged. Special muscles open them when it has to take a breath.

Sensitive whiskers

More than 400 highly sensitive whiskers on the walrus's snout enable it to locate prey by feel, mapping the exact shape and size of anything they touch.

Spectacular tusks

The tusks of adult males are longer than those of females, growing to 40 in (100 cm) or more. The male with the most impressive tusks usually outranks all the other males.

RIBBON SEAL
Histriophoca fasciata
Location: North Pacific and Arctic
Length: Up to 5¾ ft (1.75 m)

Instantly recognizable by its dramatic coat pattern, the ribbon seal breeds on Arctic pack ice around Alaska and eastern Siberia. It is specialized for movement over slippery ice, using the claws on its flippers, and is almost helpless on land.

Seals

Highly insulated with thick fat or dense fur to keep them warm underwater, seals and sea lions are well adapted for life in the icy polar regions. Many of them spend their entire lives at sea, either hunting in the near-freezing water or hauled out on the drifting pack ice.

Most polar species are true seals with backward-pointing hind limbs, which they use to drive themselves through the water. Conversely, fur seals and sea lions can rotate their hind limbs, helping their mobility on land. True seals move clumsily on land, so many breed on floating ice where they are less vulnerable to attack—although this does not deter hungry polar bears or orcas. Many ice-breeding seals are at risk from climate change, which is reducing the area covered by sea ice.

White stripes
Both males and females have a striped pattern, but the male's colors are particularly striking.

RINGED SEAL
Pusa hispida
Location: Arctic
Length: Up to 5¼ ft (1.6 m)

Widespread throughout the Arctic and nearby seas, the ringed seal owes its name to the pattern of silver-gray rings on its dark fur. Females breed in isolated, snow-covered lairs amid tumbled ice floes on the pack ice, entered from the water below. These lairs are targeted by prowling polar bears, which can detect them by smell.

Ring pattern

BEARDED SEAL
Erignathus barbatus
Location: Arctic
Length: Up to 8¼ ft (2.5 m)

Like the walrus, this Arctic seal feeds mainly on bottom-living animals, which it detects with its very long, sensitive whiskers. It lives all around the Arctic, breeding on ice floes where many fall prey to orcas and polar bears.

Newborn pup

HOODED SEAL
Cystophora cristata
Location: N. Atlantic and Arctic
Length: Up to 8⅝ ft (2.7 m)

Found in the icy seas around Greenland, the hooded seal is named for the inflatable black "hood" of the adult male, used to display to females and rivals. For maximum impact, it can also inflate the lining of one nostril like a pink balloon.

Inflatable hood

Nasal sac

HARP SEAL
Pagophilus groenlandicus
Location: N. Atlantic and Arctic
Length: Up to 5½ ft (1.7 m)

Harp seals breed in big colonies on the sea ice of eastern Canada, the Greenland Sea, and the Russian Barents Sea. Notoriously, the white-coated pups were once targeted by seal hunters, but this is now outlawed in Canada. Harp seals spend most of their lives at sea, hunting fish and shrimplike krill.

White-coated pup
The white fur is lost at the age of three weeks.

ROSS SEAL
Ommatophoca rossii
Location: Antarctic
Length: Up to 8 ft (2.4 m)

Restricted to the icy fringes of Antarctica, the Ross seal has very big eyes to help it locate squid and fish in the deep, dark water below the ice. It is a solitary, elusive animal, and its preference for thick pack ice means that it is rarely seen except by research scientists or the crews of Antarctic icebreakers.

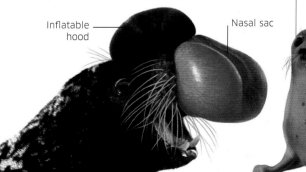

23 mph (37 km/h)—the speed a **leopard seal can swim** through the water.

Crabeater seals are one of the **most abundant** large mammals in the world.

153

ANTARCTIC FUR SEAL
Arctocephalus gazella
Location: Mainly subantarctic
Length: Up to 6½ ft (2 m)

Unlike true seals, the fur seals and sea lions swim using powerful strokes of their long front flippers. They also use these as legs, giving them much more mobility on land. The Antarctic fur seal ranges further south than most, hunting krill, fish, and squid in the Southern Ocean. But it avoids the iciest waters, breeding in colonies on rocky islands such as South Georgia.

Up to 6 million
Antarctic fur seals breed on South Georgia islands.

Woolly coat
A layer of dense fur beneath its outer coat keeps the seal warm.

STELLER'S SEA LION
Eumetopias jubatus
Location: Far north Pacific
Length: Up to 10⅚ ft (3.3 m)

One of six species of sea lions, this is the only species that lives in near-Arctic waters. It gathers on remote northern shores to breed, each big male claiming a territory and hoping to mate with any female that enters the area.

Female

Male

WEDDELL SEAL
Leptonychotes weddellii
Location: Antarctic
Length: Up to 10⅚ ft (3.3 m)

Weddell seals live all around Antarctica on the coastal sea ice, breeding on fast ice attached to the shore. They hunt fish and other animals in the water below the ice, using their teeth to make and enlarge vital breathing holes.

CRABEATER SEAL
Lobodon carcinophaga
Location: Antarctic
Length: Up to 8½ ft (2.6 m)

Despite its name, the crabeater seal does not eat crabs, instead it feeds on krill. The elaborately shaped, interlocking teeth of this seal form a sieve to strain mouthfuls of krill from icy Antarctic seas. Millions of crabeater seals live on drifting pack ice, where they are a prey of leopard seals.

Multicusped teeth

LEOPARD SEAL
Hydrurga leptonyx
Location: Antarctic
Length: Up to 11⅙ ft (3.4 m)

This is the only seal that regularly preys on other warm-blooded animals. Found all around Antarctica, it lurks in the water near and below ice floes, waiting to ambush penguins and smaller seals as they slip into the sea.

Leopard spots

SOUTHERN ELEPHANT SEAL
Mirounga leonina
Location: Antarctic
Length: Up to 16⅓ ft (5 m)

Elephant seals are named for the male's massive size, as well as the trunklike extension of its nose that amplifies its roaring calls. Rival males fight to mate with as many females as possible, inflicting deep gashes on opponents with their teeth.

Enormous male
A male southern elephant seal can weigh as much as a small truck.

The female can weigh five times less than the male

Ice Hunters

As the sea ice starts to form and thicken off the coast of Alaska in fall, a mother polar bear ventures out onto the edge of the ice, followed by her two young.

After orcas, polar bears are the most powerful Arctic predators. They hunt almost exclusively on the sea ice, using their acute sense of smell to detect seals from up to 0.6 miles (1 km) away. A bear can crouch for hours by a seal's breathing hole, waiting to scoop it from the water and kill it with a single bite. If sea ice fails to form because of climate change, the bears will be unable to hunt and may starve.

EMPEROR PENGUIN
Aptenodytes forsteri

Location: Antarctic shores and seas
Height: Up to 4 ft (1.2 m)

The emperor is the biggest penguin. It hunts fish and squid, diving so deeply to find them that it can stay submerged for 20 minutes. Unlike other penguins, it breeds in winter on fast ice (ice attached to the shore); the males incubate the eggs on their feet to prevent them from freezing.

Penguins

Often seen as clumsy and even comical when they are on land, penguins are transformed into fast, agile, highly effective hunters when they dive underwater.

Found only in the Southern Hemisphere, penguins are the most specialized of all ocean birds. Every part of a penguin's body is adapted for hunting underwater, and it is as efficient a hunter as any seal. Their excellent insulation allows them to hunt in icy Antarctic seas that teem with fish and shrimplike krill. While few species nest on the shores of Antarctica itself, others form huge breeding colonies on the bleak, rocky islands that dot the Southern Ocean.

Tight grip
Like other penguins, an Adélie has bristlelike projections from its tongue and palate that help it grip slippery prey in its beak. The direction of the bristles stops the prey from wriggling out and pushes it toward the penguin's throat.

Fish cannot escape due to the inward-facing bristles

KING PENGUIN
Aptenodytes patagonicus

Location: Subantarctic
Height: Up to 37³⁄₈ in (95 cm)

Although the king penguin looks very like the emperor penguin, it has a different way of life. It hunts in open water at the fringes of the Southern Ocean, and forms huge breeding colonies in spring on subantarctic islands such as South Georgia.

Chicks have brown down feathers

MACARONI PENGUIN
Eudyptes chrysolophus

Location: Antarctic and subantarctic
Height: Up to 28 in (71 cm)

This is one of seven species of crested penguins, all adorned with flamboyant yellow feathers on their heads. It is one of the most common penguins, with millions of pairs nesting on the Antarctic Peninsula and subantarctic islands. It mainly eats krill, plus small fish and squid.

10 ft (3 m)—the **height an Adélie penguin can leap out of the sea** to land on an ice floe.

22 mph (36 km/h)—**the top speed** of a gentoo penguin through the water.

157

Adélie penguin

Living further south than most other penguin species, the Adélie breeds on ice-free Antarctic shores in summer and spends the rest of the year at sea. It preys mainly on krill, seizing them one by one with its sharp bill, and when it has caught enough, it rests on drifting pack ice and icebergs.

Torpedo shape
Thick, warm feathers slicked back against its body give the penguin a streamlined shape.

Underwater flight
Penguins use their short, densely feathered wings to "fly" through the water.

Vital protection
A white breast makes the Adélie hard to spot against the pale sky, when viewed from below by predators such as the leopard seal.

BIRD

ADÉLIE PENGUIN

Pygoscelis adeliae

Location: Antarctic shores and seas

Length: Up to 28 in (71 cm)

Diet: Krill, fish, and squid

GENTOO PENGUIN
Pygoscelis papua
Location: Antarctic and subantarctic
Height: Up to 32 in (81 cm)

Found in the seas and islands around Antarctica, the gentoo has an unusually long tail. It can swim faster than any other penguin and uses its speed to catch a variety of prey. It has a loud trumpeting call, given with its head thrown back and beak pointing skyward.

CHINSTRAP PENGUIN
Pygoscelis antarcticus
Location: Antarctic and subantarctic
Height: Up to 30³⁄₈ in (77 cm)

A million pairs of chinstrap penguins nest on volcanic Zavodovski Island in the far south of the Atlantic. Here, the heat of the active volcano melts the snow, helping incubate their eggs in the chilly subantarctic climate. Another 3 million pairs breed on ice-free shores and islands all around Antarctica.

ROCKHOPPER PENGUIN
Eudyptes chrysocome
Location: Subantarctic islands and seas
Height: Up to 24³⁄₈ in (62 cm)

These small, yellow-crested subantarctic penguins nest on rocky coasts where they must leap from rock to rock to reach the sea. There are two very similar species, which breed on remote shores and islands as far north as Tristan da Cunha in the Atlantic.

158 polar oceans ○ **POLAR SEABIRDS**

50 million—the estimated **number of breeding pairs** of **Wilson's storm petrel** living around **Antarctica**.

Light and dark
The plumage is very variable, ranging from dark brown on its tail and wings to almost white on its head.

SOUTHERN GIANT PETREL
Macronectes giganteus
Location: Southern Ocean
Length: Up to 39 in (99 cm)

Although they are closely related to the albatrosses, and look similar, the giant petrels have many behavioral differences. Giant petrels are mainly scavengers that live on scraps picked up from the breeding colonies of seals and penguins. They also prey upon helpless young and kill and eat any injured adults they find. If threatened, they spray foul-smelling oil at their enemies.

Tubenose
As with all petrels, the bill is formed of nine distinct plates, with tubular nostrils lying along the top. This gives these birds the name "tubenose."

WHITE-CHINNED PETREL
Procellaria aequinoctialis
Location: Southern Ocean
Length: Up to 22¾ in (58 cm)

Mainly black, but often with a white patch beneath its bill, the white-chinned petrel hunts at sea for krill, small fish, and squid, which it seizes from just below the surface of the salty seawater. In the process, it swallows a lot of salt, and like other petrels it expels the excess from a special salt gland connected to its tubular nostrils.

Well built
The white-chinned petrel has a large, bulky body.

Pale bill

SOUTH POLAR SKUA
Catharacta maccormicki
Location: Antarctic
Length: Up to 21⅝ in (55 cm)

A notorious pirate, the south polar skua harasses other seabirds as they return to their breeding sites and steals their fish. It nests on Antarctic shores in summer, but when winter closes in, it leaves for the north Atlantic and north Pacific.

White flash
This mainly brown skua has distinctive white wing patches.

SNOW PETREL
Pagodroma nivea
Location: Antarctic
Length: Up to 15¾ in (40 cm)

This beautiful petrel is well named, not only because it is pure white but because it breeds mainly on the snowy continent of Antarctica. It ranges farther south than any other bird and has even been seen over the frozen wastes of the South Pole. At sea, it feeds mainly among the pack ice, resting on icebergs.

Snow white feathers

Wilson's storm petrel could be one of
the most numerous seabirds on Earth.

Fluttering wings
A storm petrel has a distinctive fluttering, hovering flight as it searches the ocean for food.

BLACK-BROWED ALBATROSS
Thalassarche melanophris
Location: Southern Ocean
Length: Up to 36⅝ in (93 cm)

Widespread throughout the Southern Hemisphere, the black-browed albatross is smaller than some other albatrosses but is just as skilled at soaring for hours over the waves with barely a wingbeat. It nests in colonies on remote islands, each pair raising a single chick.

Downy chick

WILSON'S STORM PETREL
Oceanites oceanicus
Location: Oceans worldwide
Length: Up to 8 in (20 cm)

No bigger than a songbird, this fragile-looking petrel lives on some of the wildest, windiest seas on the planet. Despite this, it is hugely successful, with millions nesting on rocky islets around Antarctica. It has a curious habit of pattering its feet on the ocean surface as it gathers the small planktonic animals that form its food.

60,000 The **number of tiny copepods** eaten each day by a **songbird-sized little auk**.

159

KING EIDER
Somateria spectabilis
Location: Arctic shores
Length: Up to 24¾ in (63 cm)

Wintering on coastal waters all around the Arctic Ocean, the king eider is a diving sea duck that feeds on bottom-living animals such as crabs and clams. In spring, it moves onto land, nesting around the lakes that form when the winter snow melts.

Camouflaged female

Polar Seabirds

In the polar regions, and especially around the frozen desert of Antarctica, the seas contain far more food than the land. A wide variety of seabirds come to prey upon the teeming animal life.

Many of these birds remain at sea for much of the year but return to the fringes of the land in spring to nest, lay eggs, and rear their young. Most of them hunt marine life, but others are scavengers or even pirates that ambush other birds and steal their food.

Colorful breeding male

LONG-TAILED SKUA
Stercorarius longicaudus
Location: Arctic, subantarctic
Length: Up to 20¾ in (53 cm)

Also known as the long-tailed jaeger, this is a predator and pirate, like most other skuas, often stealing the prey of other seabirds as they return from hunting at sea. But unlike many skuas, it is a slender, elegant bird, with slim, pointed wings and long, whippy tail streamers. It breeds all around the High Arctic but spends the northern winter over warmer oceans south of the equator.

Whip tail
Both sexes have long tail feathers when fully adult.

ARCTIC TERN
Sterna paradisaea
Location: Arctic and Antarctic
Length: Up to 14⅛ in (36 cm)

This graceful seabird breeds in the Arctic but spends the northern winter feeding in the oceans around Antarctica. This epic migration means that the Arctic tern travels further each year than any other animal.

THICK-BILLED MURRE
Uria lomvia
Location: Arctic, N. Atlantic, and N. Pacific
Length: Up to 17 in (43 cm)

Auks are the northern counterparts of penguins, hunting at sea in the same way by using their wings to swim underwater—although, unlike penguins, they are able to fly. The thick-billed murre is the largest living species of auk; it nests in dense colonies on sheer cliffs facing Arctic seas.

Unique adaptation
The spotted eggs have pointed ends and vary from white to blue in color.

LITTLE AUK
Alle alle
Location: Arctic, N. Atlantic, and N. Pacific
Length: Up to 8 in (20 cm)

A tiny relative of the thick-billed murre, this hunts underwater in the same way and flies low over the sea with fast whirring wingbeats. It breeds in colonies on the shores of Arctic islands, each pair nesting in a rocky crevice or beneath a boulder.

Stubby wings

IVORY GULL
Pagophila eburnea
Location: Arctic
Length: Up to 19 in (48 cm)

The ivory gull is the only gull with pure white plumage. It is rarely seen south of icy Arctic seas, hunting at the edge of the pack ice in winter and breeding on ice-free Arctic shores in summer. As well as taking fish and other animals, it scavenges the remains of polar bear kills.

Pure white
Adult ivory gulls are white, but as young birds, they have black spots.

Sleek Swimmer

Swooping up from the depths toward a gap in the Antarctic sea ice, an emperor penguin displays its effortless mastery of the underwater world.

Able to dive to 1,800 ft (550 m) or more below the floating ice in search of fish, squid, and other prey, the emperor penguin holds the record for the deepest-diving seabird. Special adaptations allow it to conserve oxygen in its body, enabling it to stay submerged for an incredibly long time. Dives of more than 20 minutes have been observed.

OCEANS AND US

Beautiful and bountiful, the world's oceans provide people with many vital sources of food, energy, and recreation. However, these vast yet vulnerable expanses are under serious threat from climate change, high levels of pollution, and other forms of harmful human impact.

HUMAN IMPACT

Earth's oceans are an essential part of human life. Not only do oceans help regulate Earth's climates, but they are also vital for food, transportation, trade, and energy. Although the oceans may appear to be a limitless resource, they are not. Marine life is being killed off by pollution, and overfishing has reduced some fish species to near extinction. Scientists are striving to understand more about the oceans so that we are better placed to protect marine life in the future world.

COASTAL COMMUNITIES

The oceans provided convenient transportation and trade routes for early civilizations. This gave rise to settlements along the coast, from small fishing villages to important trading posts. Today, one-third of the world's population lives along shores, and this proportion is rising. Eight out of 10 of the world's largest cities, from New York to Shanghai (below), are on the coast.

OCEAN RESOURCES

The oceans contain a wealth of resources that we rely on each day. Offshore oil and gas fuel our cars and heat our homes, and metals are used in industry. Marine life provides us with not only food but also ingredients for medicines, skin care, and other products.

Minerals and metals

For centuries, people have evaporated seawater to obtain salt, such as the sea salt harvested in this Thai lagoon. The seas are also rich in other resources, which we are only just beginning to exploit. Sand, gravel, and limestone are essential supplies for the construction industry, and gold and diamonds are also extracted from the seabed. Still untouched are manganese nodules and black smokers on the seafloor, which contain copper, nickel, titanium, and other metals. Deep-ocean muds offer a future source of some rare metals used for cell phones and computers.

Fishing

Our early ancestors gathered seaweed and shellfish from shores, caught fish, and hunted seals for food. Later, they fished from boats and began simple freshwater fish farming. Today, 3.2 billion people rely on seafood for 20 percent of their animal protein intake, and marine fish farming is growing. Commercial fishing now amounts to more than 87 million tons (79 million metric tons) a year, and people across the world are eating more seafood than ever before.

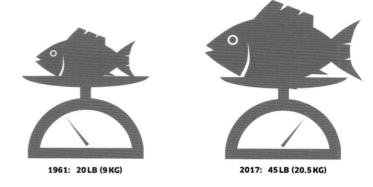

1961: 20 LB (9 KG)   **2017: 45 LB (20.5 KG)**

AVERAGE ANNUAL FISH CONSUMPTION PER PERSON

Energy sources

Modern oil exploration began on land more than 100 years ago but rapidly moved offshore into shallow coastal waters. More than half of current oil and gas discoveries are beneath the deep oceans, with drilling in water depths of up to 6,600 ft (2,000 m) and reaching as far as 23,000 ft (7,000 m) below the seafloor. More than 60 percent of commercial energy still comes from oil and gas, but sustainable sources, such as offshore wind farms (right), are steadily increasing, and power from tides and waves is also being harnessed across the world.

SEA CARGO

The oceans have provided vital trade routes for more than 2,000 years. Today, more than 50,000 cargo ships carry everything from cars to toys and oil to clothes, docking at ports across the world. Supertankers and giant container ships are among the largest vessels ever built for the high seas.

UNDERWATER CABLES

The first transatlantic telegraph cable was laid in 1858. Now parts of the oceans are a busy network of communications cables, oil and gas pipelines, and other seafloor installations. Today, 99 percent of all internet data is transmitted by submarine cables that stretch across oceans, laid as deep as Mount Everest is high. Special ships are used to lay cables, while remotely operated submarine vehicles are used to check for any problems.

LEISURE AT SEA

One of the world's largest industries is tourism, which accounts for 10 percent of world trade. Many tourists seek sun-drenched beaches, water sports, and sailing marinas. Remote ocean islands and colorful coral reefs are prized destinations for snorkeling and diving. Oceangoing cruise ships—the largest carrying more than 6,000 passengers—reach some of the remotest parts of the ocean, from around Antarctica to the islands of the South Pacific.

OCEANS IN DANGER

A fast-growing world population, crowded coastlines, extraction of oil and metals, global trade, and a booming tourist industry are all having a profound impact on the world's oceans. Tons of waste, sewage, and plastics are dumped into the seas each year. The oceans are warming, losing oxygen, and becoming more acidic. Marine ecosystems are fragile, coral reefs are dying, and resources are limited—the oceans are under threat as never before.

Pollution

Semi-enclosed seas, like the Baltic, Mediterranean, and Black Sea, and those closest to megacities and industry, such as the Yellow and East China seas, are most at risk from pollution. Some are so polluted with sewage (right), oil, toxic chemicals, and fertilizer runoff that their marine life is largely dead or dying. Inland seas, such as the Caspian Sea and the Great Lakes of North America, will find it hard to ever recover from more than a hundred years of pollution.

Habitat loss

The two sea habitats that are suffering extreme loss are coral reefs and mangrove wetlands. Together, they are home to around one-third of all marine species. More than 30 percent of these habitats has already gone and another 50 percent is at risk.

Climate change

The effects of global warming on the oceans are dramatic. Warmer waters contribute to the loss of coral reefs and lead to more extreme weather. As glaciers and ice sheets melt, sea levels rise, impacting on low-lying islands and nations.

CONSERVATION

The negative human impact on the oceans can be managed if action is taken fast. There are thousands of Marine Protected Areas, such as the Channel Islands off California (right), for the conservation of life and resources—but more are urgently needed. Oil-slick dispersal projects, plastic waste retrieval, and beach cleanup operations are all helping protect the world's seas.

Oil Rig

Most of the energy used to power our homes, industry, and transportation comes from fossil fuels, such as coal, oil, and natural gas. More than a third of oil and gas reserves are extracted from deep below the sea.

Oil and gas formed over millions of years from the remains of dead plankton buried under layers of sand and silt at intense heat and pressure. Oil rigs are used to drill for and extract these precious fuels. Offshore rigs are some of the biggest structures ever built.

Tension-leg oil platform
There are many types of oil rigs. Tension-leg platforms are floating structures used in water that is 660–6,600 ft (200–2,000m) deep. They are tethered to the ocean floor by strong cables. Oil from deep under the seabed is pumped up to the platform through long riser pipes. It is later transported to shore for processing by tanker or pipeline. Large crews maintain operations on the platform 24 hours a day, in harsh conditions.

Helicopter
Crew is transported to and from the rig by helicopter.

Living quarters
A rig can accommodate up to 500 workers, who typically work 12-hour shifts but spend four weeks onshore for every four on the rig.

Drilling tower
Also known as a derrick, this holds the equipment used to drill and pump oil from the underwater well.

Crane winches supplies up to platform from boats

Flare stack

Gas flare
Pockets of gas found trapped above the oil are burned, or "flared off," if a rig is not set up to transport gas. Increasingly, this gas is captured, to avoid waste and pollution.

Floating columns
Four huge columns support the large platform above the water.

Anchor system
Steel cables secure the floating platform to the seabed.

Helicopter landing pad

Lifeboat
The rig has lifeboats for evacuation in an emergency.

30 days—the **maximum stay** for workers on an **oil rig** without **shore leave**.

500 million barrels—the **minimum amount** of oil in a **super-giant oil field**.

10–20 million years—the **average time** that **oil** or **gas takes** to form.

167

Drilling through rock

To find offshore oil, first a survey exploring the rocks below the seabed is done to identify a potential site, then a mobile drilling rig is moved into position. A series of pipes designed to drill down through the rock to the oil, known as a drill string, is lowered to the seabed. If oil is found, the site is converted for production. Some rigs drill to depths of more than 23,000ft (7,000m) below the ocean floor.

Drilling riser holds drill string and carries mud to surface

SEABED

SEDIMENTARY LAYERS OF ROCK

OIL-RESISTANT LAYER OF ROCK

Blowout preventer controls oil flow and seals well

Wellhead

Drill string

Natural gas

Oil trapped by rock

Water

Sea life
Fish and other marine animals may shelter beneath the rig, although oil drilling and extraction can disrupt wildlife and the environment.

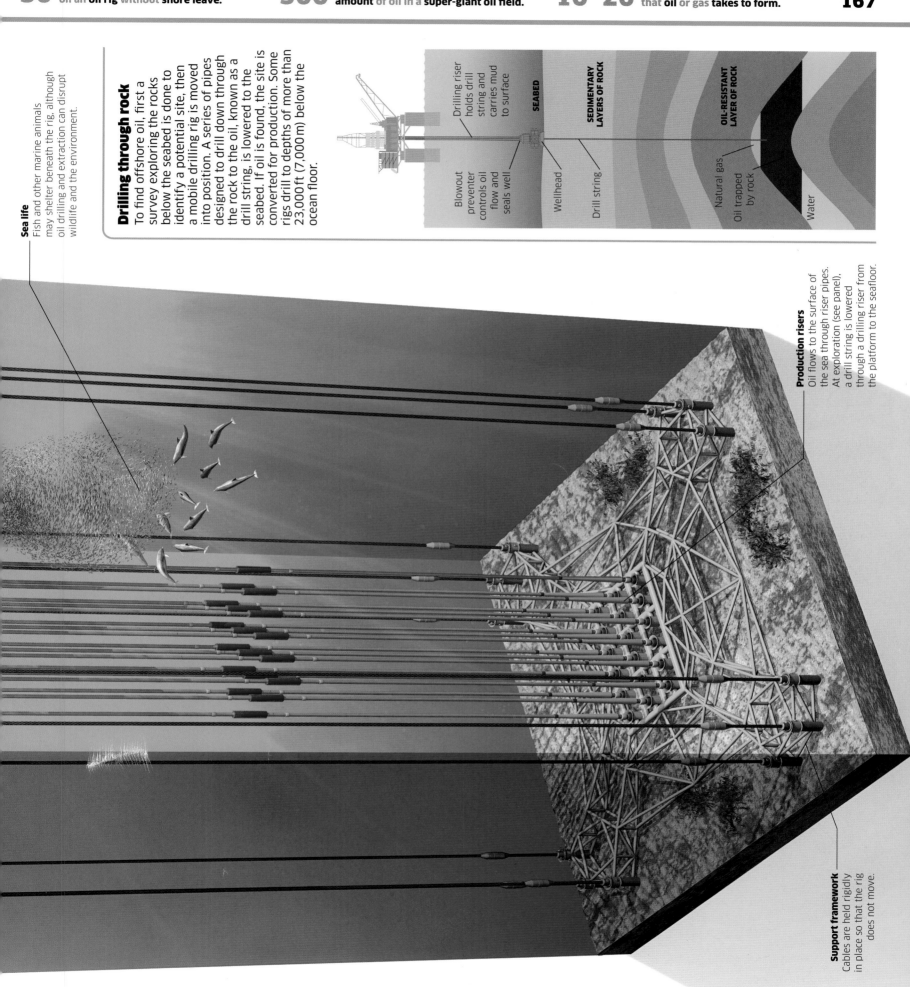

Production risers
Oil flows to the surface of the sea through riser pipes. At exploration (see panel), a drill string is lowered through a drilling riser from the platform to the seafloor.

Support framework
Cables are held rigidly in place so that the rig does not move.

Wind Power

A cleaner, safer, and sustainable alternative to fossil fuels, such as coal, is to harness the energy of the winds that blow across the oceans.

A wind power station, or wind farm, is a group of tall steel towers topped with rotating blades like those of a windmill. As the blades spin in the wind, they turn a generator, which converts this mechanical energy into electricity. Offshore wind farms are more efficient than onshore ones, since sea winds are stronger and steadier than winds on land.

Wind farm

Offshore wind farms, such as the one seen here, are sited in fairly shallow water no more than 19 miles (30 km) from the coast. The largest have more than a hundred turbines, the bases of which are sunk into the seafloor. An offshore electrical substation transfers the power to the grid on the mainland.

Jack-up vessel
These specialized turbine-installation vessels have metal "legs" that lower and attach to the seafloor. It takes the onboard engineers less than two days to install a turbine. Then the legs are jacked back up, and the vessel moves on to place the next turbine in position.

Nacelle
This sits on top of the tower and houses the generator that turns the motion of the rotor blades into electricity.

Crane
A huge crane carried on the jack-up boat lifts the components of a turbine into place.

Rotor blades
Up to 266 ft (81 m) long, each blade equals the wingspan of an Airbus A380—the world's largest passenger plane.

Towers ready for installation

Main tower
The tower is made from tubular steel and stands up to 328 ft (100 m) high.

Access ladder
This allows workers arriving by boat access for inspection and maintenance.

Power cable
A cable sends the electrical power generated at each turbine to the wind-farm substation.

Underwater base
A steel foundation called a monopile is driven deep into the seabed and wedged in with concrete to secure the turbine.

Just one of the **biggest wind turbines** can produce enough electricity to power **600 homes**.

By 2050, some experts believe that **one-third** of the **world's electricity** will be **generated by wind farms**.

169

Tidal power

Moving water is also used to generate electricity. Tides are a huge potential source of renewable energy. Large, low-lying dams called tidal barrages (pictured) generate electricity from the power of tides. However, turbines placed in a fast-flowing body of water, or tidal stream, are more widely used.

Wave power

Harnessing the power of waves to generate electricity is still underdeveloped. In 2000, the first small-scale project was launched off the coast of Scotland. This uses floating cylinders (pictured) containing motors that are activated by wave motion. The motors power a generator that produces electrical energy.

Substation
This structure collects electrical power generated by the turbines and feeds it directly to a conversion station.

Conversion station
The station converts the electrical current into the most efficient form for transmission to an onshore station.

Giant rotor blades spin this shaft

Generator converts the motion of the spinning shaft into electrical energy

Mechanism turns the rotor blades to face into the wind

Inside the nacelle
The nacelle is the heart of the turbine, where wind is harnessed to create electricity. This structure contains the mechanisms that are set in motion by the turning rotor blades. A nacelle can be large enough to have a helipad on top.

Fish Farming

Around the world, people are eating more fish than ever before. Just under half of the fish we eat is reared in farms rather than caught in the wild.

Also known as aquaculture, fish farming is one of the fastest-growing food industries in the world. Many fish farms are located inland and rear freshwater species, but about 35 percent of all farmed fish comes from marine or coastal fish farms. In addition to fish, large numbers of shellfish, such as oysters and mussels, and seaweed are grown for human consumption.

Farmed fish
The fish in this farm are European sea bass. Other widely farmed marine fish are amberjacks and yellowtails. Fed on nutrient-rich pellets, these fish thrive in farm conditions.

Buoy holds circular net in place

Wild fish

Multispecies farm

Most fish farms rear only one species at a time, but this modern farm in the Mediterranean is cultivating several types of marine life at once. Fish are reared in a net enclosure close to the shore, and the waste they produce provides nutrients for sea urchins and mussels growing nearby. Strings of seaweed help maintain healthy, oxygen-rich water.

1 billion—the number of people who **rely on seafood** as their **main source of protein**.

33 million tons (30 million metric tons)—the amount of **seaweed** farmed each year, used for food and as an **additive** in products such as **toothpaste and paints**.

171

Buoys floating on the surface keep ropes taut

Harvesting boat
A boat harvests seaweed by winching the ropes up from the sea.

Flowing current
The current flows from the fish pen toward the mussels and seaweed, bringing fish waste laden with nutrients.

Weights anchor ropes supporting seaweed and shellfish

Seaweed
Large quantities of seaweed are harvested each year for food and as an ingredient in other products.

Mussels
Mussels grow on ropes suspended from floating buoys. They feed on waste from the fish, sea cucumbers, and sea urchins, filtering nutrients from the water.

Sea cucumbers
Sea cucumbers on the seabed feed on fish waste that floats down from above. This keeps the enclosure clean, and the sea cucumbers can be harvested for food.

Net enclosure
The net is suspended from a floating frame, keeping the fish enclosed in one small area.

Sea urchins
Sea urchins are invertebrates with a spiny outer case. Their soft bodies inside are considered a delicacy in many parts of the world. Overharvested in the wild, they are often cultivated in farms.

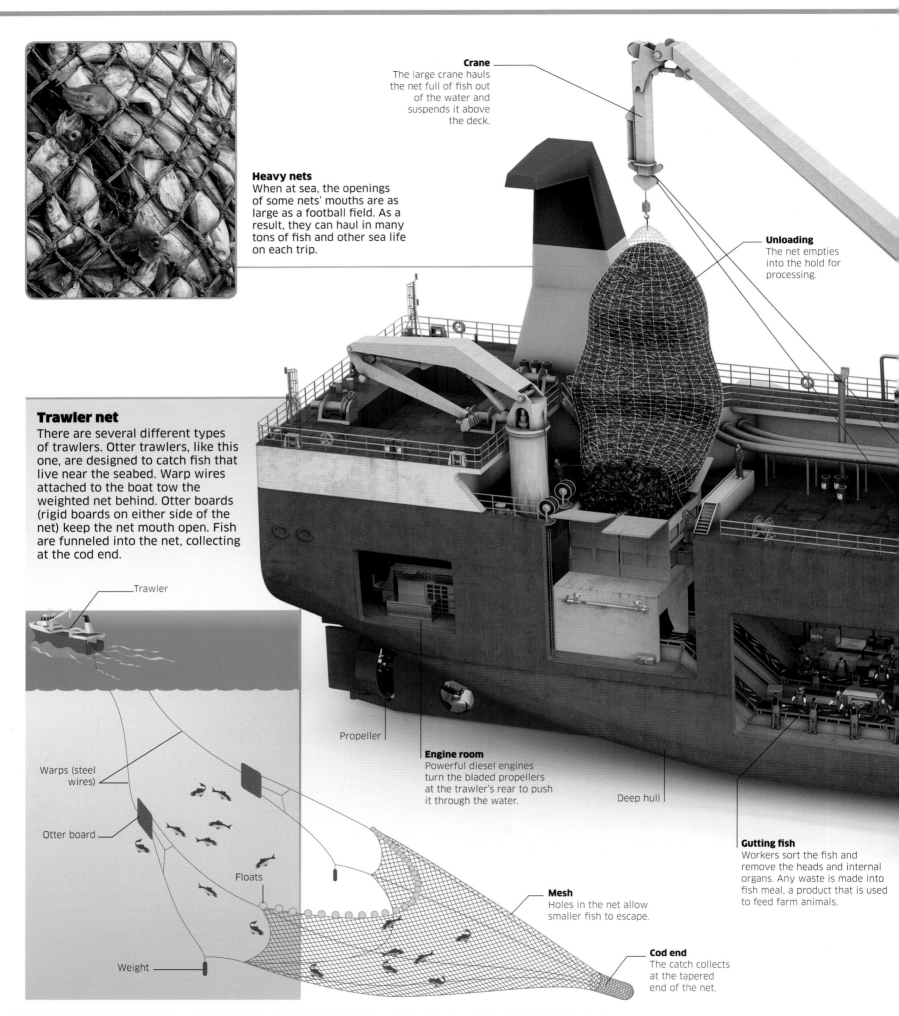

Crane
The large crane hauls the net full of fish out of the water and suspends it above the deck.

Heavy nets
When at sea, the openings of some nets' mouths are as large as a football field. As a result, they can haul in many tons of fish and other sea life on each trip.

Unloading
The net empties into the hold for processing.

Trawler net
There are several different types of trawlers. Otter trawlers, like this one, are designed to catch fish that live near the seabed. Warp wires attached to the boat tow the weighted net behind. Otter boards (rigid boards on either side of the net) keep the net mouth open. Fish are funneled into the net, collecting at the cod end.

Trawler

Warps (steel wires)

Otter board

Floats

Weight

Propeller

Engine room
Powerful diesel engines turn the bladed propellers at the trawler's rear to push it through the water.

Deep hull

Mesh
Holes in the net allow smaller fish to escape.

Gutting fish
Workers sort the fish and remove the heads and internal organs. Any waste is made into fish meal, a product that is used to feed farm animals.

Cod end
The catch collects at the tapered end of the net.

4.6 million–the number of **fishing vessels** in operation worldwide. More than **80 percent** of these are **small boats** less than **40 ft (12 m)** long.

472 ft (144 m)–the **length** of the world's **largest** fishing vessel, the **Annelies Ilena**.

173

Factory freezer trawler

This oceangoing fishing trawler hauls a large catch in its net and unloads it into the ship's hull. Different-sized nets are towed at different depths to catch particular fish species. Below decks, the fish are cut, processed, boxed, and frozen all while out at sea.

Radar
Radar navigation equipment helps the ship avoid other vessels in foggy conditions.

Sleeping quarters
Beds and storage lockers are provided for the 30–50-strong crew, who may be at sea for up to six weeks at a time.

Fishing Trawler

Braving stormy seas and long ocean voyages, sturdy trawler ships drag large nets through the water. Thousands of fish can be caught by a single sweep of a net.

In 2018, 87.4 million tons (79.3 million metric tons) of fish were caught in the world's oceans. The boats that helped land this catch range from small, simple vessels to large oceangoing factory ships, which process and freeze their catches on board so they can stay at sea for weeks on end.

Wheelhouse
The wheelhouse is where the crew navigate and check weather and sea forecasts.

Mess room
The crew eat and relax in the mess room.

Filleting and skinning
The skin and major bones of the fish are removed to produce ready-to-sell fish fillets. Some types of fish are kept whole with just the head removed.

Storing boxed fish
Within hours of being caught, packaged fish are stored in freezer compartments deep in the ship's hull. This preserves the catch until the ship returns to dock.

More than one-third of all fish stocks
are now overfished–
taken more quickly than the fish can reproduce so numbers cannot recover.

Stilt Fishing

Perched precariously on wooden sticks bound together by twine, Sri Lankan fishermen work above the waters for hours at a time using simple rods and lines.

This unique style of fishing began after the Second World War, when food shortages and overfishing in the most popular areas prompted some fishermen to seek out new spots. They first stood on shipwrecks but later erected stilts to raise themselves above the water so as not to disturb the small herring and mackerel they hoped to catch.

176 oceans and us · **SHIPS**

75 mph (121 km/h)—the fastest **speed sailing record,** set by the racing yacht *Vestas Sailrocket 2* in 2012.

Ships

People may have taken to the seas as long as 60,000 years ago, perhaps on primitive rafts. Today, the oceans carry all types of vessels, from tugs to tankers and sailing boats to submarines.

Over half of the world's 100,000-strong fleet are merchant ships carrying trade goods, while about 10 percent are naval vessels. Cruise ships and fishing boats make up most of the rest. Vessels such as oil tankers and container ships, which are some of the largest ships on the ocean, are the most efficient way of transporting bulk fuel and heavy goods around the world.

The bridge, or control room of the ship, is always manned by one or more officers

CONTAINER SHIP
Speed: Up to 23 mph (37 km/h)
Length: Up to 1,312 ft (400 m)

SPEED BOAT
Speed: Up to 100 mph (160 km/h)
Length: Up to 50 ft (15 m)

Small, high-powered motor boats are popular for cruising and sports such as fishing and racing. The world water speed record was set in 1978 by a boat called the *Spirit of Australia*, which reached 317.6 mph (511.1 km/h) powered by turbo-jet propulsion. Many modern speed boats can easily average 100 mph (160 km/h) over calm seas.

Propulsion is provided by an outboard motor

RACING YACHT
Speed: Up to 75 mph (120 km/h)
Length: Up to 50 ft (15 m)

A racing yacht is a medium-sized sailing boat with a lightweight hull and a tall mast to carry large sails. From weekend regattas to Olympic events, yacht racing is highly popular. The Ocean Race, contested over 39,000 miles (72,000 km), is one of the sport's greatest challenges.

Large sail called a spinnaker catches the wind

TUGBOAT
Speed: Up to 17 mph (27 km/h)
Length: Up to 98 ft (30 m)

Powerful and sturdily built, tugboats are the workhorses of harbors and river estuaries. They are built to maneuver other vessels by pushing, pulling, and towing, often working in teams around the largest ships.

Tugs carry equipment such as towlines and lifting gear

SEARCH AND RESCUE BOAT
Speed: Up to 46 mph (74 km/h)
Length: Up to 115 ft (35 m)

Maritime search and rescue teams operate a range of vessels for coastal and deep-sea missions. The boats are fast, robust, highly maneuverable, and can withstand very rough seas. Many even right themselves if they are overturned by freak waves.

Powerful searchlight

HOVERCRAFT
Speed: Up to 85 mph (137 km/h)
Length: Up to 190 ft (58 m)

These vessels skim on a cushion of air over water, land, mudflats, beaches, and ice floes. The air currents that lift them are blown beneath the craft by fans. Hovercrafts were once common as commercial ferries but are now mostly used for military and leisure purposes.

Skirt prevents air from escaping

The true giants of the seas, container ships transport bulk cargoes of loose products, such as construction materials and coal, and carry all kinds of nonperishable items in huge steel containers. These ships need specialized ports and take nearly 6 miles (10km) to slow down and stop.

AIRCRAFT CARRIER

Speed: 45mph (72km/h)
Length: Up to 1,122ft (342m)

This vessel is the largest warship and usually the most important ship in a naval fleet. It is a floating airbase with a huge flight deck for takeoffs and landings. Aircraft carriers can hold war planes, such as bombers and fighters, as well as helicopters and reconnaissance planes.

Angled deck assists take off

CRUISE SHIP

Speed: Up to 35mph (56km/h)
Length: Up to 1,188ft (362m)

Cruise liners offer luxury vacations, taking tourists to exotic locations such as the islands of the Caribbean or the Indian Ocean, the Norwegian fjords, or the icy seas off Antarctica. Some cruise liners rank among the largest ships ever built, carrying more than 6,000 passengers and 2,000 crew.

TALL SHIP

Speed: Up to 17mph (27km/h)
Length: Up to 364ft (111m)

High-masted, wooden-hulled sailing ships plied the seas for exploration, trade, warfare, and scientific discovery for more than four centuries. They were slowly replaced by steel-hulled steam ships in the mid-1800s, but some are still built today for tourism and racing.

A fully rigged tall ship carries square sails on two or three masts

SUBMARINE

Speed: 23mph (37km/h)
Length: Up to 574ft (175m)

A submarine can patrol underwater for months at a time, adjusting its air- or water-filled ballast tanks to dive lower or rise to the surface. Submarines have been essential to naval warfare since World War I. Today, they may be heavily armed with nuclear missiles.

Conning tower
This structure rising from the hull houses the sub's navigation and communication equipment.

RESEARCH VESSEL

Speed: Up to 23mph (37km/h)
Length: Up to 689ft (210m)

Many ocean research expeditions have taken place over the past 250 years. Modern research vessels are equipped with laboratories and specialized instruments, and some carry small self-guiding vessels for underwater investigations.

The polar research vessel RSS *Sir David Attenborough*

OIL TANKER

Speed: 23mph (37km/h)
Length: Up to 1,504ft (458m)

Tankers come in all sizes and include the biggest ships ever built. Some are longer than New York's Empire State Building is tall: roughly four football fields end-to-end. These supertankers are designed to transport liquids and have the capacity to carry more than four million barrels of crude oil.

Pollution

Every year, human activities expose the planet's vulnerable oceans to increasing amounts of pollution. Harmful substances and materials enter ocean waters, threatening marine life and upsetting the delicate balance of ocean ecosystems.

This pollution takes many forms, from air pollution, some of which falls back to Earth, to plastic waste. Some pollutants disperse more easily than others, but in large amounts, all damage the oceans. Oil is toxic to life, but small amounts from natural seeps degrade faster than harmful major spills. Raw sewage and runoff farm waste release excess nutrients, which make algae grow, and disease-causing germs into the water. Toxic chemicals from pesticides and industrial waste can enter the food chain as they build up in the bodies of living creatures.

Pollution hot spots

Human impact along densely populated coasts can produce a wide range of different ocean pollutants. Whether it's washed, blown, dumped, or the result of an accident, much of the pollution reaching the ocean was produced originally on land.

Effluent
Raw sewage can lead to the rapid growth of algae, which can release poisons into the water.

Washed-up waste
Waves frequently draw ocean pollutants and waste back to shore, contaminating coastlines.

Factories
Greenhouse gas emissions contribute to global warming and ocean acidification, while waste water runoff may contain toxic chemicals.

Gold mining
Toxic compounds of cyanide and arsenic, used to extract gold from ore, can enter water sources and reach the sea.

Crop dusting
Harmful pesticides may be blown by winds out to sea, and fertilizer runoff can trigger harmful algal blooms.

Sewage pipes
In some places, underground pipes pump untreated sewage directly into the sea, polluting the water and harming life.

Garbage islands

Plastic waste and other garbage dumped on land and washed into rivers can flow out to sea. There, circulating currents known as gyres may cause it to congregate, forming large, floating islands of garbage such as this waste mass engulfing Roatán Island in the Caribbean Sea. With typical lifetimes of up to 500 years before they biodegrade, waste plastics pose major problems for ocean life. They trap and kill marine animals and prevent sunlight from reaching phytoplankton that rely on light to produce food. In addition, this plastic debris breaks down into microplastics—tiny particles of plastic—which can then enter the food chain.

80 percent of **microplastics** in the oceans come from **plastic waste dumped on land** that then **washes into oceans**.

179

Oil spills
If wrecked, an oil tanker can discharge thousands of gallons of oil into the sea.

Ghost fishing
Thousands of fishing nets are lost or dumped in the oceans every year. These entangle, suffocate, and kill tens of thousands of turtles, fish, seals, and other marine life.

Nuclear waste
Low-level radioactive waste has been dumped at more than 50 sites in the Atlantic and Pacific oceans.

Wrecked airplane
The fuel from wrecks of ships and planes disperses rapidly, and the sunken vessels can become artificial reefs for marine life. Up to 2,000 shipping containers holding a range of contaminants are lost overboard every year.

Gas pipeline
Underwater pipes transfer gas from place to place. Damage or corrosion to pipes can lead to liquefied natural gas contaminating the seawater.

Ferry boat
Marine pollution is worst in seas that are partially enclosed by land, such as the Mediterranean, and near coasts, where busy shipping lanes and ferry routes are streaked with oil and diesel.

Fur, feathers, and oil
Oil destroys the ability of fur and feathers to repel water and so keep sea mammals and birds warm. It can also kill if swallowed. Vast amounts of oil enter the ocean every year from leaks, spills, and natural seepage. In 2010, the Deepwater Horizon oil well spilled more than 4 million barrels (636 million liters) of oil, forming a 57,500 sq mile (149,000 sq km) slick in the Gulf of Mexico, devastating marine life.

Eating plastic waste
Lots of plastic waste ends up in the sea and washes up on beaches. Seabirds often mistake the colored plastics for food. It can lodge in their throat or gut, killing them. Around one million seabirds and 100,000 marine animals die this way each year.

Plastic Pollution

In the garbage-strewn waters of Verde Island Passage in the Philippines, a crab struggles to escape from a single-use plastic cup.

This expanse of water is one of the most biodiverse regions of marine life in the world, with dozens of new species discovered there every year. Sadly, many of the sea creatures are under threat from the rising tide of plastic waste that is dumped or washed into the ocean, which traps, entangles, or chokes helpless animals. These floating garbage tips also impact more than two million people in the region, who depend on the waters for their livelihood.

Climate Change

Even though the oceans are vast, the changes that humans are making to the planet and its climate are having a devastating impact beneath the waves.

As we cut down forests and burn fossil fuels, such as coal and oil, levels of carbon dioxide in the atmosphere are rising. Carbon dioxide is known as a greenhouse gas because it traps the sun's heat. More of it traps more heat, warming up the world and its seas, and even turning the oceans acidic. Not only does climate change threaten to flood coastlines and change weather patterns, but many kinds of marine life are less likely to survive—including spectacular reef-building corals.

Ocean acidification

Seawater is far more acidic today than it was before industrialization began. This is because excess carbon dioxide—from clearing forests and burning fossil fuels for energy, transportation, and industry—dissolves in the water, making it more acidic. Acid in the oceans reacts with minerals in the shells of marine creatures, releasing the minerals into the water, leaving the shells thinner and more fragile and making it harder for the creatures to rebuild them.

Deforestation
As land is cleared of trees for farming, industry, and urban growth, less carbon dioxide is absorbed from the atmosphere and more is released into it.

The world's oceans absorb
22 million tons
(20 million metric tons) of carbon dioxide every day.

A forested world
High levels of tree cover on land help absorb carbon dioxide, reducing the amount entering the atmosphere and reaching the oceans.

Colorful corals
Brightly colored corals thrive in low-acidity water, extracting readily available minerals from the water to strengthen their structures.

Rich reefs
Coral reefs support rich and abundant marine life, including vivid clownfish, damselfish, and butterflyfish.

Body building
Shellfish such as crabs and sea urchins extract the minerals they need from water to build their hard shells, or exoskeletons.

1 Healthy seas
Before the widespread burning of coal, oil, and gas, lower levels of carbon dioxide in the atmosphere and oceans meant that seawater was far less acidic. In this environment, coral and other forms of marine life were able to build and maintain their skeletons and other hard structures, and fish flourished.

Mutual benefit
Corals protect and get some nourishment from algae living in them, which—like trees—use light energy to make food from carbon dioxide.

2 Present day
Warmer oceans carry less oxygen, making it harder for certain animals to thrive. Migration patterns may be affected as changes in temperature disrupt ocean currents. More acidic water weakens shells and rocky corals and stops the eggs of ocean creatures—such as fish—from developing properly.

525 billion tons (475 billion metric tons) of **carbon dioxide** have been **absorbed by the oceans** since the start of the **Industrial Revolution.**

25 percent of all **marine species** live in and around **coral reefs.**

183

Climate disruption

The oceans help control climates. They absorb carbon dioxide, reducing its greenhouse effect, and their currents circulate warm tropical waters with cold polar ones, preventing extremes. Warmer waters make devastating storms, such as Hurricane Dorian (pictured right), likely and could disrupt the climate.

Rising seas

Many low-lying islands, coastal towns, and cities around the world could become uninhabitable if sea levels continue to rise. This is a result of melting ice caps and glaciers and of seawater expanding as it gets warmer. Here, a boy rides his bike through floodwaters on the Pacific island of Tuvalu.

Factories
Industries, homes, and transportation burn fossil fuels, such as oil and coal, for power. When this happens, the fuel reacts with oxygen in the air to create carbon dioxide. A growing human population and rising demand may see industries maintain or even increase emissions despite the known threats.

Emptier oceans
Plankton and fish populations may be affected, while numbers of some kinds of jellyfish that are tolerant of more acidic and warmer waters may rise.

Growing grasses
Seagrasses absorb carbon dioxide so may help combat ocean acidification.

Dying corals
Warmer waters cause coral bleaching, as stressed corals expel the tiny algae that live in them and give them their vibrant colors. Without the algae to help feed them, corals may die.

Weakened shells
The shells and hard skeletons of sea urchins and other creatures are weakened and made more vulnerable to injury by the more acidic water.

3 Looking ahead
If fossil fuel burning continues and carbon dioxide emission rates are not lowered, the oceans could become 150 percent more acidic by 2100. Corals, shellfish, and other hard-shelled marine species may struggle to survive. However, some soft-bodied animals, such as jellyfish, may actually thrive.

Broken reefs
Coral reefs may be damaged beyond repair by bleaching and acidification. This makes them unable to build their skeletons, meaning that they can no longer support such a rich abundance of life.

184 oceans and us ○ **OCEAN WATCH**

5,000 The approximate **number of plastic items** found on **every 1 mile** (1.6 km) of beach in the UK.

Ocean Watch

The oceans are under threat from pollution, climate change, and overfishing. One of the ways we can conserve the oceans for future generations is by first studying them.

The major challenge of monitoring the world's oceans is their sheer scale. Oceans cover 71 percent of the planet's surface and can reach depths of more than 35,760 ft (10,900 m). To cover this range, researchers are increasingly turning to technology for assistance. This allows experts to collect large amounts of data from different areas and depths in the ocean and then compare this information over time to assess what changes are occurring and why.

Monitoring the oceans

In order to protect and conserve the ocean, scientists are using a range of devices to gather vital information about the oceans—from anchored buoys and tide gauges to unmanned vehicles that can roam thousands of miles per mission. Some instruments measure the water's temperature and chemistry, while underwater robots monitor marine life at close hand.

Tower next to the tide house monitors winds and air temperature

SoFi
This soft-bodied robot that resembles a fish passes through coral reefs without disturbing the marine life. Its sensors and high-definition video cameras film and monitor the condition of shallow-water coral.

Tide gauge station
These scientific stations measure and record the height of the surrounding water, producing accurate records of sea levels and high and low tides. Some stations also contain sensors that measure wind and air temperature.

Side-mounted fins alter their angle to help SoFi rise or fall

Beach cleanups

Scientists are not the only people monitoring oceans and coastal communities. There are worldwide efforts to clean up beaches, as seen by these students who are removing waste—much of it plastic bottles and shopping bags—from a beach in the Indonesian village of Ujong Blang.

Shark tagging

Individual creatures, such as this young blacktip reef shark, can be monitored by fitting a tag to their body. Tags communicate with satellites to track the location, direction, and depth of the shark so that researchers can learn more about its migrating, feeding, and breeding habits.

Tag attached to first dorsal fin

4,078 The number of **Argo floats** deployed at sea, as of March 2020.

80 percent—the **area of the world's oceans** that have yet to be **fully observed and mapped.**

185

Satellite sensing
Satellites are used to monitor the ocean surface. They measure the heat energy emitted from the ocean, and this data can be gathered to build up global sea surface temperature maps that are useful in climate change research.

Argo float
Thousands of these temperature and salinity (salt) measuring devices form a global network. In a 10-day cycle, each float descends to a depth of up to 6,600 ft (2,000 m). When it resurfaces, it transmits its data via satellite to researchers on land.

Survey ships
These vessels can deploy buoys, floats, and underwater robots. They can also take multiple water samples from different depths using a circular frame, called a rosette, containing niskin bottles (pictured below the water's surface).

Smart buoy
Powered by solar panels, this buoy is packed with sensors that measure the wind and other weather conditions above the surface. Submerged sensors can measure the ocean's chemistry, such as its acidity and oxygen levels.

Echo Voyager
Guided by motion sensors and using sonar to detect obstacles in its path, Boeing's Echo Voyager is an unmanned underwater vehicle (UUV). Scientists deploy it to patrol and monitor the condition of seabeds in deep waters.

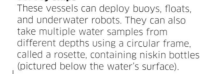

Rosette typically holds 12 or 24 niskin bottles

Each float takes around six hours to descend from the surface to 3,280 ft (1,000 m)

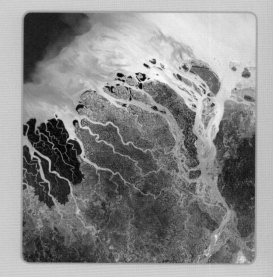

OCEAN MAPS

Humans have always explored and mapped the world's oceans, but recent technology has allowed us to see and understand these vast regions as never before. From the tropical Pacific to the chilly Arctic, each of the five oceans is home to unique geographical features, habitats, and creatures.

GLOBAL OCEAN

The world's oceans are one vast expanse of water stretching around the globe, divided into five main areas: the Arctic, the Atlantic, the Indian, the Pacific, and the Southern oceans. Near coastlines, parts of these can be grouped into smaller seas—bodies of water usually partially surrounded by land.

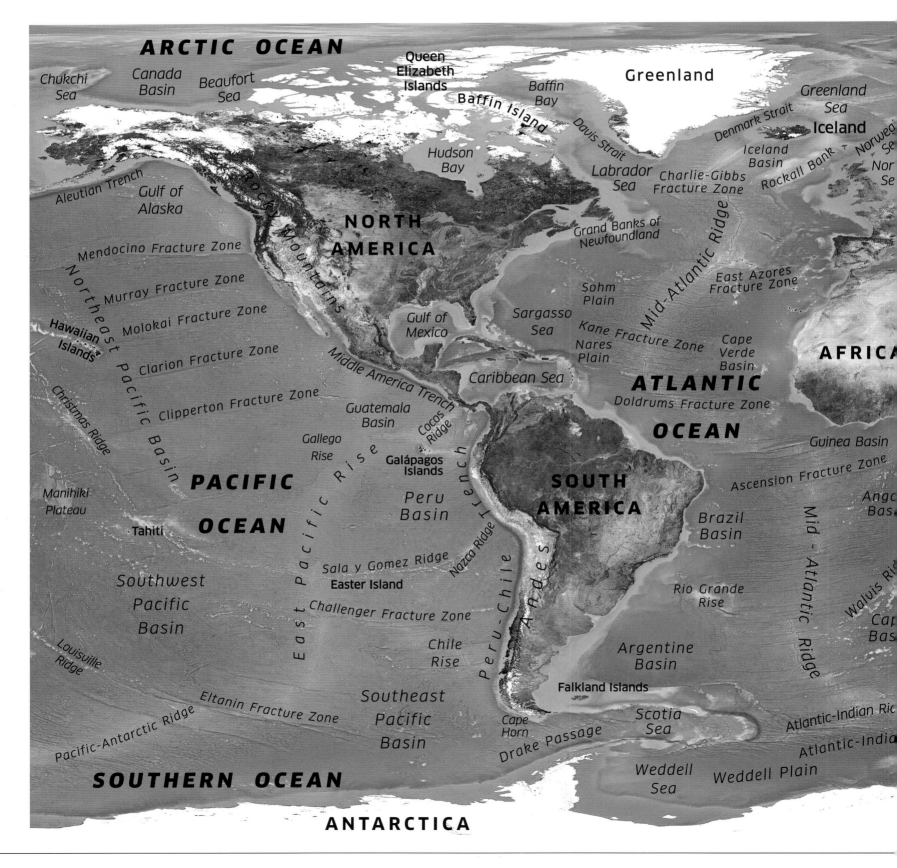

ARCTIC OCEAN

Chukchi Sea · Canada Basin · Beaufort Sea · Queen Elizabeth Islands · Baffin Bay · Greenland · Greenland Sea · Baffin Island · Davis Strait · Denmark Strait · Iceland

Aleutian Trench · Gulf of Alaska · Hudson Bay · Labrador Sea · Charlie-Gibbs Fracture Zone · Iceland Basin · Rockall Bank · Norwegi Se · Nor Se

Rocky Mountains · NORTH AMERICA · Grand Banks of Newfoundland · Mid-Atlantic Ridge

Mendocino Fracture Zone · Sohm Plain · East Azores Fracture Zone

Northeast Pacific Basin · Murray Fracture Zone · Sargasso Sea · Kane Fracture Zone · Cape Verde Basin · AFRICA

Hawaiian Islands · Molokai Fracture Zone · Gulf of Mexico · Nares Plain

Clarion Fracture Zone · Middle America Trench · Caribbean Sea · ATLANTIC OCEAN · Doldrums Fracture Zone

Christmas Ridge · Clipperton Fracture Zone · Guatemala Basin · Cocos Ridge

Gallego Rise · Galápagos Islands · Guinea Basin

Manihiki Plateau · PACIFIC OCEAN · East Pacific Rise · Peru Basin · SOUTH AMERICA · Ascension Fracture Zone · Ango Bas

Tahiti · Brazil Basin · Mid-Atlantic Ridge

Sala y Gomez Ridge · Nazca Ridge · Andes · Rio Grande Rise · Walvis Rid

Southwest Pacific Basin · Easter Island · Peru-Chile Trench · Cap Bas

Louisville Ridge · Challenger Fracture Zone · Chile Rise · Argentine Basin

Eltanin Fracture Zone · Southeast Pacific Basin · Falkland Islands · Atlantic-Indian Ric

Pacific-Antarctic Ridge · Cape Horn · Scotia Sea · Atlantic-India

Drake Passage · Weddell Sea · Weddell Plain

SOUTHERN OCEAN

ANTARCTICA

THE PACIFIC OCEAN
IS THE BIGGEST AND
ALSO THE DEEPEST OCEAN.
IT ALSO HAS THE LONGEST
COASTLINE AT 84,298 MILES
(135,665 KM) LONG.

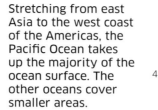

Ocean areas
Stretching from east
Asia to the west coast
of the Americas, the
Pacific Ocean takes
up the majority of the
ocean surface. The
other oceans cover
smaller areas.

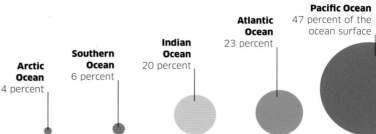

Arctic Ocean 4 percent

Southern Ocean 6 percent

Indian Ocean 20 percent

Atlantic Ocean 23 percent

Pacific Ocean 47 percent of the ocean surface

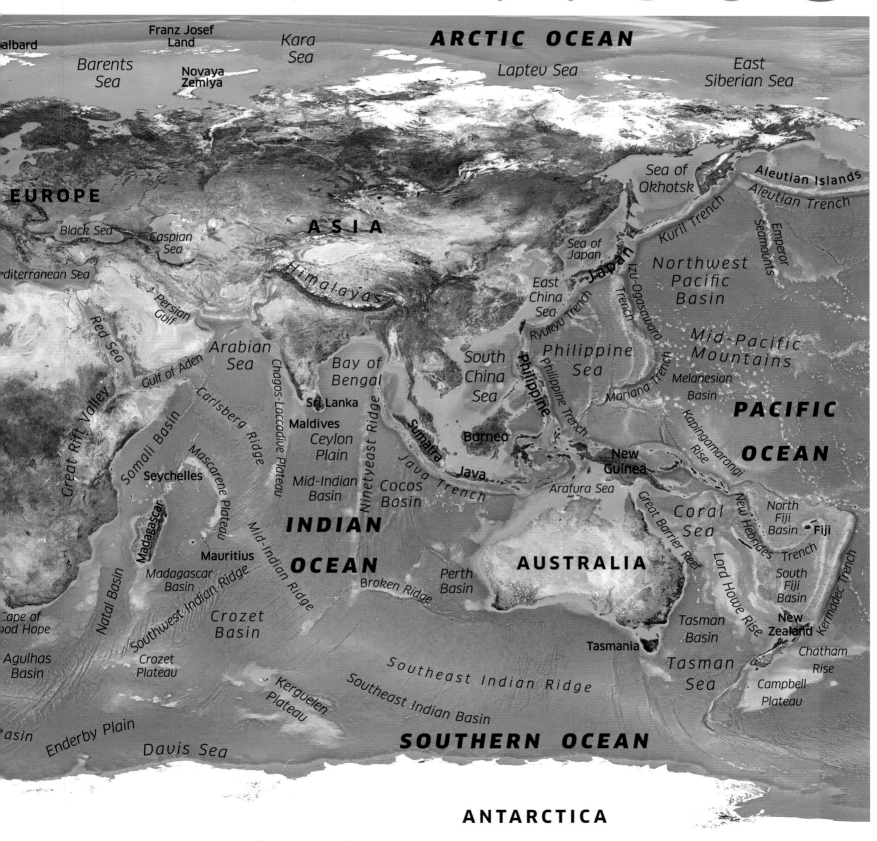

ARCTIC OCEAN

Svalbard · Franz Josef Land · Kara Sea · Laptev Sea · East Siberian Sea

Barents Sea · Novaya Zemlya

EUROPE · Black Sea · Caspian Sea · Mediterranean Sea

ASIA · Himalayas · Sea of Okhotsk · Aleutian Islands · Aleutian Trench

Persian Gulf · Red Sea · Gulf of Aden · Arabian Sea

Sea of Japan · Japan · Kuril Trench · Emperor Seamounts · Northwest Pacific Basin

East China Sea · Ryukyu Trench · Izu-Ogasawara Trench · Mid-Pacific Mountains

Great Rift Valley · Carlsberg Ridge · Chagos-Laccadive Plateau · Bay of Bengal · South China Sea · Philippine · Philippine Sea · Philippine Trench · Mariana Trench · Melanesian Basin · PACIFIC OCEAN

Somali Basin · Seychelles · Mascarene Plateau · Sri Lanka · Maldives · Ceylon Plain · Sumatra · Borneo · Kapingamarangi Rise

Madagascar · Mid-Indian Basin · Ninetyeast Ridge · Cocos Basin · Java · New Guinea · New Hebrides · North Fiji Basin · Fiji

Mauritius · Mid-Indian Ridge · INDIAN OCEAN · Arafura Sea · Great Barrier Reef · Coral Sea · Fiji Trench · South Fiji Basin · Kermadec Trench

Natal Basin · Madagascar Basin · Southwest Indian Ridge · Broken Ridge · Perth Basin · AUSTRALIA · Lord Howe Rise · Tasman Basin · New Zealand

Cape of Good Hope · Crozet Basin · Tasmania · Tasman Sea · Chatham Rise

Agulhas Basin · Crozet Plateau · Kerguelen Plateau · Southeast Indian Ridge · Campbell Plateau

Basin · Enderby Plain · Davis Sea · Southeast Indian Basin · SOUTHERN OCEAN

ANTARCTICA

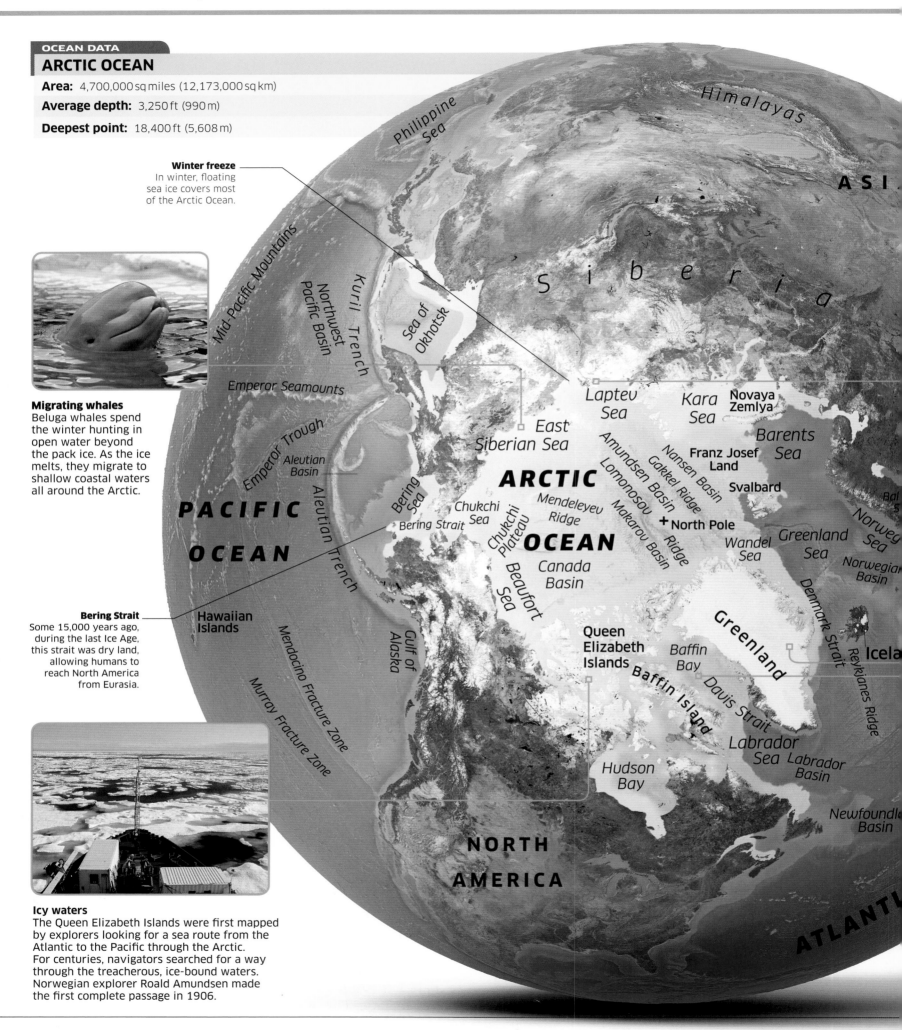

OCEAN DATA
ARCTIC OCEAN
Area: 4,700,000 sq miles (12,173,000 sq km)
Average depth: 3,250 ft (990 m)
Deepest point: 18,400 ft (5,608 m)

Winter freeze
In winter, floating sea ice covers most of the Arctic Ocean.

Migrating whales
Beluga whales spend the winter hunting in open water beyond the pack ice. As the ice melts, they migrate to shallow coastal waters all around the Arctic.

Bering Strait
Some 15,000 years ago, during the last Ice Age, this strait was dry land, allowing humans to reach North America from Eurasia.

Icy waters
The Queen Elizabeth Islands were first mapped by explorers looking for a sea route from the Atlantic to the Pacific through the Arctic. For centuries, navigators searched for a way through the treacherous, ice-bound waters. Norwegian explorer Roald Amundsen made the first complete passage in 1906.

Himalayas

Philippine Sea

ASIA

Siberia

Mid-Pacific Mountains

Northwest Pacific Basin

Kuril Trench

Sea of Okhotsk

Laptev Sea

Kara Sea

Novaya Zemlya

Barents Sea

Emperor Seamounts

East Siberian Sea

Amundsen Basin

Nansen Basin

Gakkel Ridge

Franz Josef Land

Svalbard

Emperor Trough

Aleutian Basin

ARCTIC

Mendeleyev Ridge

Lomonosov Ridge

Makarov Basin

Norweg Sea

PACIFIC

Bering Sea

Chukchi Sea

Chukchi Plateau

+North Pole

Wandel Sea

Greenland Sea

Bal
5

Aleutian Trench

Bering Strait

OCEAN

Canada Basin

Norwegia Basin

OCEAN

Beaufort Sea

Greenland

Denmark Strait

Hawaiian Islands

Gulf of Alaska

Queen Elizabeth Islands

Baffin Bay

Reykjanes Ridge

Icela

Mendocino Fracture Zone

Baffin Island

Davis Strait

Labrador Sea

Labrador Basin

Murray Fracture Zone

Hudson Bay

NORTH AMERICA

Newfoundla Basin

ATLANTI

13 percent—the present **rate** at which **summer sea ice** in the Arctic Ocean is **shrinking** each decade.

1,500 The **number** of **lives lost** when the ocean liner **RMS** *Titanic* hit an **iceberg** that drifted south from **Baffin Bay** in 1912.

191

Arctic Ocean

Lying around the North Pole and virtually surrounded by the continents of North America and Eurasia, the Arctic Ocean is the smallest of the world's oceans. In winter, it freezes over to create a vast sheet of floating ice.

The ocean floor is expanding at the Gakkel Ridge, near the North Pole, where tectonic plates are pulling apart. The ridge is flanked by deep ocean, surrounded by shallow shelves extending from the continents, which are dotted with islands. Most of these islands are connected by sea ice in winter, but the ice melts away in summer to leave a relatively small—and shrinking—area of ice around the North Pole.

Lena Delta
Six huge rivers pour fresh water into the Arctic Ocean—the Mackenzie, Yukon, Ob, Yenisei, Kolyma, and the Lena (seen here from space as it flows into the Laptev Sea). The rivers make the Arctic Ocean the least salty of the world's oceans.

Arctic islands
The ocean is dotted with islands such as Novaya Zemlya, Svalbard, the Queen Elizabeth Islands, Baffin Island, and Greenland (left). Rocky and icebound, vegetation on these islands is sparse.

Icebergs
Off Greenland, icebergs are formed from glaciers that have flowed from the land to the coast. In Baffin Bay, icebergs drift south with the Labrador Current, down the Davis Strait and into the North Atlantic where they are a threat to shipping.

Shrinking ice
Climate change has raised the annual average air temperature over the Arctic Ocean by 5.4°F (3°C) since 1970. This is making winter sea ice thinner and less likely to form at all. In summer, it melts faster, leaving a smaller area of ice in the far north. It may not be long before all the Arctic sea ice melts away in summer, leaving open water at the North Pole.

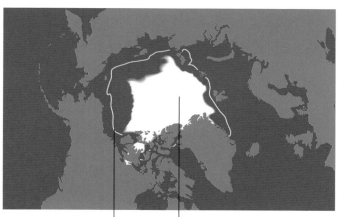

A colder past
Sea ice once extended this far in summer.

Melting away
The white area shows the sea ice in September 2019.

Top of the world
In 1958, the nuclear submarine USS *Nautilus* made the first voyage across the North Pole underneath the pack ice. More recently, similar nuclear submarines have been able to surface through the ice at the pole.

Moving waters
Polar winds blowing from the east drive an ocean current clockwise around the central Arctic Ocean as well as the cold Transpolar Drift current that diverges around Greenland. Currents also flow in the opposite direction along continental shores. The currents carry sea ice across the North Pole and south to warmer waters where it melts.

→ Cold current

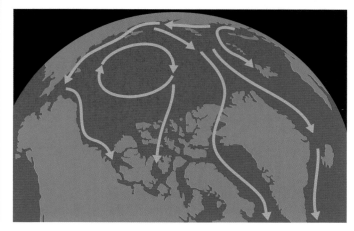

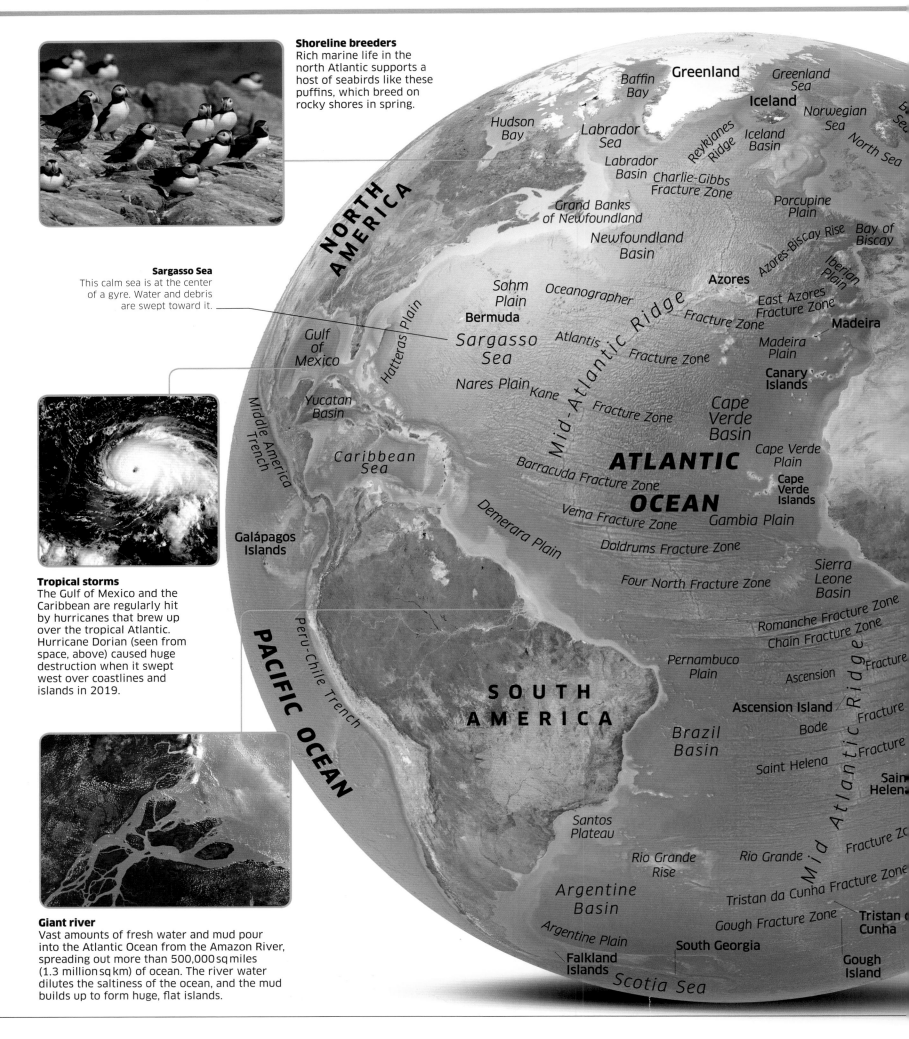

Shoreline breeders
Rich marine life in the north Atlantic supports a host of seabirds like these puffins, which breed on rocky shores in spring.

Sargasso Sea
This calm sea is at the center of a gyre. Water and debris are swept toward it.

Tropical storms
The Gulf of Mexico and the Caribbean are regularly hit by hurricanes that brew up over the tropical Atlantic. Hurricane Dorian (seen from space, above) caused huge destruction when it swept west over coastlines and islands in 2019.

Giant river
Vast amounts of fresh water and mud pour into the Atlantic Ocean from the Amazon River, spreading out more than 500,000 sq miles (1.3 million sq km) of ocean. The river water dilutes the saltiness of the ocean, and the mud builds up to form huge, flat islands.

Greenland
Greenland Sea
Baffin Bay
Iceland
Norwegian Sea
Hudson Bay
Labrador Sea
Reykjanes Ridge
Iceland Basin
North Sea
NORTH AMERICA
Labrador Basin
Charlie-Gibbs Fracture Zone
Porcupine Plain
Grand Banks of Newfoundland
Azores-Biscay Rise
Bay of Biscay
Newfoundland Basin
Azores
Iberian Plain
Sohm Plain
Oceanographer
East Azores Fracture Zone
Bermuda
Madeira
Hatteras Plain
Sargasso Sea
Atlantis Fracture Zone
Madeira Plain
Gulf of Mexico
Mid-Atlantic Ridge
Canary Islands
Nares Plain
Kane Fracture Zone
Cape Verde Basin
Yucatan Basin
Cape Verde Plain
Caribbean Sea
ATLANTIC OCEAN
Cape Verde Islands
Barracuda Fracture Zone
Middle America Trench
Vema Fracture Zone
Gambia Plain
Demerara Plain
Galápagos Islands
Doldrums Fracture Zone
Sierra Leone Basin
Four North Fracture Zone
Romanche Fracture Zone
PACIFIC OCEAN
Chain Fracture Zone
Peru-Chile Trench
Pernambuco Plain
Ascension
Fracture
Ascension Island
Fracture
SOUTH AMERICA
Brazil Basin
Bode
Fracture
Saint Helena
Mid Atlantic Ridge
Sain Helena
Santos Plateau
Fracture Zo
Rio Grande Rise
Rio Grande
Mid Atlantic Ridge
Fracture Z
Argentine Basin
Tristan da Cunha Fracture Zone
Tristan d Cunha
Argentine Plain
Gough Fracture Zone
South Georgia
Falkland Islands
Gough Island
Scotia Sea

1 in (2.5 cm) a year—the **average rate** at which the **Atlantic Ocean** is getting **wider**.

190 mph (305 km/h)—the **maximum wind speed** of the **most powerful Atlantic hurricane** on record.

193

OCEAN DATA
ATLANTIC OCEAN

Area: 41,100,000 sq miles (106,400,000 sq km)

Average depth: 10,830 ft (3,300 m)

Deepest point: 28,230 ft (8,605 m)

UROPE

Black Sea

diterranean Sea

AFRICA

a Gulf of Guinea

Angola Basin

is Ridge

e Basin

Mediterranean Sea
One of six seas linked to the Atlantic, the Mediterranean is almost completely surrounded by land.

Gulf of Guinea
The shape of the gulf is similar to the corresponding coastline of South America—evidence of the ancient continental rift.

Skeleton Coast
The cold Benguela Current in the Atlantic flows north past southwest Africa, chilling the air over the ocean. This causes fogs that strip the air of moisture, creating the coastal Namib Desert and the barren shores of what is called the Skeleton Coast. Here, the wrecks of ships that have run into rocks in the fog are strewn along the coast.

Atlantic Ocean

Extending from the icy fringes of the Arctic to the Southern Ocean around Antarctica, the vast Atlantic is the world's second-biggest ocean— and it is getting bigger every year.

The Atlantic Ocean originated as a rift that opened up through an ancient supercontinent some 180 million years ago, during the age of the dinosaurs. The ocean floor is still expanding from the rift, steadily pushing the Americas farther away from Europe and Africa. Molten rock from below Earth's crust has risen up through the rift to form the volcanic Mid-Atlantic Ridge, which snakes north to south through the entire ocean.

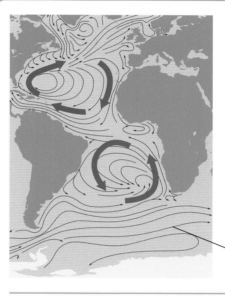

Swirling gyres
Ocean water swirls around the north and south Atlantic in huge current systems called "gyres" that flow clockwise in the north and counterclockwise in the south. They drive westward-flowing currents that carry warm water away from the tropics. Cold parts of gyres (shown here in blue) help cool the tropics, while warm parts of gyres (red) carry heat to cooler regions. Water and floating debris are pushed toward the calm centers of the gyres.

The narrow arrows indicate the direction of individual currents

Puerto Rico Trench
There are only a few areas where the ocean floor of the Atlantic is being destroyed in deep ocean trenches. The main site is the Puerto Rico Trench, where the ocean floor grinds beneath the edge of the Caribbean Plate. This activity has fueled the eruption of volcanoes, which have formed the islands of the Lesser Antilles, such as Montserrat (right).

Oceanic Iceland
The Mid-Atlantic Ridge is made up of a chain of volcanoes under the water. In the far north, an unusually active section called the Reykjanes Ridge breaks the ocean surface to form Iceland. The ridge passes through the middle of Iceland, dotting the landscape with active volcanoes. As a result, much of Iceland's landscape (left) is formed from dark basalt, a type of volcanic rock.

386,000 sq miles (1 million sq km)—the area of **ocean floor** covered by the **gigantic Bengal Fan**, to the south of the Ganges Delta.

Suez Canal
The Red Sea is a major shipping route, thanks to the Suez Canal, which links its northwestern tip with the Mediterranean. The canal is 120 miles (193 km) long and broad enough to allow the passage of ships up to 164 ft (50 m) wide.

Coral islands
The thousand-plus coral islands of the Maldives lie on the rocky ridge of the Chagos-Laccadive Plateau. Most of these are only a yard or two high, making them vulnerable to rising sea levels caused by climate change.

Living fossil
The coelacanth is a type of fish believed to have been extinct for 70 million years, until it was discovered living in the Mozambique Channel in 1938. Fish of this type were the ancestors of all land vertebrates.

Agulhas Current
The southward-flowing Agulhas Current slams into storm waves off South Africa, creating giant, very dangerous waves up to 66 ft (20 m) high.

OCEAN DATA
INDIAN OCEAN
Area: 28,400,000 sq miles (73,600,000 sq km)

Average depth: 12,760 ft (3,890 m)

Deepest point: 24,440 ft (7,450 m)

Map labels: ASIA · Himalayas · Persian Gulf · Gulf of Oman · Murray Ridge · Bay of Bengal · Andaman Islands · Saudi Arabia · Arabian Sea · Red Sea · Queen Fracture Zone · Arabian Basin · Gulf of Aden · Carlsberg Ridge · Chagos-Laccadive Plateau · Sri Lanka · Andaman Sea · Maldives · Ceylon Plain · AFRICA · Great Rift Valley · Somali Basin · Seychelles · Chagos Trench · Mid-Indian Basin · Ninetyeast Ridge · Cocos Basin · Investigator Ridge · Comoros · Mascarene Basin · Mascarene Plateau · INDIAN OCEAN · Mozambique Channel · Madagascar · Mascarene Plain · Mauritius · Réunion · Mid-Indian Ridge · Madagascar Basin · Southwest Indian Ridge · East Indiaman Ridge · Broken Ridge · Natal Basin · Madagascar Plateau · Cape Basin · South Africa · Mozambique Plateau · Crozet Basin · Southeast Indian Ridge · Agulhas Plateau · Crozet Plateau · Kerguelen Islands · Kerguelen Plateau · Agulhas Basin · Conrad Rise · Enderby Plain · Southern Ocean · ANTARCTICA · Diamond Fracture

110 The number of **active volcanoes** on Java, Sumatra, and nearby islands, created by the **tectonic activity** of the **Java Trench**.

1,192 The **number** of coral islands in the Maldives.

195

Indian Ocean

Lying to the south of Asia, the Indian Ocean is the warmest of the world's five oceans. Its temperature has dramatic effects on the climates of nearby countries.

The open waters of tropical oceans usually have relatively little marine life, because the warm surface water does not mix with the nutrient-rich water below. But strong monsoon winds in the northern Indian Ocean drive currents that drag nutrients to the surface, fueling the growth of plankton that support a wealth of fish and other life. River water flowing out of Asia also carries vast amounts of mineral-rich sediment into the Bay of Bengal, creating a rich marine ecosystem.

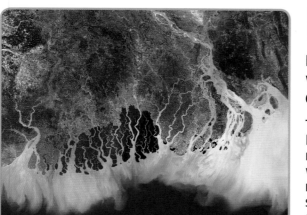

Ganges Delta
Sediment eroded from the Himalayan mountains is carried to the ocean by the Ganges River, where it forms the Ganges Delta (above). Lying above sea level, the delta is the top of the submarine Bengal Fan, a vast buildup of silt that is so heavy it distorts Earth's crust.

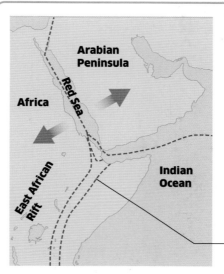

Java Trench
The northeastern edge of the ocean floor is grinding beneath Asia, creating the deep Java Trench. This is one of the world's most active volcanic and earthquake zones, creating volcanoes like Krakatoa (pictured above) and triggering the catastrophic 2004 Asian tsunami.

Cold frontier
The cold waters of the Antarctic Circumpolar Current—the largest current that swirls around Antarctica—mark the southern boundary of the Indian Ocean.

Expanding seas
The floor of the Indian Ocean is expanding where tectonic plates in Earth's crust are pulling apart. Along the line of the rift, a mid-ocean ridge has formed. This ridge extends north into the Red Sea, where it is pushing Arabia away from Africa, making the Red Sea grow wider every year. The Red Sea Rift is also linked to the East African Rift, which is ripping Africa apart.

The dotted line shows the location of the rifts

Monsoon rain
In summer, hot, dry air over the lands of Asia draws moist air from the Indian Ocean. Huge rain clouds form, spilling torrential rain over the land that often causes flooding (pictured right). In winter, cool air sinks over Asia and pushes dry air southward, reversing the wind system and causing droughts.

Cyclone chaos
The low-lying Ganges Delta is vulnerable to storm surges driven by tropical cyclones that sweep north up the funnel-shaped Bay of Bengal. In 2008, Cyclone Nargis caused catastrophic flooding in this way.

Map labels: East China Sea, Philippine Sea, Philippine Trench, PACIFIC OCEAN, Sulu Sea, Celebes Sea, Borneo, Sunda Shelf, Banda Sea, Arafura Shelf, North Australian Basin, Trench, Plateau, AUSTRALIA, South Australian Basin, Arabian Peninsula, Red Sea, Africa, East African Rift, Indian Ocean

Tropical typhoons
The tropical Pacific is regularly swept by huge revolving storms. Known as typhoons or tropical cyclones, they are the same as Atlantic hurricanes, and just as devastating in their impact. The most intense storm ever recorded was Typhoon Tip in October 1979, with winds reaching up to 190 mph (305 km/h).

Aleutian Trench
This deep trench marks where the ocean floor is plunging beneath Alaska.

Mariana Trench
The ocean floor here lies almost 7 miles (11 km) below the waves.

Coral reefs
South Pacific shores are bordered by beautiful coral reefs (see pp.98–99). The Great Barrier Reef—famous for its rich diversity of animal life—extends along the coast of northeastern Australia for 1,430 miles (2,300 km).

OCEAN DATA
PACIFIC OCEAN

Area: 54,500,000 sq miles (141,120,000 sq km)

Average depth: 14,163 ft (4,317 m)

Deepest point: 36,014 ft (10,977 m)

Pacific Ocean

The biggest and deepest ocean, the Pacific covers about a third of the world's total surface area and extends nearly halfway around the globe.

Larger than all the continents combined, and accounting for almost half of the total area of the world's oceans and seas, the Pacific is truly gigantic. Yet it was once even bigger—while other oceans, such as the Atlantic, are expanding, the Pacific is gradually getting smaller, carrying America closer to Australia, Japan, and China.

Map labels: Bering Sea · Gulf of Alaska · Aleutian Trench · Kuril Trench · Emperor Seamounts · Chinook Trough · Mendocino Fract · Murray Fract · Northwest Pacific Basin · Hawaiian Ridge · Mol · Mid-Pacific Seamounts · Hawaiian Islands · Clarion Frac · East Mariana Basin · Mariana Trench · Micronesia · Central Pacific Basin · PACIFIC OCEAN · Caroline Islands · Melanesian Basin · Melanesia · Line Islands · Papua New Guinea · Solomon Islands · Samoa · Polynesia · Coral Sea · Fiji · Tahiti · AUSTRALIA · South Fiji Basin · South West Pacific Basin · Lord Howe Rise · Kermadec Trench · Louisville Ridge · Agass · Tasman Sea · New Zealand · Mer · Campbell Plateau · Eltanin Fracture Zo · ANTARCTICA

25,000 The **number of islands** in the tropical south **Pacific**, forming the **realm of Oceania**.

171 million cubic miles (714 million cubic km)—the **approximate volume of ocean water in the Pacific**—half of the world's total.

197

Kelp forests

Extensive submerged forests of giant kelp—a type of seaweed (see pp.74–75)—line the cooler coastal waters of North and South America, which are rich in nutrients. With fronds growing up to 164 ft (50 m) from the seabed to the surface, they are home to a wide variety of animals, including fish, sea lions, and sea otters.

Galápagos Islands

Although these volcanic islands lie on the equator, they are swept by the cold waters of the Peru Current. These waters are rich in nutrients that support plankton, fish, seabirds, and other wildlife such as this seaweed-eating Galápagos marine iguana.

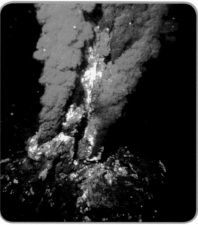

Black smoker

The East Pacific Rise is a fast-spreading mid-ocean ridge dotted with underwater hot springs known as black smokers (see pp.64–65), which gush superheated, mineral-rich water into the cold, dark ocean depths. The smokers support amazing communities of organisms that get all their energy from the chemicals in the water, instead of from sunlight.

Pacific Ring of Fire

The Pacific is shrinking because the ocean floor is being destroyed at the edges, where it is slipping beneath other plates making up Earth's crust. This process—called subduction—has created a ring of deep ocean trenches all around the outer edges of the Pacific from New Zealand to Chile. Along these subduction zones are at least 450 volcanoes, which surround the ocean and form the "Pacific Ring of Fire."

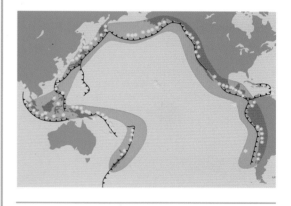

Hot spot volcanoes

Most volcanoes occur near plate boundaries. However, the ocean floor of the Pacific is also dotted with isolated volcanoes that have erupted over hot spots beneath Earth's crust. Hot spots are fixed spots in the mantle where magma is especially hot. Movement of the crust over these hot spots creates chains of volcanic islands and submerged seamounts. The longest, the Emperor Seamount Chain, which includes the Hawaiian Islands, stretches 3,730 miles (6,000 km).

Volcanic islands
The deepest point in the Southern Ocean is the South Sandwich Trench. Here, one slab of ocean floor is grinding beneath another. The collision has created a chain of volcanic islands.

Rocky refuge
The northernmost tip of Antarctica, known as the Antarctic Peninsula, thaws in summer. This allows it to support breeding colonies of birds, such as Adélie penguins, that cannot nest on the ice.

Ross Ice Shelf
The continental ice sheets of Antarctica extend over coastal seas to form deep ice shelves. The vast Ross Ice Shelf covers 193,363 sq miles (500,809 sq km)—the size of France.

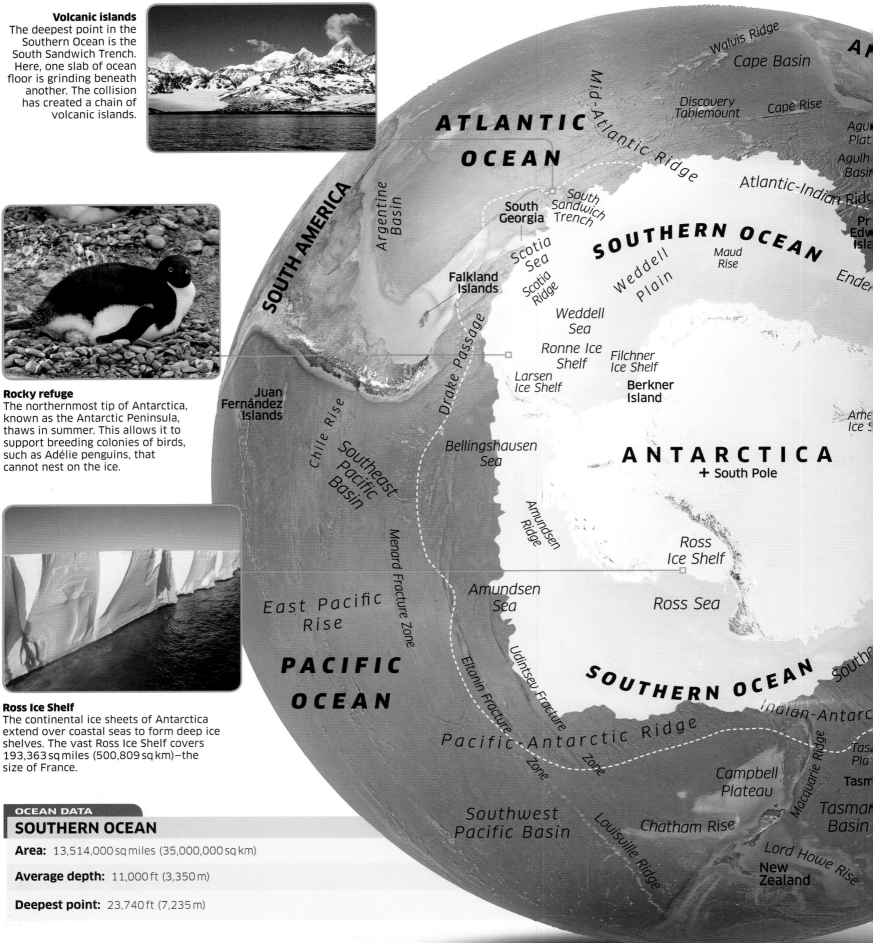

ATLANTIC OCEAN

SOUTH AMERICA

Walvis Ridge

Cape Basin

Discovery Tablemount

Cape Rise

Mid-Atlantic Ridge

Atlantic-Indian Ridge

Argentine Basin

South Sandwich Trench

South Georgia

SOUTHERN OCEAN

Scotia Sea

Maud Rise

Weddell Plain

Falkland Islands

Scotia Ridge

Weddell Sea

Drake Passage

Ronne Ice Shelf

Filchner Ice Shelf

Larsen Ice Shelf

Berkner Island

Juan Fernández Islands

Chile Rise

Bellingshausen Sea

ANTARCTICA
+ South Pole

Southeast Pacific Basin

Amundsen Ridge

Ross Ice Shelf

East Pacific Rise

Menard Fracture Zone

Amundsen Sea

Ross Sea

PACIFIC OCEAN

Eltanin Fracture Zone

Udintsev Fracture Zone

SOUTHERN OCEAN

Pacific-Antarctic Ridge

Indian-Antarctic

Macquarie Ridge

Campbell Plateau

Southwest Pacific Basin

Louisville Ridge

Chatham Rise

Lord Howe Rise

New Zealand

Tasman Basin

OCEAN DATA

SOUTHERN OCEAN

Area: 13,514,000 sq miles (35,000,000 sq km)

Average depth: 11,000 ft (3,350 m)

Deepest point: 23,740 ft (7,235 m)

10,000 miles (16,000 km)—the **distance** that some **albatrosses** can fly in a single journey.

Antarctic coastal seas are often **deep** because **Earth's crust** has been **distorted** by the colossal **weight** of the **ice sheets**.

199

Southern Ocean

The Southern Ocean, which surrounds the frozen Antarctic continent, is the stormiest, iciest, most hostile ocean on Earth, yet it abounds with marine life.

Apart from the shores of Antarctica, the Southern Ocean has no obvious boundaries. Its northern frontier is the Antarctic Convergence, where the cold Antarctic Circumpolar Current sinks beneath the warmer waters of the south Pacific, south Atlantic, and south Indian oceans. The boundary is not visible, but it is obvious to anyone heading south on a ship, as the temperature suddenly drops from about 43°F (6°C) to near freezing point.

Crozet Islands
The Crozet Islands and other subantarctic isles are home to breeding albatrosses. The wandering albatross, pictured above, spends most of its life in flight, riding the storm-force Antarctic winds, but it comes to land to nest.

Winter ice
The extent of winter sea ice is shown in gray.

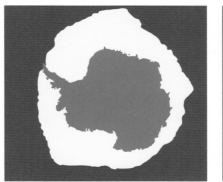

Giant icebergs
Huge tabular (flat-topped) icebergs break away from the Antarctic ice shelves and drift with the currents. This one, known as iceberg D28, broke away from the Amery Ice Shelf in 2019. Seen here from space, it had an area of 630 sq miles (1,632 sq km).

Antarctic Convergence
The white dotted line marks the boundary of the ocean at the Antarctic Convergence.

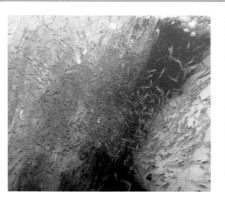

Food-rich waters
The Antarctic Circumpolar Current flows east around the continent. At its inner boundary, close to Antarctica itself, deep, nutrient-rich water is drawn to the surface from near the ocean floor. The nutrients fuel the growth of clouds of microscopic algae. These in turn feed vast pinkish swarms of krill—the staple prey of penguins, crabeater seals, and baleen whales.

Frozen ocean
When the air over the Southern Ocean chills down with the onset of winter, the sea starts to freeze over. By September, sea ice covers some 7 million sq miles (18 million sq km)—more than the area of Antarctica itself. In spring, the sea ice starts to melt away, shrinking to less than 1 million sq miles (2.6 million sq km) in February.

Sea ice extent in September

Sea ice extent in February

Drowned continent
The continent of Antarctica lies beneath vast ice sheets, up to 2.5 miles (4 km) thick at their deepest parts. These continental ice sheets are made of fresh water—in fact, they contain around 70 percent of all the fresh water on Earth. Much of the bedrock beneath lies below sea level, so if there was no ice, large areas of the continent would be underwater, as this map shows.

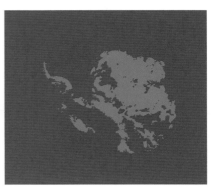

Map labels: ambique Ridge, Natal Basin, Conrad Rise, Southwest Indian Ridge, Crozet Plateau, Crozet Islands, Crozet Basin, Mid-Indian Ridge, Kerguelen Plateau, Kerguelen Island, Heard and McDonald Islands, INDIAN OCEAN, Southeast Indian Ridge, Broken Ridge, Southwest Indian Ridge, un Basin, South Australian Basin, Great Australian Bight, AUSTRALIA

Glossary

ABDOMEN
In crustaceans and insects, the rear part of the body.

ADAPTATION
The way an organism becomes more suited to its environment through evolution.

ALGAE
Plantlike organisms that usually live in water and use energy from sunlight to make their own food. The largest algae are seaweeds, while the smallest are part of the plankton.

ALGAL BLOOM
A large concentration of algae in one area. Algal blooms can be harmful to other life.

ANAL FIN
A fin on the belly of a fish, just in front of its tail, used for keeping the fish stable as it swims.

ANTENNAE
A pair of sense organs that can detect movements and chemicals in the water.

AQUACULTURE
The cultivation of fish and other marine species, usually for food.

ARTHROPOD
An invertebrate animal with an external skeleton and jointed legs.

ATMOSPHERE
The air that surrounds Earth, which contains gases such as oxygen and carbon dioxide.

ATOLL
A ring of coral reef that surrounds a lagoon.

BACTERIA
Microscopic organisms that are made of only one cell.

BAIT BALL
A tightly packed ball of small fish swimming closely together as a defense against predators.

BALEEN
A mesh of bristly plates in the mouths of some types of whales, used for sieving and trapping tiny food particles from seawater.

BEAK
In marine mammals, such as some whales and dolphins, a projecting snout similar to the beak of a bird.

BELL
The muscular, baglike body of a jellyfish.

BIODIVERSITY
The variety of all living things found on Earth or in a particular area, measured by numbers of different species.

BIOLUMINESCENCE
Emitting a natural light. It is seen in animals that live in the deep, dark zones of the ocean where sunlight cannot penetrate.

BIVALVE
A type of mollusk, such as an oyster or a mussel, that has a shell made up of two halves joined by a hinge.

BLOWHOLE
The nostril on the top of the head of a cetacean, through which it breathes air at the ocean surface.

BLUBBER
A thick layer of fat beneath the skin of some marine mammals, including whales and seals, that provides insulation in cold oceans.

BONY FISH
A fish that has a skeleton made of bone, rather than of cartilage. Around 90 percent of all fish in the oceans are classed as bony.

BRIDGE
Of a ship, the area at the front from which the ship is steered.

BUOY
A floating marker anchored to the seabed by a chain or cable.

BUOYANCY
The ability to float.

BYCATCH
Fish and other marine life that are caught accidentally in fishing nets cast to catch other species. Bycatch is often thrown dead or dying back into the sea.

CALF
The young of a whale, dolphin, or manatee.

CAMOUFLAGE
The ability of an organism to blend in with its environment.

CARAPACE
The hard upper shell of a turtle or of a crustacean such as a crab.

CARBON DIOXIDE
A gas that forms a small part of the atmosphere and is found in water in dissolved form. Some living things, such as algae and plants, can use it to make food.

CARCASS
The dead body of an animal.

CARNIVORE
An animal that eats other animals.

CARTILAGE
A tough, springy material that in some fish, such as sharks, forms the skeleton instead of bone. These fish are known as cartilaginous fish.

CAUDAL FIN
The fin that makes up a fish's tail.

CAY
A low island made of coral sand.

CELL
The smallest unit of life. Some organisms, such as bacteria, consist of just one cell. Larger forms of life may consist of trillions of different types of cells that perform various functions.

CEPHALOPOD
An animal belonging to the group of marine mollusks that includes squid, octopus, and cuttlefish.

CETACEAN
A whale, dolphin, or porpoise.

CLIMATE
The most common weather conditions in an area over a period of time.

CLIMATE CHANGE
The process of gradual change to Earth's climate due to human activity.

COLONY
A group of organisms living together. A colony of tiny organisms may work together to perform the functions of one creature, such as a salp or a siphonophore. These are known as colonial animals.

COMPOUND EYE
A type of eye found in some crustaceans and most insects that is made up of many separate units, each with its own lens.

CONSUMER
An animal that consumes other organisms to gain energy, as opposed to producing energy itself.

CONTINENTAL SHELF
The submerged edge of a continent that lies beneath shallow coastal seas.

COPEPOD
Species of small crustacean, many of which are part of the ocean plankton.

CORE
The innermost part of a planet. Earth has a liquid outer core and a solid inner core, both made of iron and nickel.

CORROSION
The wearing away of an object due to substances reacting chemically.

COUNTERSHADING
A pattern of coloration where an animal is darker on top and lighter underneath. This means that seen from above, the animal blends in with the dark water below, but seen from below, it blends in with the sunlit surface.

CRUST
The rocky outermost layer of Earth.

CRUSTACEAN
An animal with a hard external skeleton and paired, jointed legs, such as a crab or shrimp.

CURRENT
A continually flowing path of water, usually generated by the wind.

CYCLONE
Also known as a hurricane or typhoon, a weather phenomenon over the oceans where high-speed winds spin around and produce heavy rain.

DELTA
The fan-shaped area at the mouth of a river where it meets the sea. The shape is formed by sediments carried and deposited by the river.

DENTICLES
Tiny scales, shaped like teeth, covering the skin of a shark. Denticles reduce the drag of water, allowing the shark to swim fast and silently.

DIATOM
A type of algae made of a single cell, belonging to the phytoplankton.

DORSAL FIN
A fin on a marine animal's back.

EARTHQUAKE
A violent shaking of Earth produced by two tectonic plates sliding against each other at a fault.

ECHOLOCATION
A way of locating nearby objects by sending out sounds and receiving the echoes. Used by dolphins and other marine animals, and by land animals such as bats.

ECOSYSTEM
A community of living organisms that interact with each other and with their environment.

EGG
The female reproductive cell. Also the objects laid by birds, fish, and insects, which contain a developing embryo.

ENERGY
What all living things need to live and grow. Most gain this by eating other organisms or from a source such as sunlight.

EQUATOR
The imaginary circle around the middle of Earth, dividing the planet into the Northern and Southern hemispheres (halves).

EROSION
When particles of sediment produced by eroded rock get carried away, for example, by water or wind.

ESTUARY
The place where a river meets the sea.

EVOLUTION
The gradual process of change in living things between generations over millions of years.

EXOSKELETON
The hard external skeleton of a crustacean or insect.

EXTINCTION
The disappearance from Earth of the last living representative of a species.

FAST ICE
Sea ice that is frozen to the shore.

FAULT
A crack in Earth's surface where the rocks on either side have shifted in relation to each other, either upward, downward, or sideways. This movement can cause earthquakes.

FILTER-FEEDING
A method used by some whales in which they strain seawater through fringed plates in their mouths to trap small prey.

FISH
A large group of animals that breathe through gills and usually have bodies designed for swimming. There are three main classes of fish: bony fish, cartilaginous fish (sharks and rays), and jawless fish (lampreys).

FLUKE
The tail fin of a cetacean.

FOOD CHAIN
The order in which organisms, from microscopic life-forms to top predators, pass on to each other the energy they obtain from food.

FOSSIL
The preserved remains or traces of once-living animals and plants. The most common fossils are bones that have been buried and changed into stone over millions of years.

FOSSIL FUEL
A substance formed from the remains of ancient organisms that burns easily to release energy. Coal, oil, and gas are fossil fuels.

FRACTURE ZONE
A long valley in the ocean floor, which cuts through an undersea mountain ridge where the rocks are at different depths.

FRY
Young fish.

GASTROPOD
One of a group of mollusks that includes snails and slugs.

GENERATOR
A machine that converts motion into electrical energy.

GEOLOGY
The study of Earth's rocks and their history.

GILL RAKERS
Projections from the gills of a fish, used for trapping food particles.

GILLS
The organs used by fish and other animals for breathing underwater.

GLACIER
A moving mass of ice, formed from accumulated snow. Some glaciers flow like rivers. Others are vast ice sheets such as those covering Antarctica.

GRAVITY
The force that attracts one object to another and prevents things from floating off into space.

GYRE
A circular pattern of ocean currents.

HABITAT
The area where an organism naturally makes its home.

HEMOGLOBIN
The oxygen-carrying substance found inside red blood cells.

HERBIVORE
An animal that feeds on plants.

HOLDFAST
The rootlike structure used by seaweeds to attach themselves to a rock or the seabed.

HOT SPOT
A fixed point beneath Earth's surface where the mantle is particularly hot.

HYDRAULIC
Powered by the pressure of water.

HYDROTHERMAL VENT
A crack in the ocean floor from which extremely hot and chemical-rich water rises.

ICEBERG
A large floating fragment of ice that has broken off a glacier or ice shelf.

ICE FLOE
A slab of floating ice.

ICE SHEET
A very large mass of permanent ice that covers land.

ICE SHELF
Part of an ice sheet that extends over the ocean.

INTERTIDAL ZONE
The area on a beach between the highest and lowest points reached by the tide.

INVERTEBRATE
An animal without a backbone.

KERATIN
A tough material that makes up body parts such as the baleen plates in some whales and hair and fingernails in humans.

KRILL
Tiny, shrimplike crustaceans that drift in huge numbers in the oceans and provide vital food for many marine animals.

LAGOON
A stretch of water almost cut off from the sea. Also refers to the shallow water inside a coral atoll.

LARVA
The immature form of an animal that hatches from an egg.

LATERAL LINE
A row of sense organs running along the head and sides of a fish, which allow the fish to detect movement in the water.

LAVA
Molten rock from inside Earth, which is forced to the surface during a volcanic eruption.

LITHOSPHERE
The outer layer of Earth, made from the solid upper part of the mantle and the brittle outer crust.

LURE
A part of an animal's body used to attract prey, such as the luminous "fishing rod" of a deep-sea anglerfish.

MAGMA
Hot, liquid rock that is found beneath Earth's surface.

MAMMAL
One of a group of warm-blooded vertebrates, with females that feed their young with milk.

MANTLE
The layer of Earth between the central core and the outermost layer, the crust. Also the muscular, often cloaklike cover that protects the internal organs of a mollusk.

MARINE
Relating to the ocean or sea.

MICROPLASTICS
Very small pieces of plastic that result from the breakdown of plastic waste, which can be harmful to marine life.

MID-OCEAN RIDGE
A large chain of underwater mountains that stretches around the globe. It is longer than any mountain range on land.

MIGRATION
The regular, usually yearly, journey made by an animal to and from different regions to feed and breed.

MINERAL
A solid material occurring naturally in Earth. Most rocks are made from minerals. Minerals can be found dissolved in seawater.

MOLLUSK
One of a group of animals that includes slugs and snails, bivalves, and octopus and their relatives.

MOLT
The way an animal sheds part of its outer skin, coat, or exoskeleton.

In crustaceans, the regular shedding of the hard outer skeleton (exoskeleton) to allow the animal to grow.

MOLTEN
Hot and melted (in liquid form).

NUTRIENT
A substance essential for life to exist and grow.

OCEAN BASIN
A region lying beneath the ocean surface, which may include ridges and deep-sea trenches.

ORGAN
A collection of living body tissues that does a particular job. The stomach and heart are examples of organs.

ORGANISM
A living thing, such as a plant, animal, fungus, or bacterium.

OXYGEN
A gas that is present in Earth's atmosphere and is essential to life. Oxygen has no color or smell.

PACK ICE
Large masses of floating sea ice not attached to the shore.

PARASITE
An organism that feeds on another, called the host, weakening it, and sometimes eventually killing it.

PECTORAL FINS
The front pair of fins on either side of a fish's body, which are used for steering.

PHOTOSYNTHESIS
The chemical process by which plants, algae, and some bacteria use carbon dioxide, water, and the energy from sunlight to make their own food.

PHYTOPLANKTON
Tiny organisms, for example, bacteria and plantlike algae, that drift near the surface of oceans and make their own food through photosynthesis.

PLANKTON
Organisms that drift in the ocean, instead of swimming against the

current. Most plankton are tiny, but they exist in large numbers. They are an important source of food for bigger animals.

POD
A group or school of whales or dolphins.

POLAR OCEANS
The icy oceans in Earth's cold polar regions.

POLYP
A tiny, tube-shaped animal topped with a ring of tentacles. Many types of polyps attach themselves together in large colonies on the seabed, where they slowly form coral reefs.

PREDATOR
An animal that hunts other animals for food.

PREHISTORIC
Existing before written records.

PRESSURE
The force that pushes against a particular area. In the oceans, the weight of water creates strong pressure, which increases with depth.

PREVAILING WIND
Wind that blows in a particular area from a predictable direction.

PREY
An animal that is hunted by other animals for food.

PRODUCER
An organism that makes its own food using a source of energy, such as sunlight.

PROPULSION
The act of pushing or driving something forward.

REEF
A rocky ridge below the ocean made by coral, and usually found in sunlit waters near the coast.

REPRODUCTION
The process by which organisms produce new offspring.

RESPIRATION
The chemical process within living cells that releases energy from stored food molecules. Most respiration uses oxygen, but a few organisms, such as some bacteria, can respire without using any oxygen at all.

RETINA
The layer of light-sensitive cells at the back of the eye.

RIDGE
A section of risen crust formed when two tectonic plates move away from each other.

RIFT
A place where two tectonic plates are pulling apart to create a crack in Earth's crust. At rifts, new crust is being created.

SCAVENGER
An animal that feeds on the remains of dead animals or other organic waste (waste from living organisms).

SCHOOL
A large number of fish that swim in a coordinated way. Also the name for a group of dolphins or porpoises.

SEAMOUNT
A volcano rising from the ocean floor that is not high enough to form an island.

SEDIMENT
Small particles of rock that are deposited by water.

SHOAL
A group of fish.

SILT
Fine particles of rock carried by water.

SIPHON
A fleshy tube through which a mollusk can draw in or pump out seawater. It may be used for breathing or to propel the animal along.

SIPHONOPHORE
A type of animal similar to a jellyfish, but made up of a drifting colony of parts working together. An example is the Portuguese man o' war.

SOLAR
Relating to the sun.

SONAR
Short for "sound navigation and ranging." A method that uses sound waves to detect objects and measure distances underwater.

SPAWN
The mass of eggs and sperm released by aquatic animals such as fish when they mate.

SPECIES
A group of similar organisms that can interbreed and produce fertile offspring.

SPERM
Male cells of animals that fertilize female eggs, enabling them to develop into a new organism.

STREAMLINED
Having a shape that moves easily through water or air.

SUBDUCTION
When one tectonic plate moves beneath another. In areas where subduction is occurring, crust is being destroyed.

SWASH
The movement of water up the beach as a wave breaks. The movement of water back down the beach is called backwash.

TECTONIC PLATE
One of the large moving sections of Earth's uppermost layer, the lithosphere.

TEMPERATE OCEAN
Region of the ocean between the cold polar seas and the warm tropics.

TENTACLE
In marine animals such as jellyfish and sea anemones, a flexible extension of the body. Tentacles are used for feeling and grasping and may contain stinging cells to stun or kill prey.

TIDAL RANGE
The difference between sea level at high and low tide.

TOXIN
A poisonous substance.

TRANSFORM FAULT
A zone on the seabed where two adjoining rocky plates slide past one another horizontally.

TROPICAL OCEAN
Region of the ocean around the equator. Tropical waters are warm.

TSUNAMI
An enormous, rapidly rising ocean wave caused by an earthquake or volcanic activity under the sea. Tsunamis travel very fast and can cause widespread devastation when they hit coastlines.

TURBINE
A machine turned by the force of wind or water to generate energy such as electricity.

UPWELLING ZONE
An area of the sea where strong currents carry cold water from the depths of the ocean to the surface.

VERTEBRATE
An animal with a backbone.

VOLCANO
An opening in Earth's crust that provides an outlet for magma (hot, molten rock) when it rises to the surface.

WATER VAPOR
Water in the form of gas, produced during the natural cycle of evaporation. The vapor rises from the oceans and other water sources such as rivers, moving up into the atmosphere where it cools to form clouds and falls again as rain.

WEATHERING
When wind, water, or air break down rock into smaller pieces.

ZOOPLANKTON
Tiny animals that together with microscopic plantlike organisms make up the masses of plankton that float in the oceans.

ZOOXANTHELLAE
The algae that live inside the tissues of corals and some other marine organisms.

Index

Acknowledgments

The publisher would like to thank the following people for their assistance in the preparation of this book: Rachael Grady and Kit Lane for design assistance; Ann Baggaley, Ashwin Khurana, Georgina Palffy, and Selina Wood for editorial assistance; DTP designer Rakesh Kumar, Jackets Editorial Coordinator Priyanka Sharma, and Managing Jackets Editor Saloni Singh; Nic Dean for picture research; Hazel Beynon for proofreading; and Helen Peters for the index. Special thanks to Clive Gifford for additional text.

Smithsonian Enterprises:
Kealy E. Gordon, Product Development Manager
Jill Corcoran, Director, Licensed Publishing
Brigid Ferraro, Vice President, Consumer and Education Products
Carol LeBlanc, President

The publisher would like to thank the following for their kind permission to reproduce their photographs:

(Key: a-above; b-below/bottom; c-center; f-far; l-left; r-right; t-top)

1 Fotolia: Strezhnev Pavel (c/ocean background). **3 Fotolia:** Strezhnev Pavel (cb/ocean background). **15 Alamy Stock Photo:** Ryan M. Bolton (tr); B Christopher (tc). **20-21 Martin Harvey Photography:** (c). **25 Alamy Stock Photo:** James O'Sullivan (br). **naturepl. com:** Philip Stephen (tr). **31 Fotolia:** Strezhnev Pavel (ca/sea background). **33 Dorling Kindersley:** Linda Pitkin (cr/shark). **34 Alamy Stock Photo:** Paulo Oliveira (cl). **NOAA:** (tc). **36 Science Photo Library:** Carolina Biological Supply Co, Visuals Unlimited (cl); Steve Gschmeissner (bl). **36-37 Nat Geo Image Collection:** David Liittschwager (c). **37 Alamy Stock Photo:** blickwinkel (cr); Underwater (tr). **ESA:** (br). **38 Shutterstock:** Sergey Uryadnikov (tl). **39 Doug Perrine:** (br). **47 Alamy Stock Photo:** RDW-Underwater (bl). **48 123RF. com:** Naveen kawa (clb/size comparison). **49 Dorling Kindersley:** Professor Michael M. Mincarone (tr). **50 Alamy Stock Photo:** BIOSPHOTO (bl). **53 Dorling Kindersley:** Harry Taylor / Natural History Museum, London (cla/size comparison). **56-57 TandemStock.com:** Christian Vizl. **59 Science Photo Library:** Michael Ready / Visuals Unlimited, Inc. (tr). **65 Ocean Networks Canada:** (tr). **69 Alamy Stock Photo:** Zacarias Pereira da Mata (bc). **mauritius images:** Alaska Stock Doug Lindstrand (tr). **Nat Geo Image Collection:** Maria Stengel (br). **naturepl.com:** Nick Upton (bl). **70 Fotolia:** Strezhnev Pavel (cl/sea background). **73 Alamy Stock Photo:** Jane Gould (cl); Seaphotoart (tl); Rasmus Loeth Petersen (clb); Scubazoo (bl). **Ambient Recording GmbH / ambient.de:** (cr). **naturepl. com:** Georgette Douwma (bc, br). **74 Alamy Stock Photo:** Arterra Picture Library (clb); pzAxe (bl); Amy Cicconi (cl); ITAR-TASS News Agency (tl). **75 Alamy Stock Photo:** Richard Mittleman / Gon2Foto (tr). **Getty Images:** Brent Durand (br); Steven Trainoff PhD (cr). **77 Kevin W. Conway:** (br). **78 Alamy Stock Photo:** Nature Picture Library (bl). **naturepl.com:** Alan James (cl). **79 123RF.com:** tudor antonel adrian / tony4urban (cr). **81 Dorling Kindersley:** Linda Pitkin (tc/size comparison). **83 naturepl.com:** Constantinos Petrinos (br). **84 Alamy Stock Photo:** Reinhard Dirscherl (cl). **Dorling Kindersley:** Linda Pitkin (cla). **85 Dreamstime. com:** Andrey Armyagov / Cookelma (clb/size comparison). **86-87 Alamy Stock Photo:** Nature Picture Library (c). **88 Alamy Stock Photo:** Ethan Daniels (br); Beth Swanson (bl). **89 Alamy Stock Photo:** Dennis Sabo (br). **92 Science Photo Library:** Ted Kinsman (cra). **94 Alamy Stock Photo:** ImageBROKER (bl/size comparison). **95 Alamy Stock Photo:** dotted zebra (bc). **Dorling Kindersley:** Terry Goss (cr/size comparison). **99 Alamy Stock Photo:** mauritius images GmbH (br); RGB Ventures (cr). **100 Alamy Stock Photo:** WaterFrame (tl). **Dreamstime.com:** Soren Egeberg (cl). **101 Prof. Nico J. Smit:** (br). **103 123RF. com:** Visarute Angkatavanich / bluehand (c). **104-105 Getty Images:** Reinhard Dirscherl / ullstein bild (c). **110 Alamy Stock Photo:** Bill Brooks (ca/both); Harold Stiver (cl); Jesse Kraft (bl). **111 Alamy Stock Photo:** Arterra Picture Library (bc); maisie hill (clb); Nature Picture Library (bl); blickwinkel (cb); Nikolay Mukhorin (br). **112 naturepl.com:** Visuals Unlimited (tc). **113 Getty Images:** ankh-fire (cr). **116-117 Shutterstock:** Eduardo Sousa (c). **118 Alamy Stock Photo:** Chris Ison (tl). **119 Getty Images:** apomares (cr). **Shane Gross:** (br). **120 Alamy Stock Photo:** Nature Picture Library (br). **121 123RF.com:** Marek Poplawski / mark52 (tr). **Shutterstock:** Michael Nolan / Splashdowndirect (bc). **123 Alamy Stock Photo:** Nature Picture Library (bc); Martin Strmiska (tl). **124 Alamy Stock Photo:** Henry Ausloos (cla). **125 Alamy Stock Photo:** EyeEm (br). **Getty Images:** Home-brew Films Company (bc). **naturepl. com:** Pete Oxford (tl). **126 Alamy Stock Photo:** blickwinkel (cl). **127 Alamy Stock Photo:** blickwinkel (br). **128-129 NASA:** (c). **130 Alamy Stock Photo:** mark Colombus (tl). **131 Alamy Stock Photo:** All Canada Photos (tr); ImageBROKER (tc). **Getty Images:** Education Images (bc). **133 Dorling Kindersley:** E. J. Peiker (cb/size comparison). **134 Fotolia:** Strezhnev Pavel (cl/sea background penguin, cr/sea background algae). **136 Dreamstime.com:** Aomvector (c/3 globes). **NASA:** Goddard Media Studios (bc, br). **137 ESA. Getty Images:** Gallo Images (bl). **138 naturepl.com:** Doug Allan (tl). **139 Alamy Stock Photo:** blickwinkel (bl). **141 Alamy Stock Photo:** Minden Pictures (tc). **Andrill Project, University of Nebraska-Lincoln:** (tr). **145 naturepl. com:** Mark Carwardine (br). **146 Alamy Stock Photo:** Minden Pictures (tl). **148 123RF. com:** Simone Gatterwe / Smgirly (bc). **149 Alamy Stock Photo:** Nature Picture Library (tr). **150 Alamy Stock Photo:** Michael S. Nolan (bl); WaterFrame (tl). **Dreamstime. com:** Vladimir Melnik / Zanskar (cr/size comparison). **151 Alamy Stock Photo:** Arterra Picture Library (tr). **153 Alamy Stock Photo:** Gianni Marchetti (bl). **Dorling Kindersley:** Alan Burger (cl/size comparison, tc/size comparison). **154-155 naturepl.com:** Steven Kazlowski. **156 Dorling Kindersley:** Hanne Eriksen / Jens Eriksen (clb/size comparison). **Dreamstime. com:** Jan Martin Will (tl/size comparison). **157 123RF. com:** leksele (tr/size comparison). **Dreamstime. com:** Eric Chen / Heartwarmer (cr/size comparison); Jan Martin Will (bc). **158 Dorling Kindersley:** Hanne Eriksen / Jens Eriksen (bl/size comparison). **159 123RF. com:** jager (cr/size comparison). **Dreamstime. com:** Luis Leamus (crb/Arctic Tern). **160-161 Nat Geo Image Collection:** Paul Nicklen (c). **164 Alamy Stock Photo:** Nigel Cattlin (bl); Niels Quist 2 (br). **165 Alamy Stock Photo:** agefotostock (bc); Lee Rentz (br); Justin Chevallier (cb); Global Warming Images (crb). **Getty Images:** bfk92 (cla); Mint Images (clb); cmturkmen (cra). **166 Alamy Stock Photo:** STOCKFOLIO® (tc). **168 Alamy Stock Photo:** Martin Lüke (cl). **169 Alamy Stock Photo:** Ange (tl). **kollected. com:** (bc). **Wave Energy Scotland:** Pelamis Wave Power Ltd (tr). **170 Alamy Stock Photo:** WaterFrame (tr). **171 Alamy Stock Photo:** agefotostock (br). **172-173 TurboSquid:** 3dshtorm / Dorling Kindersley (c). **172 naturepl. com:** Jeff Rotman (tl). **173 Getty Images:** Universal Image Group (bl). **174-175 Magnum Photos:** Stev McCurry (c). **178 Caroline Power:** (bl). **179 Alamy Stock Photo:** agefotostock (br); Jens Metschurat (bc). **naturepl. com:** Jordi Chias (tr). **180-181 Greenpeace:** Noel Guevara (c). **183 Getty Images:** Mario Tama (tl). **NASA:** Christina Koch (tc). **184 Alamy Stock Photo:** Cultura Creative Ltd (bc). **Getty Images:** Zikri Maulana / SOPA Images / LightRocket (bl). **186 Alamy Stock Photo:** Universal Images Group North America LLC (cr). **Getty Images:** (cl). **190 Alamy Stock Photo:** mauritius images GmbH (cla). **Getty Images:** The Washington Post (bl). **191 Alamy Stock Photo:** NASA (cl); US Navy Photo (cr). **Getty Images:** Karlheinz Irlmeier (clb); Hubert Stadler (bl). **192 Alamy Stock Photo:** Susan & Allan Parker (tl). **Getty Images:** (cl); Universal Images Group (bl). **193 Alamy Stock Photo:** Jon Arnold Images (br); Lubos Paukeje (bc). **194 Alamy Stock Photo:** Stock Connection Blue (cla); Guido Vermeulen-Perdaen (tl). **Science Photo Library:** Peter Scoones (cb). **195 Alamy Stock Photo:** Eddie Gerald (br); Universal Images Group North America LLC (tl); Tjetjep Rustandi (clb); Filip Jedraszak (crb). **196 Alamy Stock Photo:** ImageBROKER (cl); NG Images (tl). **197 Alamy Stock Photo:** Photo Resource Hawaii (br); Jeff Rotman (tc); Science History Images (bc). **naturepl. com:** Tui De Roy (c). **198 Alamy Stock Photo:** Martin Almqvist (tl); Michel & Gabrielle Therin-Weise (cla); Nature Picture Library (clb). **199 Alamy Stock Photo:** Juniors Bildarchiv GmbH (tl); National Geographic Image Collection (ca). **ESA**

Cover images: *Front and Back:* **Dreamstime.com:** Allexxandar; *Front:* **Alamy Stock Photo:** Stephen Frink Collection / Masa Ushioda cb; **Dreamstime. com:** Andreykuzmin t/ (Ocean surface), Richard Brooks cra, Linda Bucklin c/ (Shipwreck), Valentyna Chukhlyebova cb/ (Diver), Digitalbalance clb, Taviphoto tr; *Back:* **123RF. com:** Mike Price / mhprice clb, Willyambradberry c; **Dreamstime.com:** Seadam bc; **Nat Geo Image Collection:** Paul Nicklen cra; *Spine:* **Alamy Stock Photo:** Stephen Frink Collection / Masa Ushioda (Turtle); **Dreamstime.com:** Richard Brooks (School of fish)

All other images © Dorling Kindersley
For further information see: **www.dkimages.com**